LABORATORY AND FIELD EXERCISES IN SPORT AND EXERCISE BIOMECHANICS

Laboratory and Field Exercises in Sport and Exercise Biomechanics is the first book to fully integrate practical work into an introduction to the fundamental principles of sport and exercise biomechanics.

The book concisely and accessibly introduces the discipline of biomechanics and describes the fundamental methods of analysing and interpreting biomechanical data, before fully explaining the major concepts underlying linear kinematics, linear kinetics, angular kinematics, angular kinetics and work, energy and power. To supplement chapters, the book includes nineteen practical worksheets which are designed to give students practice in collecting, analysing and interpreting biomechanical data, as well as report writing. Each worksheet includes example data and analysis, along with data recording sheets for use by students to help bring the subject to life.

No other book offers students a comparable opportunity to gain practical, hands-on experience of the core tenets of biomechanics. *Laboratory and Field Exercises in Sport and Exercise Biomechanics* is, therefore, an important companion for any student on a Sport and Exercise Science or Kinesiology undergraduate programme, or for any instructors delivering introductory biomechanics classes.

James Watkins is Professor of Biomechanics in the College of Engineering at Swansea University, UK.

LABORATORY AND FIELD EXERCISES IN SPORT AND EXERCISE BIOMECHANICS

James Watkins

Routledge
Taylor & Francis Group

LONDON AND NEW YORK

First published 2018
by Routledge
2 Park Square, Milton Park, Abingdon, Oxon OX14 4RN

and by Routledge
711 Third Avenue, New York, NY 10017

Routledge is an imprint of the Taylor & Francis Group, an informa business

© 2018 James Watkins

British Library Cataloguing-in-Publication Data
A catalogue record for this book is available from the British Library

Library of Congress Cataloging-in-Publication Data
A catalog record for this book has been requested

ISBN: 978-1-138-23469-7 (hbk)
ISBN: 978-1-138-23470-3 (pbk)
ISBN: 978-1-315-30631-5 (ebk)

Typeset in Bembo
by Apex CoVantage, LLC

To Shelagh

CONTENTS

FIGURES

TABLES

PREFACE

All movements and changes in movement are brought about by the action of forces. The two most common types of force are pushing and pulling, but there are many variations such as lifting a book from a table, holding a pen, turning a door handle, catching a ball, kicking a ball and throwing a discus. These are all examples of the human body applying a force to an object in order to move it or change the way it is moving, i.e. change its speed and/or direction of movement.

Human movement is brought about by the musculoskeletal system under the control of the nervous system. The skeletal muscles pull on the bones to control the movements of the joints and, in doing so, control the movement of the body as a whole. By coordination of the various muscle groups, the forces generated by our muscles are transmitted by our bones and joints to enable us to apply forces to the external environment, usually by our hands and feet, so that we can adopt upright postures (counteract the constant tendency of body weight to collapse the body), transport the body and manipulate objects, often simultaneously. Consequently, the capacity of the body to move and carry out all of the activities that constitute daily living depends upon the capacity of the musculoskeletal system to generate and transmit forces. The forces generated and transmitted by the musculoskeletal system are referred to as internal forces. Body weight and the forces that we apply to the external environment are referred to as external forces. At any point in time we cannot change body weight and, as such, body weight is a passive external force. The external forces that are actively generated are active external forces. The active external forces are determined by the internal forces. Biomechanics is the study of the forces that act on and within living organisms and the effect of the forces on the size, shape, structure and movement of the organisms. The musculoskeletal components (muscles, bones, joints between the bones) normally continuously adapt their size, shape and structure to more readily withstand the time-averaged internal forces exerted on them in daily living. Structural adaptation is the branch of biomechanics concerning the effect of internal forces on the size, shape and structure of the components of the musculoskeletal system.

Biomechanics of movement is the branch of biomechanics concerning the effect of external forces on the movement of the body. In sport and exercise, every time a teacher, coach, trainer, instructor or therapist attempts to improve an individual's technique (the way that the arms, legs, trunk and head move in relation to each other during the performance of a particular movement, such as a forward roll in gymnastics, a jump shot in basketball or walking with the aid of crutches), s/he is trying get the individual to change the internal forces (changes in the magnitude and/or duration and/or timing of muscle forces) to change the magnitude, duration and timing of the active external forces which, in turn, determine the quality of performance.

Biomechanics of movement is an essential component in the professional preparation of sports coaches, athletic trainers, physical education teachers, physical fitness instructors and physical therapists. In addition to the study of scientific theory underlying biomechanics of movement, professional preparation in these fields normally involves a considerable amount of laboratory and field work designed to enhance conceptual understanding and develop good practice in performance assessment. In accordance with this approach, the purpose of the book is to engage students in laboratory and field exercises to

- Develop knowledge and understanding of the fundamental concepts underlying the biomechanics of movement.
- Facilitate practice in observation and measurement of performance, analysis of individual and group results and report writing.
- Facilitate practice in operating standard laboratory and field equipment used in biomechanical assessment of performance and biomechanics research.
- Develop an appreciation of the importance of good practice in performance analysis in laboratory and field situations.

The book comprises seven chapters. Chapter 1 introduces the fundamental concepts of force, mechanics, biomechanics and forms of motion, and describes the mechanical units of measurement in the metric system of units. Chapter 2 describes the fundamental methods of analyzing and interpreting biomechanical data, in particular, measures of central tendency, measures of variability, correlation, reliability and validity. Chapters 3 to 7 describe the biomechanics of linear kinematics (Chapter 3), linear kinetics (Chapter 4), angular kinematics (Chapter 5), angular kinetics (Chapter 6) and work, energy and power (Chapter 7). Chapters 3 to 7 highlight one or more Practical Worksheets concerning the biomechanical concepts and principles covered in the respective chapter. There are 19 Practical Worksheets. The Practical Worksheets are designed as laboratory and field exercises to accompany the lecture programme in a first level undergraduate course in biomechanics of sport and exercise. Each worksheet describes the objectives of the worksheet, the equipment required and the method of collecting and analyzing the data. In addition, each worksheet includes example data obtained by students, analysis of the data and presentation of the results in tables and figures.

No previous knowledge of biomechanics is assumed. All of the biomechanical concepts are explained from first principles. To aid learning, the book features a content overview and objectives at the start of each chapter, a large number of applied examples with illustrations, references to guide further study and an extensive index.

ACKNOWLEDGEMENTS

I thank all of the staff at Routledge who have contributed to the commissioning and production of the book. I also thank my academic colleagues and the large number of undergraduate and graduate students who have helped me, directly and indirectly, over many years, to develop and organize the content of the book.

1

INTRODUCTION TO BIOMECHANICS

All movements and changes in movement are brought about by the action of forces. The two most common types of force are pulling and pushing. Human movement is brought about by our skeletal muscles which pull on our bones to control the movements of our joints and, in doing so, enable us to apply forces to the external environment so that we can perform all of the movements that constitute daily living, in particular, maintaining upright postures, transporting the body and manipulating objects. Biomechanics is the study of the forces that act on and within living organisms and the effect of the forces on the size, shape, structure and movement of the organisms. The purpose of this chapter is to introduce the concepts of force, mechanics, biomechanics, forms of motion and mechanical units of measurement.

Objectives

After reading this chapter, you should be able to do the following:

1 Describe the two ways that forces tend to affect bodies.
2 Describe the four subdisciplines of mechanics.
3 Describe the two fundamental forms of motion.
4 Convert units of measurement between the International System (SI) and the British imperial system.

Force

All bodies, animate and inanimate, are continuously acted upon by forces. A force can be defined as that which alters or tends to alter a body's state of rest or type of movement. The forces that act on a body arise from interaction of the body with its environment. There are two types of interaction: contact interaction which produces contact forces, and attraction interaction which produces attraction forces (Watkins 2014).

Contact interaction refers to physical contact between the body and its environment. In contact interactions, the forces exerted by the environment on a body are referred to as contact forces. The environment consists largely of three main types of physical phenomena: solids, liquids and gases. In sport and exercise, the main sources of contact forces are implements (e.g. balls, rackets), the ground (e.g. walking, running, jumping), water (e.g. swimming, diving, rowing), air (e.g. skydiving, ski jumping, downhill skiing) and the forces exerted by opponents, usually in the form of pushes and pulls.

Attraction interaction refers to naturally occurring forces of attraction between certain bodies that tend to make the bodies move toward each other and to maintain contact with each other after contact is made. For example, electromagnetic attraction force maintains the configuration of atoms in molecules and the configuration of molecules in solids, liquids and gases. Similarly, a magnetized piece of iron attracts other pieces of iron to it by the attraction force of magnetism. The human body is constantly subjected to a very considerable force of attraction, i.e. body weight, the force due to the gravitational pull of the earth. It is body weight that keeps us in contact with the ground and which brings us back to the ground should we leave it, for example, following a jump into the air.

BOX 1.1

All bodies, animate and inanimate, are continuously acted upon by forces which arise from interaction of the body with its environment. The environment exerts two kinds of force, contact forces and attraction forces.

Mechanics

Forces tend to affect bodies in two ways:

- Forces tend to deform bodies, i.e. change the shape of the bodies by, for example, stretching (pulling force), squashing (pushing force) and twisting (torsion force).
- Forces determine the movement of bodies, i.e. the forces acting on a body determine whether it moves or remains at rest and determine its speed and direction of movement if it does move.

Mechanics is the study of the forces that act on bodies and the effects of the forces on the size, shape, structure and movement of the bodies. The actual effect that a force or combination of forces has on a body, i.e. the amount of deformation and change of movement that occurs, depends upon the size of the force in relation to the mass of the body and the mechanical properties of the body. The mass of a body is the amount of matter (physical substance) that makes up the body. The mass of a body is the product of its volume and its density. The volume of a body is the amount of space that the mass occupies and its density is the concentration of matter (atoms and molecules) in the mass, i.e. the amount of mass per unit volume. The greater the concentration of mass, the larger the density. For example, the density of iron is greater than that of wood, and the density of wood is greater than that of polystyrene. Similarly, with regard to the structure of the human body, bone is more dense than muscle and muscle is more dense than fat.

The mass of a body is a measure of its inertia, i.e. its resistance to start moving if it is at rest and its resistance to change its speed and/or direction if it is already moving. The larger the mass, the greater the inertia and, consequently, the larger the force that will be needed to move the mass or change the way it is moving. For example, the inertia of a stationary soccer ball (a small mass) is small in comparison to that of a heavy barbell (a large mass), i.e. much more force will be required to move the barbell than to move the ball.

Whereas the effect of a force on the movement of a body is largely determined by its mass, the amount of deformation that occurs is largely determined by its mechanical properties, in particular, its stiffness (the resistance of the body to deformation) and strength (the amount of force required to break the body). For a given amount of force, the higher the stiffness and the greater the strength of a body, the smaller the deformation that will occur.

BOX 1.2

Mechanics is the study of the forces that act on bodies and the effects of the forces on the size, shape, structure and movement of the bodies.

Subdisciplines of mechanics

The different types and effects of forces are reflected in four overlapping subdisciplines of mechanics: mechanics of materials, fluid mechanics, statics and dynamics. Mechanics of materials is the study of the mechanical properties of materials including, for example, the stiffness and resilience of materials used to make running tracks and other playing surfaces and the strength of bone, muscle and connective tissues. Fluid mechanics is the study of the movement of liquids and gases, such as blood flow in the cardiovascular system, and the effect of liquids and gases on the movement of solids, such as the movement of the human body through water and air.

Statics is the study of bodies under the action of balanced forces, i.e. the study of the forces acting on bodies that are at rest or moving with constant speed in a particular direction. In these situations the resultant force (the net effect of all the forces) acting on the body is zero. Figure 1.1 shows a book resting on a table. Since

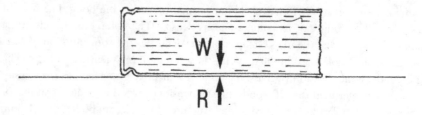

FIGURE 1.1 The forces acting on a book resting on a table. W = weight of the book; R = force exerted on the book by the table.

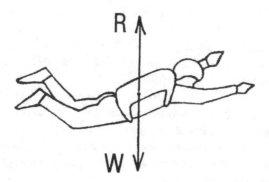

FIGURE 1.2 The forces acting on a skydiver. W = weight of the skydiver, clothing and parachute; R = air resistance.

the book is at rest, there are only two forces acting on the book (discounting the force exerted by the surrounding air which is negligible), the weight of the book W acting downward and the upward reaction force R exerted by the table. The magnitudes of W and R are the same, but they act in opposite directions and, therefore, cancel out, such that the resultant force acting on the book is zero.

Figure 1.2 shows a skydiver falling to earth. After jumping out of the aeroplane she is accelerated downward (her downward speed increases) by the force of her weight W. However, as her downward speed increases, so does the upthrust of air on the underside of her body, i.e. the air resistance R. After falling for a few seconds R will be equal in magnitude, but opposite in direction to W. Consequently, the resultant force acting on the skydiver will be zero and provided that she does not alter the orientation or shape of her body, she will continue to fall with constant speed until she opens her parachute.

Dynamics is the study of bodies under the action of unbalanced forces, i.e. bodies moving with non-constant speed. In this situation the resultant force acting on the body will be greater than zero, i.e. the body will be accelerating (speed increasing) or decelerating (speed decreasing) in the direction of the resultant force. For example, Figure 1.3a shows a sprinter in the set position, i.e. when the body is at rest. In this situation the resultant force acting on the sprinter will be zero. However, following the starting signal, the sprinter accelerates away from the blocks under the

a.   b.

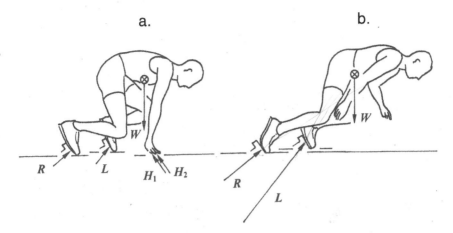

FIGURE 1.3 The forces acting on a sprinter in the set position (a) and just after the start (b). H_1 and H_2 = forces acting on the hands; W = weight of the sprinter; L = force exerted on the left foot; R = force exerted on the right foot.

action of the resultant force acting on his body, i.e. the resultant of his body weight and the forces acting on his feet (Figure 1.3b). The determination of resultant force is described in Chapter 3.

Kinematics is the branch of dynamics that describes the movement of bodies in relation to space and time (Greek *kinema*, movement). A kinematic analysis describes the movement of a body in terms of distance (change in position), speed (rate of change of position) and acceleration (variability in the rate of change of position). Kinetics is the branch of dynamics that describes the forces acting on bodies, i.e. the cause of the observed kinematics (Greek *kinein*, to move).

Biomechanics

Biomechanics is the study of the forces that act on and within living organisms and the effect of the forces on the size, shape, structure and movement of the organisms. Biomechanics of sport and exercise is the study of the internal forces (muscle forces and the forces in bones and joints that result from transmission of the muscle forces through the skeleton), the external forces (e.g. ground reaction force) that result from the internal forces, the effects of the internal forces on the size, shape and structure of the musculoskeletal components (structural adaptation) and the effects of the external forces on the movement of the body (biomechanics of movement) in sport and exercise.

Forms of motion

There are two fundamental forms of motion: linear motion and angular motion. Linear motion, also referred to as translation, occurs when all parts of a body

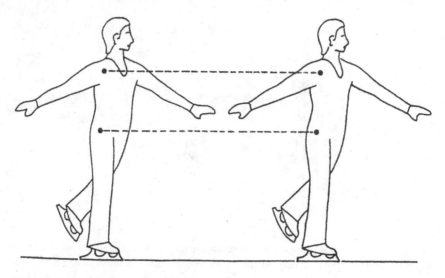

FIGURE 1.4 Rectilinear motion in skating.

move the same distance in the same direction in the same time. In all types of self-propelled human movement, such as walking, running and swimming, the orientation of the body segments to each other continually changes and, therefore, pure linear motion seldom occurs in human movement. The human body may experience pure linear motion for brief periods in activities such as skating (Figure 1.4) and ski jumping (Figure 1.5). When the linear movement is in a straight line, the motion is called rectilinear motion (Figure 1.4 and 1.5a). When the linear movement follows a curved path, the motion is referred to as curvilinear motion (Figure 1.5b).

Angular motion, also referred to as rotation, occurs when a body or part of a body, such as an arm or a leg, moves in a circle or part of a circle about a particular line in space, referred to as the axis of rotation, such that all parts of the body move through the same angle in the same direction in the same time. The axis of rotation may be stationary or it may experience linear motion (Figure 1.6). Figure 1.7 shows a gymnast rotating about a horizontal bar. Provided that the orientation of the body segments to each other does not change, the gymnast as a whole and each of the body segments will experience angular motion about the bar. Most whole body human movements are combinations of linear and angular motion. For example, in walking, the movement of the head and trunk is fairly linear, but the movements of the arms and legs involve simultaneous linear and angular motion as the body as a whole moves forward. Similarly, in cycling, the movement of the trunk, head and arms is fairly linear, but the movements of the legs involve simultaneous linear and angular motion. The movement of a multi-segmented body, like the human body, which involves simultaneous linear and angular motion of the segments, is usually referred to as general motion.

(a)

(b)

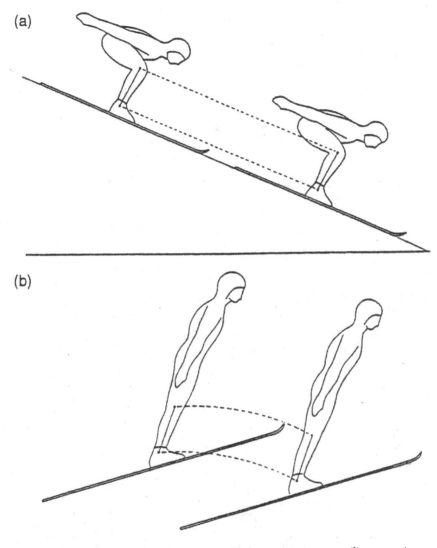

FIGURE 1.5 Linear motion. A ski jumper is likely to experience rectilinear motion on the runway (a) and curvilinear motion during flight (b).

BOX 1.3

There are two fundamental forms of motion: linear motion and angular *rotation* motion. Most whole body human movements are combinations of linear and angular motion.

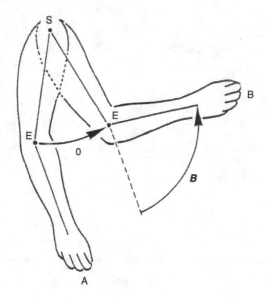

FIGURE 1.6 Angular motion. As the arm swings from position A to position B, the upper arm rotates through an angle θ about the transverse (side-to-side) axis S through the shoulder joint, and the lower arm and hand rotate through an angle β about the transverse axis E through the elbow joint.

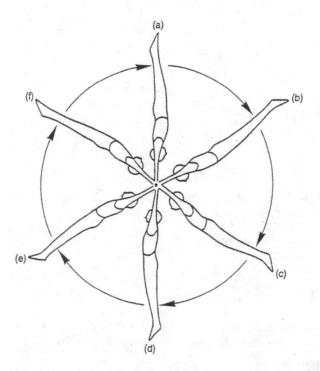

FIGURE 1.7 A gymnast rotating about a horizontal bar.

Units of measurement

Commerce and scientific communication are dependent on the correct use and interpretation of units of measurement. With the advent of the industrial revolution in the eighteenth century and the progressive increase in international trade that resulted from it, the need for uniformity in measurement became increasingly evident. At that time, one of the most widely used systems of units was the British imperial system, but lack of clarity and consistency with regard to definitions and symbols for many variables resulted in resistance to the use of this system internationally (Rowett 2004). The metric system of measurements originated in France around 1790. The name of the system is derived from the base unit for length, i.e. the metre, which was defined as one ten-millionth of the distance from the equator to the North Pole. In contrast to the British imperial system, each unit in the metric system has a unique definition and a unique symbol. Largely for this reason, the metric system progressively gained ground internationally. The metric system was officially adopted in the Netherlands and Luxembourg in 1820 and in France in 1837. In 1875, many of the industrialized countries signed the Treaty of the Metre which established the International Bureau of Weights and Measures (BIPM for *Bureau International des Poids et Mesures*) and a single system of units, the international system of units, to include all physical and chemical, metric and non-metric units. The system is usually referred to as the SI system after its French language name *Systeme International d'Unites*. The SI system is now the most widely used system of units, especially in science and international commerce. The system is maintained and updated by the BIPM as new units are proposed and accepted. The system now consists of a large number of units, but all of the units are derived from a set of base units. The base units for mechanical variables in the SI system are the metre (length), the kilogram (mass) and the second (time). These three units give rise to a subsection of the SI system called the metre-kilogram-second (m-kg-s) system. The corresponding subsection of the British imperial system is the foot-pound-second (ft-lb-s) system. These two sub-systems are shown in Table 1.1. With the exception of a few examples, the m-kg-s system is used throughout this book.

BOX 1.4

The international system of units (SI system) includes all physical and chemical, metric and non-metric units. It is the most widely used system of units, especially in science and international commerce.

TABLE 1.1 Mechanical units and (symbols) of measurement

Quantity	British imperial system	SI system
Distance	foot (ft)	metre (m)
Time	second (s)	second (s)
Speed	feet per second (ft/s)	metres per second (m/s)
Acceleration	feet per second per second (ft/s²)	metres per second per second (m/s²)
Mass	pound (lb)	kilogram (kg)
Linear momentum	pound feet per second (lb·ft/s)	kilogram metres per second (kg·m/s)
Force	poundal (pdl) 1 pdl = 1 lb × 1 ft/s²	newton (N) 1 N = 1 kg × 1 m/s²
Weight★	pound force (lbf) 1 lbf = 1 lb × 32.2 ft/s² = 32.2 pdl	kilogram force (kgf) 1 kgf = 1 kg × 9.81 m/s² = 9.81 N
Pressure	pounds force per square inch (lbf/in²)	pascal (Pa) (1 Pa = 1 N/m²)
Angular distance	radian (rad)	radian (rad)
Angular speed	radians per second (rad/s)	radians per second (rad/s)
Angular acceleration	radians per second per second (rad/s²)	radians per second per second (rad/s²)
Moment of inertia	pound foot squared (lb·ft²)	kilogram metres squared (kg·m²)
Angular momentum	pound foot squared per second (lb·ft²/s)	kilogram metres squared per second (kg·m²/s)
Turning moment	poundal foot (pdl·ft)	newton metre (N·m)
Energy and work	foot poundal (ft·pdl)	joule (J) (J = N·m)
Power	horsepower (hp) 1 hp = 550 ft lb/s★★	watt (W) (W = J/s)

★ pound force (lbf) and pound weight (lbwt) are different names for the same unit, i.e. the weight of a mass of 1 lb.

★ kilogram force (kgf), kilopond (kp) and kilogram weight (kgwt) are different names for the same unit, i.e. the weight of a mass of 1 kg.

★★ The horsepower symbol is usually written as ft lb/s, but the 'lb' is actually 'lbf' (pound force). Consequently, the correct symbol for horsepower is ft lbf/s (foot pounds force per second). Fortunately, the horsepower is rarely used in biomechanics.

Unit symbols in the SI system

Units in the SI system are represented by symbols which are derived according to mathematical rules, rather than abbreviations that follow grammatical rules (Rowett 2004). The mathematical rules include:

- A symbol is not followed by a full-stop (period) except at the end of a sentence.
- The letter 's' is not added to a symbol to indicate more than one. For example, 2 kilograms is reported as 2 kg, not 2 kgs.
- Superscripts are used to indicate 'squared' or 'cubed'. For example, 4 square metres is written as 4 m^2, not 4 sq m.
- A raised dot (also referred to as a middle dot, centred dot and half-high dot), a decimal point or a space is used to indicate multiplication of one SI unit by another. For example, the symbol for a newton metre is N·m, N.m or N m, but not Nm. The raised dot format is used in this book.
- A forward slash or raised dot with a negative power is used to indicate division of one unit by another. For example, the symbol for metres per second is m/s or m·s^{-1}. However, only one slash or raised dot is permitted. For example, the symbol for metres per second per second is m/s^2 or m·s^{-2}, not m/s/s. The slash format is used in this book.
- A space is placed between the number and the associated symbol. For example, 2.4 kg and 3.25 s are correct, but 2.4kg and 3.25s are incorrect. In addition, the signs for percentage and degrees Celsius, which are widely used in scientific literature although they are not part of the SI system, should be spaced, as in 7.6 % and 5.5 °C. However, angle symbols (degrees °, minutes ' and seconds ") should be closed up; an angle is correctly reported as 53° 32' 23".
- In numbers with five or more digits on either side of the decimal point, groups of three digits are separated by a space instead of a comma (which is used as a decimal point in some countries) as, for example, 10,000 m or 0.123 46 kg.

Conversion of units

Whereas most countries use the SI system, units from the British imperial system are still widely used in the UK and the USA. These units include, for example, inches (in), feet (ft), yards (yd) and miles (as in miles per hour, mph) for distance, and pound (lb) and ton for mass. Table 1.2 shows some frequently used equivalences between SI and British imperial system units.

To convert units, it is necessary to replace the units to be converted by their numerical equivalent in the units required. For example, the maximum speed of elite male sprinters in a 100 m race is approximately 12 m/s. This is equivalent to a speed of 26.84 mph:

As 1 m/s = 2.2369 mph (Table 1.2),
then 12 m/s = 12 × 2.2369 mph = 26.84 mph

Similarly, the standard road vehicle speed limit in built-up areas in the UK is 30 mph. This is equivalent to a speed of 48.28 km/h:

As 1 mph = 1.609 34 km/h,
then 30 mph = 30 × 1.609 34 km/h = 48.28 km/h

TABLE 1.2 Equivalences between SI and British imperial system units

Mass

1 lb = 0.4536 kg

1 kg = 2.2046 lb

1 ton = 2240 lb = 1016.05 kg

Length

1 in = 25.4 mm (mm = millimetre: 1 m = 1000 mm)

1 in = 2.54 cm (cm = centimetre: 1 m = 100 cm)

1 in = 0.0254 m

1 ft = 0.3048 m

1 yd = 0.9144 m

1 mile = 1609.34 m

1 mile = 1.609 34 km (km = kilometre: 1 km = 1000 m)

1 cm = 0.3937 in

1 cm = 0.0328 ft

1 m = 39.37 in

1 m = 3.2808 ft

1 m = 1.0936 yd

1 m = 6.2137×10^{-4} miles = 0.000 621 37 miles

1 km = 0.621 37 miles

Angular distance

$360° = 2\pi$ rad

$1° = 0.017\ 45$ rad

1 rad = 57.296°

Time

1 s = 0.0167 min

1 s = 2.7778×10^{-4} h (hours) = 0.000 277 78 h

1 min = 60 s

1 h = 60 min

1 h = 3600 s

Force

1 kgf = 9.81 N

1 N = 0.1019 kgf

1 kgf = 2.2046 lbf

1 lbf = 0.4536 kgf

1 lbf = 4.4498 N

1 N = 0.2247 lbf

1 tonf (ton force) = 2240 lbf

1 tonf = 1016 kgf

1 tonf = 9964 N

Speed

1 m/s = 3.2808 ft/s

1 m/s = 2.2369 mph (miles per hour)

1 m/s = 3.6 km/h

1 km/h = 0.277 78 m/s

1 ft/s = 0.3048 m/s

1 ft/s = 0.6818 mph

1 mph = 0.4470 m/s

1 mph = 1.609 34 km/h

1 km/h = 0.6214 mph

Area

$1\ m^2 = 10.7639\ ft^2$

$1\ m^2 = 1550\ in^2$

$1\ m^2 = 1.1960\ yd^2$

$1\ yd^2 = 0.8361\ m^2$

$1\ ft^2 = 0.0929\ m^2$

$1\ in^2 = 0.000\ 645\ 16\ m^2 = 6.4516 \times 10^{-4}\ m^2$

Surface area of a sphere $= 4\pi \cdot r^2$ where $r =$ radius of the sphere

Volume

$1\ yd^3$ (cubic yard) $= 0.764\ 555\ m^3$ (cubic metre)

$1\ ft^3$ (cubic foot) $= 0.028\ 316\ m^3$

$1\ in^3$ (cubic inch) $= 16.387\ cm^3$

$1\ m^3 = 35.3144\ ft^3$

$1\ m^3 = 1.307\ 95\ yd^3$

$1\ cm^3 = 0.061\ 023\ 7\ in^3$

1 l (litre) $= 10^3\ cm^3 = 1000$ ml (millilitres)

$1\ m^3 = 10^6\ cm^3 = 10^3$ l

$1\ l = 10^{-3}\ m^3$

Volume of a sphere $= 4\pi \cdot r^3/3$ where $r =$ radius of the sphere

Volume of an ellipsoid $= 4\pi \cdot a \cdot b^2/3$ where $a =$ length radius and $b =$ width radius

Pressure

$1\ Pa$ (pascal) $= 1\ N/m^2$

$1\ Pa = 0.000\ 144\ 988\ lbf/in^2 = 1.449\ 88 \times 10^{-4}\ lbf/in^2$

$1\ lbf/in^2 = 6897.15\ Pa$

1 atm (atmosphere) $= 101\ 325\ Pa = 14.69\ lbf/in^2$

Density

Water (at sea level) $= 1000\ kg/m^3$

Air (at sea level) $= 1.25\ kg/m^3$

Viscosity

1 P (poise) $= 1\ g/(cm \cdot s) = 1\ g \cdot cm^{-1} \cdot s^{-1}$

1 Pl (poiseulle) $= 1\ Pa \cdot s$ (pascal second) $= 1\ kg/(m \cdot s) = 1\ kg \cdot m^{-1} \cdot s^{-1} = 10\ P$

Water (at 20 °C) $= 0.1002\ P = 0.010\ 02\ Pl$

Air (at 20 °C) $= 0.0018\ P = 0.000\ 18\ Pl$

References

Rowett, R. (2004) *How many? A dictionary of units of measurement.* Online. Available: www.unc.edu/~rowlett/units/sipm.html 14 June 2004.

Watkins, J. (2014) *Fundamental biomechanics of sport and exercise.* London: Routledge.

2

ANALYSIS OF DATA

Data is numerical information obtained by measuring or counting something. Statistics is a branch of applied mathematics that is used to analyze data so that the meaning of the data can be interpreted and evaluated. A statistical analysis involves the application of one or more statistical procedures (specific arithmetic calculations) to produce specific numbers that describe different characteristics of the data; each of these specific numbers is called a statistic. A statistical procedure may be lengthy, especially when there is a large amount of data. However, as most statistical procedures involve arithmetic operations that will be very familiar to all secondary school students (addition, subtraction, multiplication, division, square roots), the procedures will not be mathematically difficult. The purpose of this chapter is to introduce the fundamental concepts that underlie statistical analysis and to describe the statistics required to complete the worksheets that accompany Chapters 3 to 7.

Objectives

After reading this chapter, you should be able to do the following:

1   Distinguish continuous and discontinuous data.
2   Describe the four measurement scales.
3   Describe the normal distribution curve.
4   Describe the measures of central tendency.
5   Describe the measures of variability.
6   Calculate Pearson's product moment correlation coefficient.
7   Calculate a simple regression equation.

Continuous and discontinuous data

Most of the things that we measure (e.g. joint flexibility, muscle strength, leg power) or count (e.g. number of people who attend a sports centre each week, number of people who cycle to work each day) vary over time. Consequently, these phenomena and many other things that we measure or count are called variables. In general, there are two types of variables: continuous and discontinuous. Discontinuous variables are also referred to as discrete variables. The units of a continuous scale can be subdivided (to an extent that is dependent upon the precision of the measurement instrument), whereas the units of a discontinuous scale only occur as whole units, such as the number of spectators at a football game. Most things that can be measured yield continuous data. Most things that can be counted yield discontinuous data. Measurement is the process of comparing an unknown quantity, such as someone's weight, with some standard of the same variable, such as calibrated weighing scales, and then describing the previously unknown quantity in terms of the standard. The precision of a measurement is limited by the precision of the measurement instrument. For example, most bathroom scales measure weight to 0.1 kgf, but a more sophisticated force measurement system, such as a force platform in a biomechanics laboratory, may be able to measure weight to 0.01 kgf.

BOX 2.1

In general, there are two types of variables: continuous and discontinuous. The units of a continuous scale can be subdivided, whereas the units of a discontinuous scale only occur as whole units.

Measurement scales

Different types of data contain different amounts of information. For example, the numbers of students who passed and failed a particular exam is one type of data (number of passes, number of fails). Analysis of pass/fail data is restricted to calculating percentages, in this case, the percentage of students in the group that passed the exam and the percentage of students that failed. In comparison, the actual marks obtained by the students in the exam is a different type of data which not only allows the calculation of percentage pass and percentage fail, but also allows the calculation of a number of other statistics to provide a clearer interpretation and more in-depth evaluation of the performance of the students in the exam. Consequently, the amount of information contained in a set of data depends upon the measurement scale used in the collection of the data. There are four generally accepted measurement scales (also referred to as measurement levels): nominal, ordinal, interval and ratio (Stevens 1946).

A nominal scale consists of a number of mutually exclusive categories that are qualitatively different with respect to a particular variable. For example, a nominal scale could be developed for hair colour with categories such as black, brown, blonde, red and grey. Similarly, a nominal scale could be developed for customer satisfaction with several categories ranging from very satisfied to very dissatisfied. The order of the categories in a nominal scale is not relevant as there is no quantitative difference between the categories. For example, it makes no sense to suggest that black hair is quantitatively different to brown hair. Category membership is the only information in a nominal scale of measurement

An ordinal scale, also referred to as a rank-order scale, is one in which the data can be ordered (or ranked) from low to high (or high to low) with respect to a particular variable without any knowledge of the actual differences between the ranks. For example, a group of soldiers could be arranged in order of increasing height with the number 1 assigned to the shortest soldier, the number 2 assigned to the next shortest soldier, and so on, with the highest number (rank) being assigned to the tallest soldier. When all of the soldiers had been given a rank-order number, the assigned numbers would represent an ordinal scale. By knowing the rank assigned to a particular soldier, we would not know the actual height of the soldier nor by how much he was taller or shorter than the soldiers adjacent to him. However, we would know whether he was shorter or taller than any other soldier in the group. Similarly, each runner that completes a marathon race is normally given a number that indicates the order in which she finished the race. The list of numbers assigned to the runners, from first to last, represents an ordinal scale. Each number indicates the position in which a particular runner finished the race, but not the amount of time between the runner and the runner who finished just in front or the runner who finished just behind.

In an interval scale, the data can be ranked and there is uniformity of difference between the units in the scale such that the actual difference between ranks can be accurately quantified. However, in an interval scale there is no zero. For example, temperature is measured on an interval scale where equal distances on the temperature scale indicate equal changes in heat. However, it is incorrect to say that the temperature at any particular point A on the scale is so many times hotter or colder than that at some other point B because the points A and B are not measured from true zero. The Celsius scale of temperature defines the freezing point of water as zero degrees (0 °C) and the boiling point of water as 100 degrees (100 °C), but the Celsius scale, satisfactory for measuring temperature in daily living, represents only part of the global temperature scale which extends below 0 °C and above 100 °C.

A ratio scale is the most useful measurement scale as it includes all of the characteristics of the other three scales and, in addition, has a true zero. Time is a ratio variable: 4 minutes is twice as long as 2 minutes. Age, height, weight, distance, speed, acceleration, force and power are also ratio variables.

BOX 2.2

There are four generally accepted measurement scales: nominal, ordinal, interval, ratio.

Normal distribution curve

The word score is used in different ways which include, for example, a test score, a golf score and a credit score. In statistics, a score is that which results from any act of measuring or counting. Any score taken directly, without alteration, such as measurement of body weight on a set of weighing scales, is called a raw score. In statistics, a raw score is usually denoted by the capital letter X and a collection of raw scores is often referred to as a distribution of scores. The total number of scores in a distribution of scores is usually denoted by the capital letter N. When N is large and the variable is discontinuous, it is helpful to start the process of data analysis by organizing the scores into a manageable form by (i) identifying the lowest score and the highest score in the distribution of scores, (ii) listing, in ascending order, each possible score between and including the lowest and highest scores, (iii) counting the frequency of each actual score in the distribution. The resulting distribution of frequencies is referred to as a frequency distribution. Table 2.1 shows a frequency distribution based on the heights (to the nearest whole centimetre) of 247 adult male applicants for entry to a physical fitness instructor course. The sum of the frequencies should be the same as the total number of scores, in this case, $N = 247$. In this frequency distribution the lowest score is 164 cm (5' 4 1/2") and the highest score is 194 cm (6' 4 1/2"). The difference between the highest score and the lowest score in a distribution is called the range, usually denoted in statistics by the capital letter R. The range in the distribution in Table 2.1 is 30 cm ($R = 194$ cm $- 164$ cm $= 30$ cm). Inspection of Table 2.1 indicates that the frequency of scores tends to increase from the lowest score toward the middle of the range and then decrease from the middle of the range toward the highest score. The trend is shown more clearly in Figure 2.1a which shows the frequencies plotted against the scores. In a two-dimensional graph such as Figure 2.1a, it is customary to refer to the vertical axis as the ordinate (or y axis) and the horizontal axis as the abscissa (or x axis). The roughly bell-shaped frequency distribution of scores for height in Figure 2.1a is typical of the frequency distribution of many other variables concerning body size and shape; these include body weight, leg length, waist girth, hat size, shirt size and shoe size. For these and other variables, such as IQ (intelligence quotient), the greater the number of scores in the distribution, the closer the frequency distribution tends to approximate a symmetric bell-shaped curve, referred to as the normal distribution curve, normal probability curve and Gaussian curve, as shown in Figure 2.1b. Any distribution of scores which closely approximates the normal probability curve is said to be normally distributed. Figure 2.1c shows the similarity between the frequency distribution in Figure 2.1a and the normal distribution curve.

BOX 2.3

When the total number of scores is large, many variables concerning body size and shape are normally distributed.

TABLE 2.1 Frequency distribution of the heights of 247 men. X, raw scores; f, frequency of each score; Xf, product of each score and the frequency of each score; CF, cumulative frequency of the scores from the lowest score to the highest score; $\sum Xf$, sum of all scores.

X (cm)	f (n)	Xf (cm)	CF (n)
194	1	194	247
193	0	0	246
192	1	192	246
191	0	0	245
190	1	190	245
189	3	567	244
188	2	376	241
187	4	748	239
186	6	1116	235
185	6	1110	229
184	10	1840	223
183	15	2745	213
182	18	3276	198
181	21	3801	180
180	22	3960	159
179	24	4296	137
178	22	3916	113
177	19	3363	91
176	20	3520	72
175	14	2450	52
174	9	1566	38
173	8	1384	29
172	6	1032	21
171	5	855	15
170	3	510	10
169	3	507	7
168	2	336	4
167	0	0	2
166	1	166	2
165	0	0	1
164	1	164	1

$N = 247$

$\sum Xf = 44180$

$\overline{X} = \text{Mean} = \text{sum } Xf/N = 44180/247 = 178.87 \text{ cm}$

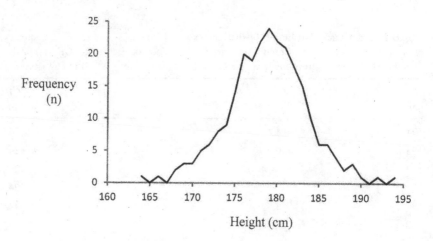

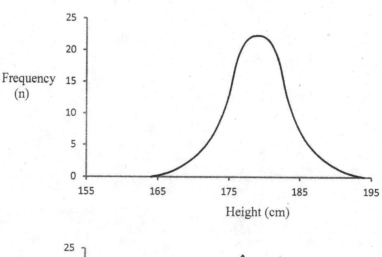

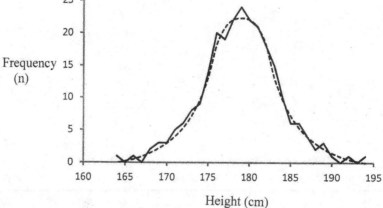

FIGURE 2.1 (a) Frequency distribution of the height of 247 men. (b) Normal distribution curve. (c) Normal distribution curve superimposed on the frequency distribution.

Measures of central tendency

As most of the scores in a distribution tend to be around the middle of the distribution, it is very common for a mid-range score to be used to reflect or represent the distribution as a whole. For example, a student may describe her whole-year academic performance in terms of an average grade or average percentage. Similarly, the socio-economy of a particular region might be described in terms of the average wage or average house price. In statistics, these measures are known as measures of central tendency. There are three measures of central tendency: mean, median and mode.

The mean, also referred to as the arithmetic mean and average, is the most useful and most widely used measure of central tendency. The mean of a distribution is calculated by dividing the sum of the scores by the number of scores, i.e.

$$\overline{X} = \frac{\sum X}{N}$$

where
$\overline{X}$ = the mean ($\overline{X}$ is read as X bar)
$\sum X$ = the sum of X (the sum of the scores)
N = the number of scores

The mean of the distribution 2, 5, 7, 5, 8, 5, 6 is 5.43, i.e.

$$\overline{X} = \frac{2+5+7+5+8+5+6}{7} = \frac{38}{7} = 5.43 \text{ (to two places of decimals)}$$

The mode of any distribution is the score that occurs most frequently. In the distribution of scores consisting of 2, 5, 7, 5, 8, 5, 6 the mode is 5 (frequency = 3). In the distribution shown in Table 2.1, the mode is 179 cm (5′ 10 1/2″) (frequency = 24). The mode tends to be the most useful measure of central tendency in the manufacture of certain goods such as clothing and footwear. For example, trouser manufacturers produce trousers to fit particular waist girth/ leg length ranges and production will be geared to the number of sales of the different ranges. As most people will be of intermediate size, most of the trousers produced will be in the intermediate range. Similarly, shoe manufacturers produce shoes to fit particular length/width ranges. As most people will be of intermediate size, most of the shoes produced will be in the intermediate range. When a distribution has one mode, it is referred to as a unimodal distribution. Some distributions may have more than one mode, i.e. two or more scores may exhibit distinct peaks in the distribution. If there are two such scores, the distribution is referred to as bimodal, and if there are three such scores, the distribution is referred to as trimodal.

The median score in a distribution is the middle score in the distribution when the distribution is listed from lowest score to highest score. In the distribution of scores consisting of 2, 5, 7, 5, 8, 5, 6, the order becomes 2, 5, 5, 5, 6, 7,

8 when the scores are listed from low to high. As there are seven scores in the distribution, the median is the fourth score in the list, i.e. 5. When there is an even number of scores in a distribution, the median is the mean of the middle two scores. In the distribution 2, 3, 5, 6, 8, 9, the median is 5.5 ($(5 + 6)/2 = 5.5$). The median is useful when there are one or more outliers in the distribution, i.e. scores that are much higher or much lower than all of the other scores in the distribution and, if included in the calculation of the mean, would be likely to result in the data being misinterpreted. For example, in the distribution 2, 3, 4, 5, 6, 7, 23, the highest score, 23, is much higher than all of the other scores. The mean of the distribution is 7.14 ($2 + 3 + 4 + 5 + 6 + 7 + 23 = 50$; $50/7 = 7.14$), but the median is 5. The median score of 5 is much more representative of the majority of the scores than the mean score of 7.14. Outliers may occur due to measurement error or to experimental error.

For ratio data, the mean is the best measure of central tendency because it is based on all of the scores in the distribution. In contrast, the mode is simply the single score that occurs most frequently and the median is a single score or the mean of only two scores in the distribution. When N is large, the distribution of scores for many human attributes including, for example, height and weight, is likely to be close to normal, i.e. the mean, median and mode will be close to each other. For example, in the distribution of the heights of 247 adult men shown in Table 2.1, the mean = 178.87 cm, the mode = 179 cm (frequency = 24) and the median = 179 cm (124th score). In a perfectly normal distribution, the mean, mode and median will be exactly the same. The most common type of deviation from a normal distribution is a skewed distribution, i.e. one in which there are a disproportionate number of scores close to one end of the distribution. Figure 2.2a shows a distribution in which most of the scores are in the lower part of the distribution. This type of distribution is described as positively skewed. A positively skewed distribution may reflect, for example, the results of an exam in which many of the students obtained a low score. In a positively skewed distribution, the mode will be lower than the median and the median will be lower than the mean. Figure 2.2b shows a distribution in which most of the scores are in the upper part of the distribution. This type of distribution is described as negatively skewed and may reflect, for example, the results of an exam in which many of the students obtained a high score. In a negatively skewed distribution, the mode will be higher than the median and the median will be higher than the mean.

BOX 2.4

There are three measures of central tendency: mean, median and mode.

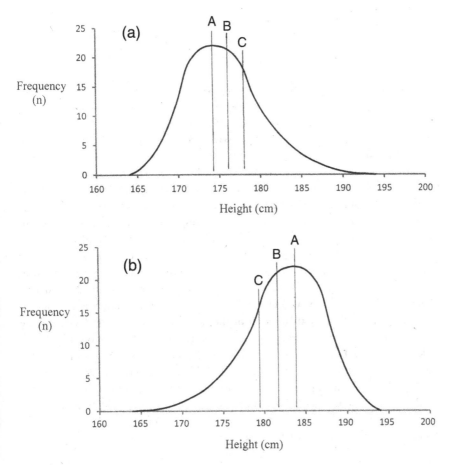

FIGURE 2.2   (a) A positively skewed distribution. (b) A negatively skewed distribution. A: mode; B: median; C: mean.

Measures of variability

A measure of central tendency provides useful but limited information about a particular distribution. For example, the average temperature in London, England, is 10.4 °C (50.8 °F), but the temperature ranges between a low of −3 °C (26.6 °F) and a high of 33 °C (91.4 °F) (Weather Online 2016). Clearly, in addition to a measure of central tendency, it would be helpful to have a measure that describes the spread or dispersion of the scores with respect to the central tendency. There are three statistics that are commonly used to indicate the spread or dispersion of scores in a distribution: range, average deviation and standard deviation. These statistics are known as measures of variability.

The range is the simplest measure of variability, but as it is based on only two scores, the lowest score and the highest score, it gives no indication of the spread of the other scores about the central tendency. The average deviation and standard deviation are both based on all of the scores in a distribution. The difference between any score in a distribution and the mean of the distribution is called the score's deviation. The deviation is symbolized by the lower case letter x and $x = X - \overline{X}$, i.e. the mean is subtracted from the score so that scores larger than the mean are associated with positive deviations and scores smaller than the mean are associated with negative deviations. Table 2.2 shows a distribution of scores consisting of the weights of 12 men. The mean of the distribution is 82.5 kgf as shown in the second column of Table 2.2. The deviations of the scores are shown in the third column of Table 2.2 together with the sum of the deviations, Σx, which is zero. In any distribution of scores, irrespective of the size of N, the sum of the positive deviations (+44.5 in Table 2.2) must equal the sum of the negative deviations (−44.5 in Table 2.2) and, therefore, the sum of the deviations must be zero. Consequently, it is not possible to calculate the average deviation based on the positive and negative deviations because the numerator of the formula for average deviation, $\Sigma x/N$, will always be zero. However, it is possible to calculate the average deviation by treating all of the deviations as absolute deviations, i.e. all deviations are considered positive, irrespective of whether a score is above or below the mean. For example, a deviation of 1.5 kgf below the mean is the same distance from the mean as a deviation of 1.5 kgf above the mean. When the signs of the deviations are ignored, the deviations become absolute deviations. The mathematical notation for an absolute value is $|n|$, where n is the number whose absolute value is to be taken. Thus, $|-5| = |5| = 5$. The average deviation must be calculated from the absolute deviations, i.e.

$$\text{Average deviation} = \frac{\Sigma |x|}{N}$$

where
$\Sigma |x| =$ the sum of the absolute deviations
$N =$ the number of scores

The fourth column of Table 2.2 shows the absolute deviations. The sum of the absolute deviations is 89, which results in an average deviation of 7.42 kgf, i.e.

$$\text{Average deviation} = \frac{\Sigma |x|}{N} = \frac{89}{12} = 7.42\,\text{kgf}$$

$$\overline{X} = 82.5 \quad \Sigma x = 0 \quad \Sigma |x| = 89 \quad \Sigma x^2 = 1155$$

TABLE 2.2 Average deviation, variance and standard deviation of the weights (X) of 12 men. AD = average deviation; VAR = variance; SD = standard deviation.

Score	X (kgf)	$x = X - \overline{X}$ (kgf)	$\lvert x \rvert$ (kgf)	x^2 (kgf^2)
1	72	−10.5	10.5	110.25
2	85	2.5	2.5	6.25
3	77	−5.5	5.5	30.25
4	67	−15.5	15.5	240.25
5	82	−0.5	0.5	0.25
6	82	−0.5	0.5	0.25
7	97	14.5	14.5	210.25
8	102	19.5	19.5	380.25
9	89	6.5	6.5	42.25
10	84	1.5	1.5	2.25
11	82	−0.5	0.5	0.25
12	71	−11.5	11.5	132.25

$$AD = \frac{\sum \lvert x \rvert}{N} = \frac{89}{12} = 7.42 \, \text{kgf}$$

$$VAR = \frac{\sum x^2}{N} = \frac{1155}{12} = 96.25 \, \text{kgf}^2$$

$$SD = \sqrt{\frac{\sum x^2}{N}} = \sqrt{96.25} = 9.81 \, \text{kgf}$$

An increase or decrease in the spread of scores will be reflected in a corresponding increase or decrease in the average deviation. Like the average deviation, the standard deviation will also increase or decrease as a result of an increase or decrease in the spread of scores. However, unlike the average deviation, the standard deviation can be used to calculate other statistics for distributions of scores that approximate normal distributions; these statistics provide a more detailed analysis of the data. As many variables concerning human characteristics and behaviours are normally distributed (as in Figure 2.1b) when N is large, the standard deviation is the most commonly reported measure of variability.

The normal distribution curve is a regular geometric figure, i.e. the symmetric bell-shaped relationship between frequency and score is embodied in a mathematical equation (not required in this book). The slope of the normal distribution curve constantly changes (Figure 2.3a). The slope is close to zero (almost parallel with the abscissa) at the low end of the range and then increases gradually to a point of maximum steepness called the point of inflection. Between the point of inflection and the peak of the curve the slope gradually decreases to zero. Between the peak of the curve and the high end of the range, the curve is a mirror image of that between the peak and the low end of the range. In a normal distribution, the distance along the abscissa between the mean of the distribution, $\overline{X}$ (the peak of the curve where the slope is zero) and the point of inflection (where the slope is steepest) is called the standard deviation (Figure 2.3a). The standard deviation, denoted in statistics by σ, the lower case Greek letter sigma, is a key element in the mathematical equation of the normal distribution curve.

The area between the normal distribution curve and the abscissa represents all of the scores in a distribution. If the standard deviation of the distribution is known, it is possible to determine the percentage of scores contained in any section of the area with respect to the abscissa. If the curve is normal, the area between the mean $\overline{X}$ and $\overline{X} + 1\sigma$ is always 34.13% of the total area, i.e. for any normally distributed set of scores, 34.13% of the scores will lie between $\overline{X}$ and $\overline{X} + 1\sigma$ (Figure 2.3b). Similarly,

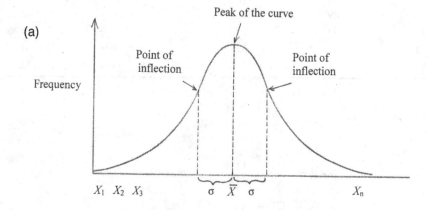

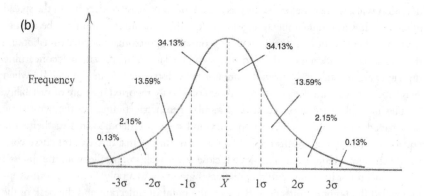

FIGURE 2.3 (a) The relationship between the mean and the standard deviation in the normal distribution curve. (b) The areas under the normal distribution curve defined by standard deviation units.

34.13% of the scores will lie between $\overline{X}$ and $\overline{X} - 1\sigma$. Standard deviations are always measured from the mean. The percentage of the total area between $+1\sigma$ and $+2\sigma$ is 13.59%, as is the percentage of the total area between -1σ and -2σ. The percentage of the total area between $+2\sigma$ and $+3\sigma$ is 2.15%, as is the percentage of the total area between -2σ and -3σ. For most practical purposes, the area contained within three standard deviation units in both directions (99.74% of the total area) can be considered to include 100% of the scores.

As described earlier, the average deviation is the mean of the sum of the absolute deviations $(\sum |x|/N)$. The standard deviation is the square root of the mean of the sum of the squared deviations, i.e.

$$\text{Standard deviation} = \sigma = \sqrt{\frac{\sum x^2}{N}}$$

where
$\sum x^2$ = the sum of the squared deviations
N = the number of scores

The fifth column of Table 2.2 shows the squared deviations together with the sum of the squared deviations (1155 kgf²). Table 2.2 also shows the mean of the sum of the squared deviations (96.26 kgf²) and the standard deviation (9.81 kgf), i.e.

$$\sum x^2 = 1155\,\text{kgf}^2$$

$$\frac{\sum x^2}{N} = \sigma^2 = \frac{1155\,\text{kgf}^2}{12} = 96.26\,\text{kgf}^2$$

$$\sqrt{\frac{\sum x^2}{N}} = \sigma = \sqrt{(96.26\,\text{kgf}^2)} = 9.81\,\text{kgf}$$

The mean of the sum of the squared deviations $(\sum x^2/N = \sigma^2 = 96.26\ \text{kgf}^2)$ is called the variance. The variance is an important statistic in detailed analyses of normally distributed data.

Some authorities maintain that the denominator in the equation for the calculation of the standard deviation should be $N-1$ rather than N. Unless N is very small, the use of $N-1$ makes very little difference to the value of the standard deviation or to interpretation of the standard deviation. Using $N-1$ is likely to give a better estimate of the standard deviation of the population from which the sample of N scores was taken (Spiegel *et al.* 2013). However, in most circumstances the user is only interested in describing the distribution of N scores, in which case, the use of N is preferred. In the distribution of scores in Table 2.2, $\sigma = 9.81$ kgf when N is used and $\sigma = 10.2$ kgf when $N-1$ is used.

The average deviation is always smaller than the standard deviation. In a perfectly normal distribution the average deviation is always 0.79788σ (Spiegel *et al.* 2013). For the distribution of scores in Table 2.2, the average deviation is 7.42 kgf and the standard deviation is 9.81 kgf, i.e. the average deviation $= 0.756\sigma$ (7.42/9.81 = 0.756) which, not surprisingly, indicates that the distribution of 12 scores is not normal. For the distribution of scores in Table 2.1, the average deviation is 3.59 cm and the standard deviation is 4.63 cm, i.e. the average deviation $= 0.775\sigma$ (3.59/4.63 = 0.775), which indicates that the distribution of 247 scores is not normal, but closer to normal than the much smaller distribution of 12 scores in Table 2.2.

In a normal distribution, 68.26% of scores would be expected to lie between -1σ and $+1\sigma$ (Figure 2.3b). The mean and standard deviation of the distribution of 247 scores in Table 2.1 are 178.87 cm and 4.63 cm, respectively. Consequently, the -1σ to $+1\sigma$ range corresponds to 178.87 ± 4.63 cm, i.e. 174.24 cm to 183.5 cm. Inspection of the first column of Table 2.1 shows that 74.5% of the scores (184 of the 247 scores: 184/247 × 100 = 74.5%) lie within the 174 cm to 183 cm range, which indicates that the distribution approximates a normal distribution (as shown in Figure 2.1c).

BOX 2.5

There are three measures of variability: range, average deviation and standard deviation.

Reliability

The usefulness of any test or measurement is determined by its validity and reliability. Validity refers to the characteristic or attribute that the measurement is supposed to assess. For example, a valid test of muscle strength will assess strength rather than, for example, muscular endurance. Similarly, a valid test of power will assess power rather than, for example, speed. Validity is covered in the next main section. Reliability refers to the consistency of a measurement, i.e. the stability of a score in repeated measurements. For example, if the height and weight of each member of a group of people are carefully measured by trained personnel using properly calibrated equipment and then measured again a few minutes later by the same personnel using the same equipment, it is likely that the second set of measures will be exactly the same as the first set of measures. Consequently, height and weight are very reliable measures when the amount of time between repeated measures is short. In adults, height is a very reliable measure over much longer periods of time as diurnal bodily changes are unlikely to affect height. However, diurnal bodily changes are likely to affect weight. Consequently, weight is a less reliable measure than height in adults. Even so, for most adults, height, weight and other anthropometric measures tend to be very reliable measures over long periods. In contrast, measures of attributes that involve considerable mental and physical effort as in, for example, tests of strength, endurance, speed and power, may vary considerably for individuals and between individuals over quite short periods due to differences in habituation, learning, motivation, fatigue and other diurnal variations. A test or measure cannot be considered valid if is it not reliable. A test or measure can be reliable but not valid.

Correlation

The reliability of a test or measure is determined by correlation, i.e. a statistical technique which expresses the strength of the relationship between two sets of scores. In this context, relationship refers to the level of agreement in the rankings of the scores and in the differences between the ranks in repeated measures; the greater the similarity in the rankings of the scores and in the differences between the ranks, the greater the reliability of the measurement. The strength of the relationship between two sets of scores is expressed numerically by a statistic called the coefficient of correlation. The coefficient of correlation ranges between +1 and −1, where +1 indicates a perfect positive correlation (an increase in score in one set of scores is associated with an equivalent increase in score in the second set of scores), zero indicates no relationship and −1 indicates a perfect negative relationship (an increase in score in one set of scores is associated with an equivalent decrease in score in the second set of scores). The most common method of calculating the coefficient of correlation is the Pearson Product Moment method (after the English statistician Karl Pearson, 1857–1936). The coefficient of correlation obtained by using the Pearson Production Moment method is the statistic referred to as Pearson's *r* (lower case letter *r*). Figure 2.4 shows

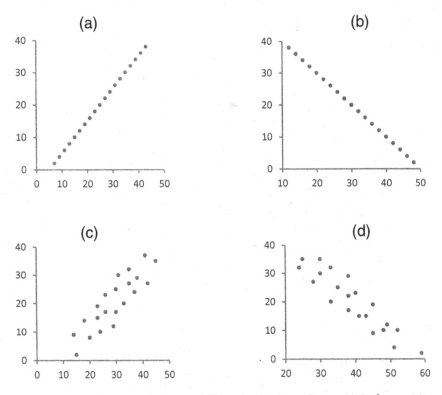

FIGURE 2.4   Scattergrams to illustrate different levels of correlation. (a) Perfect positive correlation, *r* = +1. (b) Perfect negative correlation, *r* = −1. (c) Positive correlation, r = +0.88. (d) Negative correlation, *r* = −0.92.

four scattergrams which illustrate different levels of correlation. In a scattergram, each pair of scores (first score on the x axis, second score on the y axis) is plotted as a single point. Figure 2.4a shows a perfect positive relationship ($r = +1$). Figure 2.4b shows a perfect negative relationship ($r = -1$). Figure 2.4c shows a positive relationship of $r = +0.88$ and Figure 2.4d shows a negative relationship of $r = -0.92$. The two sets of data used to plot Figure 2.4c are shown in Table 2.3 together with the calculation of r.

BOX 2.6

The strength of the relationship between two sets of scores is expressed numerically by a coefficient of correlation which ranges between −1 and +1. The most commonly reported coefficient of correlation is Pearson's r.

TABLE 2.3 Calculation of the Pearson Product Moment coefficient of correlation between two variables, X and Y. The number of scores in each set of scores is 21.

Score	X	x	x^2	Y	y	y^2	xy
1	15	−14.29	204.08	2	−18.57	344.90	265.30
2	14	−15.29	233.65	9	−11.57	133.90	176.88
3	20	−9.29	86.22	8	−12.57	158.04	116.73
4	18	−11.29	127.37	14	−6.57	43.18	74.16
5	24	−5.29	27.94	10	−10.57	111.75	55.88
6	23	−6.29	39.51	19	−1.57	2.47	9.88
7	23	−6.29	39.51	15	−5.57	31.04	35.02
8	29	−0.29	0.08	12	−8.57	73.47	2.45
9	26	−3.29	10.79	23	2.43	5.90	−7.98
10	26	−3.29	10.79	17	−3.57	12.75	11.73
11	30	0.71	0.51	17	−3.57	12.75	−2.55
12	30	0.71	0.51	25	4.43	19.61	3.16
13	33	3.71	13.80	20	−0.57	0.33	−2.12
14	37	7.71	59.51	24	3.43	11.75	26.45
15	31	1.71	2.94	30	9.43	88.90	16.16
16	35	5.71	32.65	27	6.43	41.33	36.73
17	38	8.71	75.94	29	8.43	71.04	73.45
18	32	2.71	7.37	27	6.43	41.32	17.45
19	41	11.71	137.22	37	16.43	269.90	192.45
20	45	15.71	246.94	32	11.43	130.61	179.58
21	45	15.71	246.94	35	14.43	208.18	226.74
			$\sum x^2 = 1604.29$			$\sum y^2 = 1813.14$	$\sum xy = 1507.57$

$$x = X - \overline{X}$$

$$y = Y - \overline{Y}$$

$$r = \frac{\sum xy}{\sqrt{(\sum x^2)(\sum y^2)}} = \frac{1507.57}{\sqrt{(1604.29)(1813.14)}} = \frac{1507.57}{1705.52} = 0.88$$

The most common method of assessing the reliability of a test or measure is to calculate r from two sets of scores obtained by administering the test on two occasions. This type of reliability is referred to as 'test-retest reliability' and the resulting correlation coefficient is referred to as the test's 'reliability coefficient'. In tests and measures of physical fitness, the time between test and retest should allow adequate recovery, but be short enough to prevent the second set of scores being affected by growth and development. Two or three days of rest may be required to ensure adequate recovery from some physiological tests that involve prolonged intense physical effort. However, a few minutes of rest should ensure adequate recovery from tests that are completed fairly quickly, such as single jumps or short sprints.

Standard error of measurement

Table 2.4 shows the test and retest scores for a test of peak instantaneous mechanical power output in a countermovement vertical jump with hands on hips for a group of 26 male rugby players. After a few practice trials (practice jumps) to familiarize themselves with the movement, the players performed two test trials with 5 minutes' rest between the trials. The reliability coefficient for the test was found to be $r = 0.9255$ (the plus sign is usually omitted for positive correlations). Figure 2.5 shows a scattergram of the test (x axis) and retest (y axis) scores. A reliability coefficient of $r = 0.9255$ is considered very high in the classification of Guilford (1950) (see Table 2.5) and would suggest that the test is a reliable test of peak instantaneous power in male rugby players. However, the reliability coefficient of a test does not indicate whether the test is reliable enough for its intended purpose. For example, if the test of peak instantaneous power is to be used to monitor the effects of a power training programme with a group of male rugby players, some estimate of the precision of measurement afforded by the test is required so that changes in peak instantaneous power that occur following training can be properly interpreted as real changes or measurement error. A statistic called the standard error of measurement (*SEM*) of a test provides an estimate of the precision of measurement (Thomas *et al.* 2005). The $SEM = s\sqrt{(1-r)}$, where s is the standard deviation of all of the test scores and retest scores and r is the reliability coefficient. For the

TABLE 2.4 Reliability coefficient (r) and standard error of measurement (SEM) for peak instantaneous power (W) in a countermovement vertical jump with hands on hips for 26 male rugby players

Score	Test 1	Test 2
1	3443	3634
2	3880	3916
3	3927	3686
4	4195	4258
5	4845	4383
6	4292	4436
7	3150	3279
8	4364	4670
9	4215	4087
10	4324	4269
11	2042	4299
12	4177	3950
13	5324	5439
14	3423	3351
15	5216	5421
16	3753	4150
17	5270	5175
18	4021	3994
19	4633	4771
20	4959	4992
21	5003	5172
22	4502	4488
23	4607	4119
24	5560	5775
25	3708	3808
26	5458	5885

$r = 0.9255$ (based on the method shown in Table 2.3).
$s = 683.15 =$ standard deviation of all of the test 1 and test 2 scores.
$SEM = s\sqrt{(1 - r)} = 683.15(0.2729) = 186.43$ W.

peak instantaneous power scores in Table 2.4, $s = 683.15$ W and $r = 0.9255$. Therefore,

$$SEM = 683.15 \times \sqrt{(1 - 0.9255)} = 683.15 \times \sqrt{(0.0745)}$$
$$= 683.15 \times 0.2729 = 186.43 \text{ W}$$

TABLE 2.5 Guilford's classification of the magnitude of the coefficient of correlation (*r*) (Guilford 1950)

Magnitude of r	Degree of relationship
Less than 0.20	Slight, almost negligible
0.20–0.40	Low correlation, relationship definite but small
0.40–0.70	Moderate correlation, substantial relationship
0.70–0.90	High correlation, marked relationship
0.90–1.00	Very high correlation, very dependable relationship

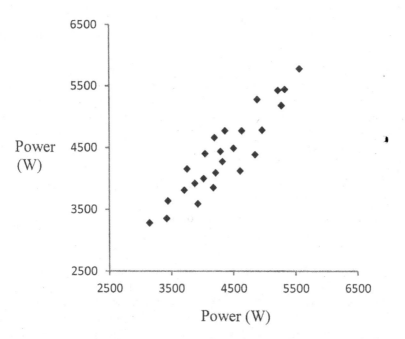

FIGURE 2.5 Scattergram of test-retest scores for peak instantaneous power (W) in a countermovement jump (hands on hips) for 26 male rugby players, 19–24 years of age.

The *SEM* is a standard deviation and in a normal distribution (Figure 2.3), 95% of the scores in the distribution lie within ±1.96σ of the mean. Consequently, the tester can be 95% confident that when the test and retest data were collected the true score of any of the 26 players was within the range of test score ± 1.96 × 186.43 W, i.e. within the range of test score ± 365.40 W. The equation for the *SEM* indicates that the higher the reliability coefficient, the lower the *SEM* and, therefore, the greater the precision of measurement.

Validity

In addition to establishing the reliability and precision of measurement of a test, it is even more important to ensure that the test is valid, i.e. that it measures what it is supposed to measure. For example, if a student took an examination and all or most of the exam questions concerned topics that were not covered in the course, the student could complain that the exam did not measure what it was supposed to measure, i.e. that it was not valid (Safrit and Wood 1995). This is an example of a lack of content validity. There are four main types of validity: content, logical, construct and criterion (Thomas *et al.* 2005).

Content validity refers to the extent that the test measures content that is representative of the knowledge, skill or ability being assessed. For example, the extent that the content of an exam represents the content covered in the course determines the content validity of the exam. Similarly, the extent that the components of a test designed to assess the ability to play soccer reflect actual playing conditions determines the content validity of the test.

Logical validity, also known as face validity, refers to tests which clearly test the ability being tested. For example, measuring the ability to stand on one leg is clearly a test of static balance and measuring the ability to sprint 5 m from a standing start is clearly a test of speed of movement.

Construct validity refers to the extent that a test measures an ability or attitude that cannot be measured directly such as anxiety, intelligence, creativity and general athletic ability (Rampinini *et al.* 2007).

Criterion validity of a test refers to the extent that the results of the test correlate with the results of a criterion test that is known to be valid. There are two main types of criterion validity: predictive and concurrent. Predictive validity refers to the extent that the results of a test predict future criterion behaviour. For example, a test of intelligence might be used to predict scholastic achievement at some future date. Similarly, a soccer skills test might be used to predict soccer playing ability at some future date. Concurrent validity refers to the extent that the results of a test predict current performance in a criterion test. For example, mechanical power output is generally regarded as an important determinant of performance in all sports that require high rates of mechanical work, such as in sprinting, jumping and throwing (Owen *et al.* 2014). Consequently, athletes in many sports are regularly subjected to tests of power output within training programmes. There is general agreement that the most valid test of human mechanical power output is peak instantaneous power output in a countermovement vertical jump (Davies and Rennie 1968). However, administration of this test requires expensive equipment and trained personnel on a one-to-one basis. Consequently, the test is impractical for the majority of athletes. Not surprisingly, many attempts have been made to develop tests that have concurrent validity with the criterion test of Davies and Rennie (1968), but which require little or no equipment and are easy to administer in non-laboratory settings (Duncan *et al.* 2008; Quagliarella *et al.* 2011). These tests are referred to as 'field tests'.

In addition to field tests to assess power output, field tests have been developed to assess other fitness components. For example, the criterion method of measuring a person's per cent body fat involves weighing the subject underwater. This requires special laboratory facilities and trained personnel not normally available to most athletes. Consequently, several field tests based on skinfold measurements have been developed to predict criterion test scores for per cent body fat (Wilmore et al. 2008). Similarly, field tests based on bench stepping and distance run in a certain time have been developed to predict criterion test measures of cardiorespiratory function (McArdle et al. 2010). In Practical Worksheet 19, the concurrent validity of a standing long jump field test is determined with respect to the Davies and Rennie (1968) criterion test of power output.

BOX 2.7

There are four main types of validity: content, logical, construct and criterion.

The correlation between the scores in a field test and the corresponding criterion test scores is referred to as the 'validity coefficient' of the field test with respect to the criterion test. The higher the validity coefficient, the more linear the relationship between the two sets of scores, i.e. the more the scattergram approximates a straight line. In a perfect positive relationship (Figure 2.4a) and a perfect negative relationship (Figure 2.4b), all of the points in the corresponding scattergram lie on the same straight line. Consequently, each score on one variable is associated with a unique score on the other variable, i.e. a score on one variable can be used to predict a score on the other variable with 100% accuracy. For example, the first three columns of Table 2.6 show the time (t), speed (v) and distance (d_1) data corresponding to a man who starts from rest and walks at a constant speed of $v = 2$ m/s along a straight, level track for a period of 10 s. As $d_1 = v \cdot t$ and v is constant, there is a perfect positive correlation between distance and time. Consequently, the scattergram of distance-time data is a straight line as shown in Figure 2.6a. After walking for 10 s at 2 m/s the man will have travelled a distance of 20 m (2 m/s × 10 s = 20 m). If, on another occasion, the man walks on the same straight, level track at a constant speed of 2 m/s for 10 s from a start point that was 12 m forward of the original start point, his distance from the original start point at any particular point in time would be given by $d_2 = v \cdot t + 12$. Figure 2.6b shows the corresponding scattergram and the straight line joining the points. After walking for 10 s the man would be 32 m from the original start point:

$$d_2 = v \cdot t + 12 = (2 \text{ m/s} \times 10 \text{ s}) + 12 \text{ m} = 20 \text{ m} + 12 \text{ m} = 32 \text{ m}$$

TABLE 2.6 Distance-time data for a man who starts from rest and walks along a straight, level track at a constant speed of 2 m/s for 10 s. d_1, starting from a reference point where distance is zero; d_2, starting from a point that is 12 m forward of the reference point.

Time (t) (s)	Speed (v) (m/s)	Distance (d_1) (m)	Distance (d_2) (m)
0	2	0	12
1	2	2	14
2	2	4	16
3	2	6	18
4	2	8	20
5	2	10	22
6	2	12	24
7	2	14	26
8	2	16	28
9	2	18	30
10	2	20	32

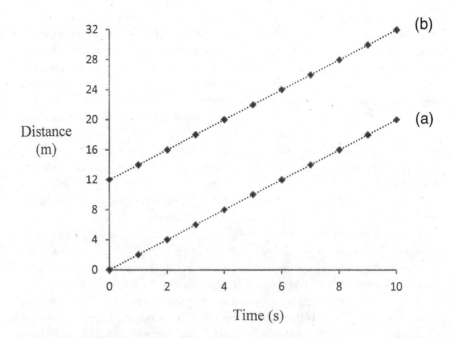

FIGURE 2.6 Distance-time graphs of a man who starts from rest and walks along a straight, level track at a constant speed of 2 m/s for 10 s. (a) Starting from a reference point where distance is zero. (b) Starting from a point that is 12 m forward of the reference point.

The equation of the line, $d_2 = v \cdot t + 12$, is a specific example of the general equation for a straight line relationship between two variables. The general equation is referred to as a linear function and is expressed as follows:

$$Y = a \cdot X + b$$

where

$Y =$ the value that is to be calculated by the equation. Y is usually referred to as the dependent variable because its value depends upon the value of X.

$X =$ the value that is known and is used to calculate Y. X is usually referred to as the independent variable.

$a =$ a multiplicative constant that defines the rate at which Y changes as X changes, i.e. the gradient of the line.

$b =$ an additive constant that gives a reference point from which changes in Y are measured. b is the value of Y when $X = 0$, i.e. the value of Y at the point where the line crosses (or intercepts) the Y axis. b is usually referred to as the intercept.

In the distance-time graph in Figure 2.6a, $b = 0$. Consequently the linear function shown in Figure 2.6a is $Y = 2X$, where Y represents distance in metres and X represents time in seconds; when $X = 0$, $Y = 0$. In the distance-time graph in Figure 2.6b, $b = 12$. Consequently the linear function shown in Figure 2.6b is $Y = 2X + 12$. In this case, when $X = 0$, $Y = 12$ m.

Regression

Unlike the perfect relationship ($r = 1$) between distance and time shown in Figure 2.6, validity coefficients between field and criterion test measures concerning physical fitness, anthropometric and behavioural variables are usually less than perfect. For example, the second and third columns of Table 2.7 show the vertical jump height scores (field test) and mechanical power output in a vertical jump scores (criterion test) for 25 young, physically active men. The corresponding scattergram (Figure 2.7) shows a clear trend for power to increase as jump height increases. This trend is reflected in the validity coefficient between the field and criterion test scores of $r = 0.7694$. The scattergram indicates that any particular jump height score is associated with a range of power scores. For example, a jump height of 0.45 m is associated with power scores in the approximate range of 3500 W to 4500 W. Consequently, based on this data, prediction of power from jump height would be subject to a margin of error. To define the margin of error, it is necessary to derive the linear function (equation of a straight line) that best represents the trend shown in the scattergram. In the absence of any other statistics, the best estimate of power for any particular jump height score would be the mean power score, i.e. 3955.82 W. This is shown as a dotted horizontal line in Figure 2.8 where $Y = 3955.82$ W.

If the relationship between the power scores and the jump height scores was perfectly linear, an increase in one standard deviation in jump height would be accompanied by an increase in one standard deviation in power. In this case, the gradient of the linear function would be equal to the standard deviation of the power scores divided by the standard deviation of the jump height scores and the linear function between power and jump height would be as follows:

$$Y = \overline{Y} + \frac{\sigma_Y}{\sigma_X}(X - \overline{X})$$

Eq. 2.1

where

Y = predicted power score
X = the jump score used to predict Y
$\overline{X}$ = the mean of the jump height scores = 0.439 m
$\overline{Y}$ = the mean of the power scores = 3955.82 W
σ_X = the standard deviation of the jump height scores = 0.053 m
σ_Y = the standard deviation of the power scores = 487.987 W

Consequently,

$$Y = 3955.82 + \frac{487.987}{0.053}(X - 0.439)$$
$$Y = 3955.82 + 9207.302\,(X - 0.439)$$
$$Y = 3955.82 + 9207.302X - 4042$$
$$Y = 9207.302X - 86.18$$

Eq. 2.2

The line corresponding to equation 2.2 is shown as the dotted oblique line in Figure 2.8. The scatter of the data points around this line is, in general, much lower than the scatter of the data points around the line $Y = 3955.82$ W, i.e. in general, the data points are much closer to the line $Y = 9207.302 - 86.18$ than they are to the line $Y = 3955.82$ W. Scatter is measured as the sum of the squared deviations of the actual Y scores from the corresponding predicted Y scores; the lower the sum of the squared deviations, the more accurate the predicted criterion test scores across the full range of possible field test scores. For each particular set of field test–criterion test data points, there is a linear function for which the sum of squared deviations is least. This line, which is called the least squares linear best fit, provides the most accurate predictions across the full range of possible field test scores. The linear function of the least squares linear best fit can be derived by adjusting the gradient of equation 2.1 by applying the validity coefficient as follows:

$$Y' = \overline{Y} + r\frac{(\sigma_Y)}{\sigma_X}(X - \overline{X})$$

Eq. 2.3

where
Y' = Y prime = predicted score from a non-perfect linear relationship
r = validity coefficient = 0.7694

Consequently,

$$Y' = 3955.82 + 0.7694 \frac{(487.987)}{0.053}(X - 0.439)$$
$$Y' = 3955.82 + 0.7694(9207.302)(X - 0.439)$$
$$Y' = 3955.82 + 7084.098X - 3109.919$$
$$Y' = 7084.098X + 845.9 \qquad\qquad \text{Eq. 2.4}$$

The line corresponding to equation 2.4 is shown as the full oblique line in Figure 2.8. When the validity coefficient is less than 1.0, the gradient of the least squares linear best fit (Equation 2.4) is always depressed or regressed relative to that of the perfect linear function (Equation 2.2). For this reason, equation 2.4 is called a regression equation. When prediction is based on a single field variable, as in equation 2.4, the process is referred to as simple regression. When prediction is based on two or more field variables, the process is referred to as multiple regression. Multiple regression is beyond the scope of this book.

TABLE 2.7 Determination of the regression line equation and standard error of the estimate (*SEE*) for predicting peak instantaneous power in a countermovement jump with hands on hips (criterion test) from height jumped in a countermovement jump with hands on hips (field test). The subjects were twenty-five, young, physically active men.

Subject	Jump height (X) (m)	Power (Y) (W)	Predicted Power (Y') (W)	$d = Y - Y'$ (W)	d^2 (W^2)
1	0.352	3373.4	3339.50	33.90	1149.04
2	0.359	3126.1	3389.09	−262.99	69164.36
3	0.391	3276.9	3615.78	−338.88	114841.22
4	0.432	3439.9	3906.23	−466.33	217463.98
5	0.462	3655.5	4118.75	−463.25	214603.60
6	0.468	4216.9	4161.26	55.64	3096.05
7	0.504	4073.8	4416.28	−342.48	117296.24
8	0.435	4027.2	3927.48	99.71	9943.55
9	0.491	4731.5	4324.19	407.31	165899.71
10	0.395	3890.4	3644.12	246.28	60654.47
11	0.362	3549.6	3410.34	139.26	19392.38
12	0.442	3647.5	3977.07	−329.57	198617.25
13	0.414	4150.9	3778.72	372.18	138520.50
14	0.446	4378.9	4005.41	373.49	139496.49
15	0.476	4570.9	4217.93	352.97	124587.36
16	0.515	4315.2	4494.21	−179.01	32044.74
17	0.475	3845.9	4210.84	−364.95	133185.98
18	0.535	4981.6	4635.89	345.71	119513.72

(Continued)

TABLE 2.7 (Continued)

Subject	Jump height (X) (m)	Power (Y) (W)	Predicted Power (Y') (W)	$d = Y - Y'$ (W)	d^2 (W²)
19	0.462	3655.5	4118.75	−463.25	214603.60
20	0.401	3464.5	3686.62	−222.12	49338.76
21	0.384	3588.4	3566.19	22.21	493.12
22	0.435	4027.2	3927.48	99.72	9943.55
23	0.521	4651.6	4536.71	114.88	13198.55
24	0.372	3890.4	3481.18	409.21	167457.36
25	0.455	4365.8	4069.16	296.64	87992.57

$$\overline{X} = 0.439 \qquad \overline{Y} = 3955.82 \qquad\qquad \sum d^2 = 2332498.20$$

$$\sigma_X = 0.053 \qquad \sigma_Y = 487.987$$

$$r = 0.7694$$

$$Y' = \overline{Y} + r\frac{(\sigma_Y)}{\sigma_X}(X - \overline{X}) = 7084.098X + 845.9$$

$$SEE = \sqrt{\frac{\sum d^2}{N}} = \sqrt{\frac{2332498.20}{25}} = \sqrt{93299.93} = 305.45 \, \text{W}$$

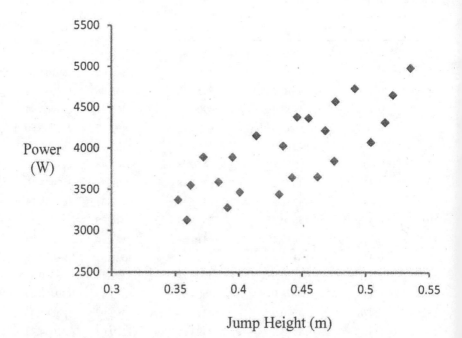

FIGURE 2.7 Scattergram of scores for vertical jump height (field test) and peak instantaneous power in a vertical jump (criterion test) for 25 physically active young men. $r = 0.7694$.

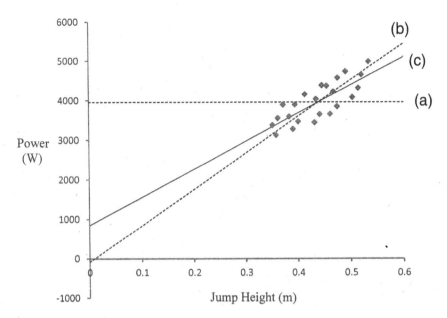

FIGURE 2.8 Simple regression. (a) The line $Y = 3955.82$. (b) The linear function $Y = 9207.302X - 86.18$ that would exist between power and jump height if the scores were perfectly related. (c) The linear function of the regression line between power and jump height, $Y = 7084.098X + 845.9$.

Standard error of the estimate

Just as the standard error of measurement provides an estimate of the precision of measurement of a test, a statistic called the standard error of the estimate (*SEE*) provides an estimate of the precision of prediction of a regression equation. The *SEE* is the standard deviation of the distribution of deviations of the actual Y scores from the corresponding predicted Y scores.

$$SEE = \sqrt{\frac{\sum d^2}{N}}$$

where
$\sum d^2$ = the sum of the squared deviations, i.e. the sum of $(Y - Y')^2$
N = the number of scores

The fourth column of Table 2.7 shows the predicted power scores based on equation 2.4. The fifth column of Table 2.7 shows the deviations of the predicted power scores from the actual power scores. The deviations are shown graphically in Figure 2.9. The sixth column of Table 2.7 shows the squares of the deviations together with the sum of the squared deviations.

$$SEE = \sqrt{\frac{\sum d^2}{N}} = \sqrt{\frac{2332498.2}{25}} = \sqrt{93299.93} = 305.45 \text{ W}$$

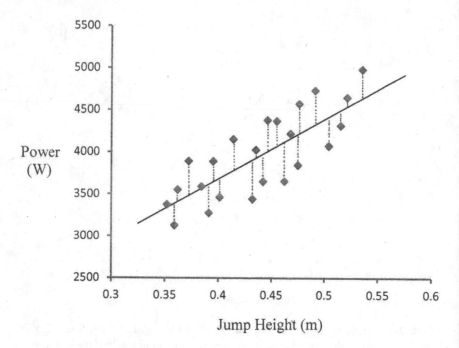

FIGURE 2.9 The deviations of the actual power scores from the corresponding predicted power scores are represented by the vertical distances between the actual power scores and the regression line. The regression line is the line through the scattergram for which the sum of the squares of the deviations is least.

In a normal distribution (Figure 2.3), 95% of the scores in the distribution lie within $\pm 1.96\sigma$ of the mean. Consequently, the tester can be 95% confident that when the field test and criterion test data were collected, the true criterion power score of any of the 25 participants was within the range of predicted power score $\pm 1.96 \times 305.45$ W, i.e. within the range of predicted power score ± 598.68 W.

BOX 2.8

Together with the standard error of the estimate, the regression line provides the most accurate estimate of a criterion test score based on a field test score.

References

Davies, C. T. M. and Rennie, R. (1968) 'Human power output', *Nature* 217:770–771.

Duncan, M. J., Lyons, M. and Nevill, A. M. (2008) 'Evaluation of peak power prediction equations in male basketball players', *Journal of Strength and Conditioning Research* 22(4):1379–1381.

Guilford, J. P. (1950) *Fundamental statistics in psychology and education*, 2nd edn. New York: McGraw-Hill Book.

McArdle, W. D., Katch, F. L. and Katch, V. L. (2010) *Exercise physiology: Energy, nutrition, and human performance*, 7th edn. Philadelphia: Lippincott Williams & Wilkins.

Owen, N., Watkins, J., Kilduff, L., Bevan, H. R. and Bennett, M. (2014) 'Development of a criterion method to determine peak mechanical power output in a countermovement jump', *Journal of Strength and Conditioning Research* 28(6):1552–1558.

Quagliarella, L., Sasanelli, N., Belgiovine, G., Moretti, L. and Moretti, B. (2011) 'Power output estimation in vertical jump performed by young male soccer players', *Journal of Strength and Conditioning Research* 25(6):1638–1646.

Rampinini, E., Bishop, D., Marcora, S., Ferrari-Bravo, D., Sassi, R. and Impellizzeri, F. M. (2007) 'Validity of simple field tests as indication of match-related physical performance in top-level professional soccer players', *International Journal of Sports Medicine* 28(2):228–235.

Safrit, M. J. and Wood, T. M. (1995) *Introduction to measurement in physical education and exercise science*, 3rd edn. St Louis, MO: Mosby-Year Book.

Spiegel, M. R., Schiller, J. J. and Srinavasan, R. A. (2013) *Probability and statistics*, 4th edn. McGraw-Hill: New York.

Stevens, S. S. (1946) 'On the theory of scales of measurement', *Science* 103(2684):677–680.

Thomas, J. R., Nelson, J. K. and Silverman, S. J. (2005) *Research methods in physical activity*, 5th edn. Champaign, IL: Human Kinetics.

Weather Online. Available: www.weatheronline.co.uk/

Wilmore, J. H., Costill, D. L. and Kenney, W. L. (2008) *Physiology of sport and exercise*, 4th edn. Champaign, IL: Human Kinetics.

3

LINEAR KINEMATICS

Kinematics is the branch of dynamics that describes the movement of bodies in relation to space and time. A kinematic analysis describes the movement of a body in terms of distance (change in position), speed (rate of change of position) and acceleration (variability in the rate of change of position). As there are two forms of motion, linear and angular, a kinematic analysis may involve linear kinematics and/ or angular kinematics. The purpose of this chapter is to introduce the fundamental mechanical concepts underlying linear kinematic analysis, in particular, linear distance, linear speed and linear acceleration. These variables are usually referred to simply as distance, speed and acceleration. Practical Worksheets 1 and 2 should be completed after reading the chapter.

Objectives

After reading this chapter, you should be able to do the following:

1 Describe the Newtonian frame of reference.
2 Describe the anatomical frame of reference.
3 Differentiate distance, speed and acceleration.
4 Describe the factors to consider when setting the frame rate, shutter speed and aperture of a video camera for recording and analyzing human movement.
5 Describe the relationship between cycle length, cycle rate and speed of movement in cyclic human locomotion.
6 Describe the effect of an increase in speed on stride length and stride rate in human walking and running.

Space and Newtonian frame of reference

In mechanics, position and change in position of a body in space is defined in relation to a Newtonian frame of reference (after Isaac Newton, 1642–1727). In a Newtonian frame of reference, the three dimensions of space (forward-backward, side-to-side, up-down) are represented by three orthogonal axes (three lines at right angles to each other) that intersect at a point called the origin (Figure 3.1). The three axes are usually referred to as X (forward-backward), Y (vertical) and Z (side-to-side) axes. Each axis has a positive and a negative sense with respect to the origin. Forward is positive and backward is negative on the X axis, upward is positive and downward is negative on the Y axis. Positive Z may be to the left or to the right giving rise to the so-called left-handed and right-handed axis systems, respectively. In the right-handed axis system, as shown in Figure 3.1, positive Z is to the right. If the thumb and first two fingers of the right hand are held at right angles to each other with the index finger pointing forward (positive X) and the second finger pointing upward (positive Y), then the thumb will point to the right (positive Z); hence the name right-handed axis system. The right-handed axis system is the most widely used system. The right-handed axis system will be used in this book.

In a Newtonian frame of reference, the position of a point is defined by the coordinates of the point with respect to the three axes, i.e. the lengths x, y and

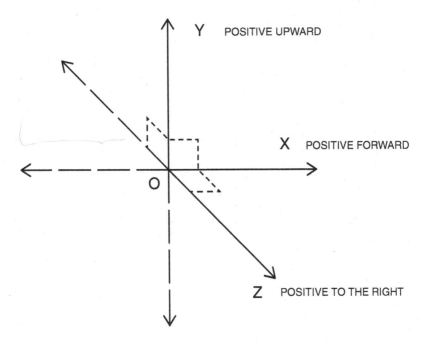

FIGURE 3.1   The right-handed axis system. O = origin.

z along the X, Y and Z axes that correspond to the point. The coordinates of a point are listed in the order x, y and z. For example, the coordinates of the points A, B and C in Figure 3.2 are $(0, 0, 2)$, $(0, 3, 2)$ and $(4, 3, 2)$, respectively. The three axes give rise to three orthogonal planes, XY, YZ and XZ (Figure 3.3). Analysis of human movement may be concerned with movement along an axis (such as the movement of the body as a whole along the X axis in a 100 m sprint), in a plane (such as the movement of the head in the XY plane in a 100 m sprint) or in three-dimensional space.

BOX 3.1

In a Newtonian frame of reference, the three dimensions of space are represented by three orthogonal axes that intersect at a point called the origin.

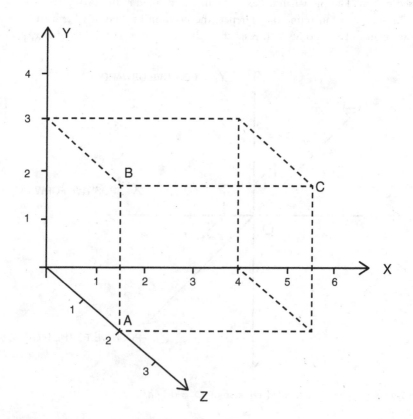

FIGURE 3.2   Coordinates of points in the right–handed axis system. A(0, 0, 2), B(0, 3, 2), C(4, 3, 2).

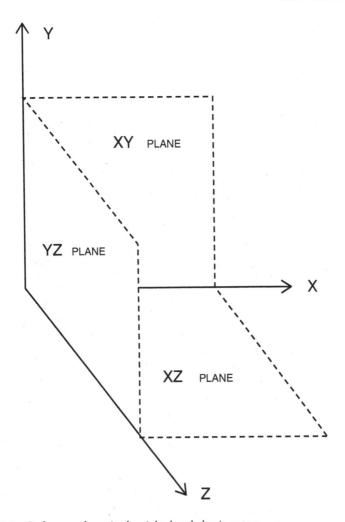

FIGURE 3.3 Reference planes in the right-handed axis system.

Anatomical frame of reference

To describe the spatial orientation of a particular part of the body in relation to another, it is necessary to use standard terminology with reference to a standard body posture. The generally accepted convention, referred to as the anatomical, relative or cardinal frame of reference, utilizes the right-handed Newtonian frame of reference axis system in relation to a standard body posture called the anatomical position. In the anatomical position, the body is upright with the arms by the sides and palms of the hands facing forward. The anatomical frame of reference (Figure 3.4) describes three principal planes (median, coronal, transverse) and three principal axes (anteroposterior, vertical, mediolateral).

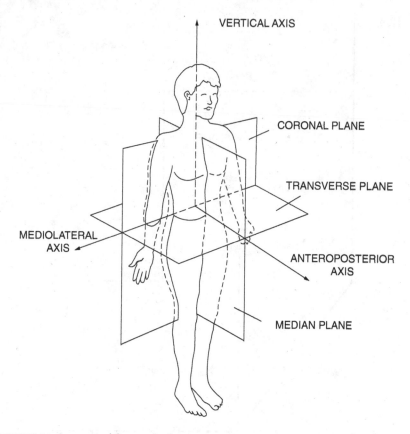

VERTICAL AXIS

CORONAL PLANE

TRANSVERSE PLANE

MEDIOLATERAL
AXIS

ANTEROPOSTERIOR
AXIS

MEDIAN PLANE

FIGURE 3.4 Anatomical frame of reference.

The median plane is a vertical plane that divides the body down the middle into more-or-less symmetrical left and right portions. The median plane is also frequently referred to as the sagittal plane; the terms sagittal, paramedian and para-sagittal (para = beside or against) are also sometimes used to refer to any plane parallel to the median plane. In this book the term sagittal is used to refer to any plane parallel to the median plane. The mediolateral axis is perpendicular to the median plane. The terms lateral and medial are used to describe the position of structures with respect to the mediolateral axis. Lateral means further away from the median plane and medial means closer to the median plane. For example, in the anatomical position, the fingers of each hand are medial to the thumbs (and the thumbs are lateral to the fingers). Lateral and medial are also used to describe the direction of forces acting in the body in a mediolateral direction. For example, a laterally directed force acting on the right foot tends to move the body to the right and a medially directed force acting on the right foot tends to move the body to the left.

The coronal plane (or frontal plane) is a vertical plane perpendicular to the median plane that divides the body into anterior and posterior portions. The anteroposterior axis is perpendicular to the coronal plane. The terms anterior (in front of) and posterior (behind) are used to describe the position of structures with respect to the anteroposterior axis. For example, in the anatomical position, the toes of each foot are anterior to the heels (and the heels are posterior to the toes). The terms ventral and dorsal are synonymous with anterior and posterior, respectively.

The transverse plane is a horizontal plane, perpendicular to both the median and coronal planes, which divides the body into upper and lower portions. The vertical axis is perpendicular to the transverse plane. The terms superior (above) and inferior (below) are used to describe the position of structures with respect to the vertical axis. For example, in the anatomical position, the head is superior to the shoulders (and the shoulders inferior to the head).

Some spatial terms apply to some segments, but not to others. For example, the terms proximal and distal are normally only used in reference to the limb segments (upper arm, forearm, hand, thigh, shank, foot). Superior parts or features of the segments (with respect to the anatomical position) are referred to as proximal, whereas inferior parts or features are referred to as distal. For example, the proximal end of the right upper arm articulates with the trunk to form the right shoulder joint. Similarly, the distal end of the right upper arm articulates with the proximal end of the right forearm to form the right elbow joint.

BOX 3.2

The anatomical frame of reference describes three principal planes (median, coronal, transverse) and three principal axes (anteroposterior, vertical, mediolateral).

Distance and speed

The length of the line between two points in three-dimensional space is referred to as the distance between the points. Similarly, the length of the path followed by a body as it moves from one position to another in three-dimensional space is referred to as the distance travelled by the body. Speed is defined as rate of change of position, i.e. the distance travelled in moving from one position to another divided by the length of time taken to change position. For example, if a cross country runner completes the race distance of 10.7 km (6.65 miles) in 37 min 2.5 s, his average speed during the run is given by:

$$\text{average speed} = \frac{\text{distance}}{\text{time}}$$

$$37 \text{ min } 2.5 \text{ s} = 2222.5 \text{ s} = 0.6174 \text{ hr}$$

$$\text{i.e. average speed} = \frac{10.7 \text{ km}}{0.6174 \text{ hr}} = 17.33 \text{ km/h} (10.77 \text{mph})$$

When the speed of an object is constant over a certain period of time, the object is said to move with uniform speed. When the speed of an object varies over a certain period of time, the object is said to move with non–uniform speed.

Analysis of the speed of human movement is important in all sports where time is the determinant of performance, such as track athletics and swimming. Knowledge of the average speed and the variation in speed of an athlete during a race can be helpful in the training of the athlete. For example, an endurance athlete aiming to run 5000 m in 13 min would need to achieve an average speed of 6.41 m/s, i.e.

$$\text{average speed} = \frac{5000\text{m}}{780\text{s}} = 6.41\text{m/s}$$

However, average lap time would probably be more useful to the athlete and coach. Since there are 12.5 laps (1 lap = 400 m) in a 5000 m race, an average speed of 6.41 m/s corresponds to an average lap time of 62.4 s/lap, i.e.

average lap time = 780 s / 12.5 laps = 62.4 s/lap

BOX 3.3

Analysis of the speed of human movement is important in all sports where time is the determinant of performance, such as track athletics and swimming.

Average speed in a marathon race

Table 3.1 shows the 5 km split times and average speeds in the 5 km splits of the winner of the 2005 women's London marathon, Paula Radcliffe (UK). Her average speed over the whole race was 5.11 m/s (11.43 mph), i.e.

$$\text{distance} = 26 \text{ miles } 385 \text{ yd} = 42.195 \text{ km}$$
$$\text{time} = 2 \text{ h } 17 \text{ min } 42 \text{ s} = 8262 \text{ s}$$
$$\text{average speed} = \frac{42195\text{m}}{8262\text{s}} = 5.11\text{m/s}$$

The distance-time data (columns 1 and 2 of Table 3.1) are plotted in the distance-time graph in Figure 3.5. The graph is close to linear, indicating little variation in speed throughout the race. This is reflected in the 5 km split times which range between 15 min 47 s and 16 min 40 s and the corresponding average speed in the 5 km splits which ranges between 5.00 m/s and 5.28 m/s. The average speed over the final 2.195 km of the race was 5.03 m/s. The average speed-time data are plotted in the average speed-time graph in Figure 3.5. As the speed data are average speeds, each data point is plotted at the mid-point of the corresponding time interval.

TABLE 3.1 Race time, time after each 5 km, 5 km split times and average speed in the 5 km splits of the winner of the 2005 women's London marathon

Distance (km)	Time (min:s)	5 km split time* (min:s)	Average speed in each 5 km split* (m/s)
5	15:47	15:47	5.28
10	32:17	16:30	5.05
15	48:34	16:17	5.12
20	64:55	16:21	5.10
25	81:03	16:08	5.17
30	97:27	16:24	5.08
35	114:07	16:40	5.00
40	130:26	16:19	5.11
42.195	137:42	7:16	5.03

*The time for the final 2.195 km of the race was 7 min 16 s resulting in an average speed of 5.03 m/s

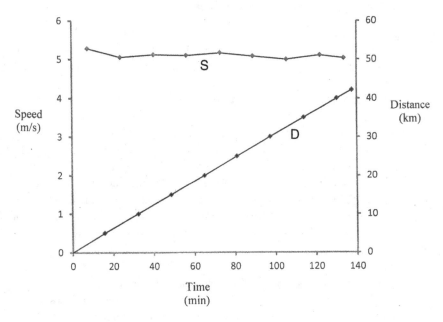

FIGURE 3.5 Distance-time graph (D) and average speed-time graph (S) of the winner of the 2005 women's London marathon. See data in Table 3.1.

Linear kinematic analysis of a 100 m sprint

Whereas an analysis of performance based on average speed is likely to be useful to athlete and coach in middle and long-distance running events, average speed is of limited value in the short sprints of 100 m and 200 m. In these events, the aim of the sprinter is to achieve maximum speed as soon as possible and then maintain it to the end of the race. Consequently, analysis of the variation in speed during the race rather than average speed is likely to provide the most useful performance indicators. These include:

- Time taken to achieve maximum speed.
- Maximum speed.
- Length of time that maximum speed is maintained.
- Difference between maximum speed and speed at the finish.

To produce a speed-time graph, it is first of all necessary to obtain distance-time data. The most frequently used method of recording sprint performance for the purpose of obtaining distance-time data is video.

Video recordings for movement analysis

A video recording consists of a series of discrete images of the subject, each separated by a fixed time interval. The time interval between images is determined by the frame rate setting of the camera, i.e. the number of images (frames) recorded per second. In the SI system of units, frequency (the rate at which a periodic event or cycle of events occurs) is measured in hertz (Hz), i.e. the number of times that the event occurs per second (1 Hz = 1/s). The minimum frame rate available on most standard digital video cameras is 25 Hz. The human eye cannot detect discrete changes in the environment that occur more frequently than approximately 15 Hz. Consequently, to the human eye, a video playing at 25 Hz appears to be continuous rather than a series of discrete images. Whereas the frame rate of a digital video camera may be 25 Hz, the way that the images are stored by the camera allows the user to view discrete images at twice the frame rate, i.e. 50 Hz. Many analyses of human movement are based on measurements taken from sequences of discrete images in video recordings.

The type of analysis that can be carried out will depend upon the frame rate (which will determine the number of discrete images of the action under consideration) and the exposure (which will determine the sharpness and brightness of the images). The required frame rate of a recording will be determined by the duration of the action under consideration. For example, whereas 25 Hz is adequate for most types of human locomotion, such as walking and running (Winter 1990), a much higher frame rate is normally needed to record high speed or short-duration events, such as impacts, adequately. For example, the contact time between clubhead and ball during a golf drive is approximately 0.0005 s, i.e. half a millisecond (0.5 ms) or one two-thousandth of a second (Daish 1972). A frame rate in the region of 10 000 Hz would provide only 5 images of this type of impact:

Number of images = frame rate × contact time
= 10 000 Hz (images/s) × 0.0005 s
= 5 images.

The contact time between a tennis racket and ball during impact is approximately 0.005 s i.e. 5 ms or one two-hundredth of a second (Daish 1972). A frame rate of 2000 Hz would provide approximately 10 images of this type of impact:

Number of images = frame rate × contact time
= 2000 Hz (images/s) × 0.005 s
= 10 images

Exposure determines the sharpness (of contours and particular reference points) and brightness of the images. Sharpness is determined by the shutter speed setting of the camera, i.e. the length of time that the image sensor of the camera is exposed to the image. The faster the shutter speed, the sharper the image. A shutter speed of 0.002 s (one five-hundredth of a second) is usually adequate to capture sharp images in fast human movement. However, the faster the shutter speed, the shorter the duration of the exposure. This has to be balanced with the aperture setting of the camera (referred to as the f-stop) which determines the amount of light entering the camera during the exposure to ensure that the images are not too light or too dark.

BOX 3.4

Many analyses of human movement are based on measurements taken from sequences of discrete images in video recordings. The type of analysis that can be carried out will depend upon the frame rate and the exposure.

Distance-time and speed-time data from video analysis

Video was used to record the performance of a 19-year-old male junior international sprinter as he sprinted 100 m with maximum effort on a straight level track (frame rate = 25 Hz; shutter speed = 0.002 s; aperture = f8). Figure 3.6 shows the layout of the camera and track. The camera was placed close to the centre of the infield area, in line with the 50 m mark on the track.

Prior to videotaping the sprint, the inside lane, i.e. the lane nearest to the camera, was marked at 10 m intervals from the start line. The sprinter was then asked to

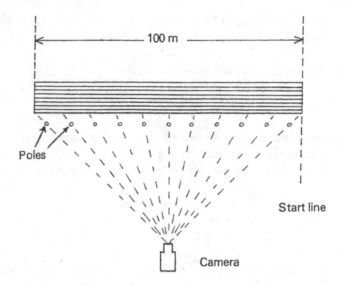

FIGURE 3.6 Layout of the video camera, track and citing poles for recording a 100 m sprint for the purpose of obtaining distance time data.

stand at the 10 m mark while a white wooden pole was placed in the infield area approximately 1 m away from the track on a line between the camera lens and the sprinter. This procedure was repeated at each of the other nine 10 m marks, the last one being the finish line. The sprinter was then videotaped as he ran 100 m flat out under normal race start conditions. By viewing the video frame by frame (50 Hz) from the start of the run, the time taken by the sprinter to run the first 10 m, the first 20 m, the first 30 m etc. up to 100 m was estimated by counting the frames and multiplying the number of frames by the frame rate, i.e. 0.02 s (1/50th of a second). The results are presented in the second column of Table 3.2. Column 3 of Table 3.2 shows the time for each successive 10 m of the sprint. Based on this data, the average speed of the sprinter in each successive 10 m is shown in column 4 of Table 3.2. For example,

$$\text{average speed over the first } 10\,\text{m} = \frac{10\,\text{m}}{1.92\,\text{s}} = 5.21\,\text{m/s}$$

Elite performance in the 100 m sprint is characterized by a rapid increase in speed just after the start followed by a more gradual increase in speed up to maximum speed, which is then maintained till the end of the race (Wagner 1998, Murase *et al.* 1976). The average speed-time data in column 4 of Table 3.2 does not indicate a smooth change in speed; indeed the data indicate marked fluctuations in speed during the last 60 m, involving two phases of increasing speed alternating with three phases of decreasing speed. This almost certainly reflects error in the distance-time data from which the average speed-time data was obtained. Timing errors could be

TABLE 3.2 Cumulative distance, cumulative time, time for each successive 10 m and average speed during each successive 10 m in a 100 m sprint by a male junior international athlete

Distance (m)	Cumulative time (s)	Time for 10 m (s)	Average speed for 10 m (m/s)
10	1.92	1.92	5.21
20	3.10	1.18	8.47
30	4.16	1.06	9.43
40	5.06	0.90	11.11
50	6.08	1.02	9.80
60	7.00	0.92	10.87
70	8.02	1.02	9.80
80	9.04	1.02	9.80
90	10.02	0.98	10.20
100	11.12	1.10	9.09

related to the variation in body position of the sprinter at each 10 m marker and the restriction of the frame rate which both create difficulties in trying to locate the same point on the body, such as the pelvic region, at each marker post. More accurate distance-time data can be obtained from a 'line of best fit' distance-time graph. The line of best fit is a line drawn through the distance-time data that more accurately reflects the normal changes in speed during a 100 m sprint, i.e. a progressive smooth change in speed (absence of marked fluctuations in speed) involving an increase in speed up to maximum speed followed by maintenance of maximum speed or slight decrease in speed toward the end of the race. Figure 3.7 shows the distance-time data (columns 1 and 2 of Table 3.2) and the corresponding line of best fit distance-time graph. Some of the distance-time data points lie on the line of best fit graph, but others do not. Very small errors in distance-time data will result in much larger errors in speed-time data derived from them.

To obtain more accurate distance-time data from the line of best fit distance-time graph, parallel lines, perpendicular to the time axis, are drawn at one-second intervals to intersect the line of best fit distance-time curve. Parallel lines, perpendicular to the distance axis, are then drawn from the points of intersection of the one-second lines with the line of best fit distance-time curve to intersect the distance axis (Figure 3.8). These lines indicate the cumulative distance after successive intervals of one second (column 2 of Table 3.3). The distance covered in each one-second interval (column 3 of Table 3.3) and, therefore, the average speed in each one-second interval (column 4 of Table 3.3) can then be calculated. Unlike the average speed-time data obtained directly from the original distance-time data (column 4 of Table 3.2), the average speed-time data obtained from the line of best fit distance-time graph (column 4 of Table 3.3) indicate that the speed of the sprinter

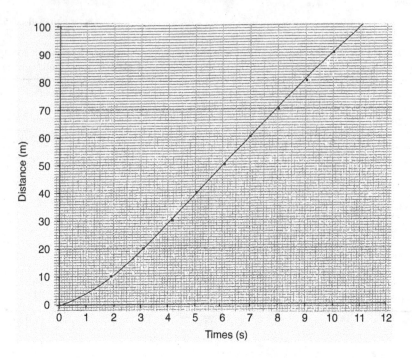

FIGURE 3.7 Distance–time data and the corresponding line of best fit distance–time graph.

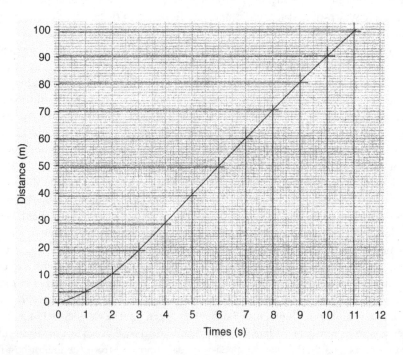

FIGURE 3.8 Method of determination of distance–time data from the line of best fit distance–time graph.

TABLE 3.3 Cumulative time, cumulative distance, distance covered in each 1 s interval and average speed in each 1 s interval in a 100 m sprint by a male junior international athlete

Time (s)	Cumulative distance (m)	Distance travelled in each second (m)	Average speed in each second (m/s)
1	3.8	3.8	3.8
2	10.3	6.5	6.5
3	18.9	8.6	8.6
4	28.7	9.8	9.8
5	39.0	10.3	10.3
6	49.5	10.5	10.5
7	60.0	10.5	10.5
8	70.4	10.4	10.4
9	80.6	10.2	10.2
10	90.3	9.7	9.7
11	99.2	8.9	8.9

increased fairly smoothly to a maximum value and then gradually decreased. This is typical of maximal effort sprinting over 100 m.

The average speed-time data obtained from the line of best fit distance-time graph (column 4 of Table 3.3) are plotted in Figure 3.9 together with the line of best fit average speed-time graph. As the average speed-time data represent average speeds, each data point is plotted at the mid-point of the corresponding time interval. The line of best fit distance-time graph is also shown in Figure 3.9. Note the shallow S shape of the distance-time graph (look along the graph at eye level). The dotted vertical line distinguishes the two main phases of the run. The first phase is characterized by a progressive increase in the slope of the distance-time graph, corresponding to a progressive increase in speed to maximum speed of about 10.5 m/s (0 s–6.4 s, 0 m–53 m). The second phase is characterized by a progressive decrease in the slope of the distance-time graph, corresponding to a steady decrease in speed to a finishing speed of approximately 8.2 m/s (6.4 s–11.12 s, 53 m–100 m). The average speed-time data in column 4 of Table 3.3 indicate a brief period of constant maximum speed (5.5 s–6.5 s), but this is not evident in the line of best fit average speed-time graph.

To show that the distance-time and speed-time graphs in Figure 3.9 were truly representative of the sprinter's performance, it would be necessary to repeat the process on a number of trials, not just the one described here. However, assuming that the graphs in Figure 3.9 were representative, it would be useful to compare the speed-time graph with that of a senior elite sprinter in order to highlight areas for improvement. Figure 3.10 shows the junior international sprinter's speed-time

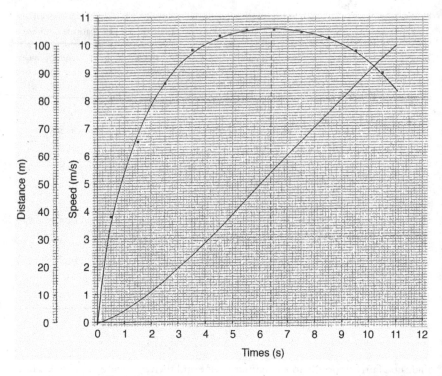

FIGURE 3.9 Line of best fit distance-time and speed-time graphs together with average speed-time data points obtained from the line of best fit distance-time graph.

graph (as in Figure 3.9) in relation to that of Carl Lewis (USA) in the final of the 100 m at the 1987 World Athletics Championships in Rome (Wagner 1998). Lewis finished second in a time of 9.93 s. Table 3.4 shows a comparison of the performances of the two sprinters. Whereas Lewis took longer to achieve maximum speed (7.5 s, 6.4 s), he was far superior to the junior athlete in relation to maximum speed (11.7 m/s, 10.5 m/s), length of time that maximum speed was maintained (2.4 s, 0 s) and finishing speed (11.7 m/s, 8.2 m/s).

Acceleration

Acceleration is defined as rate of change of speed, i.e. change in speed divided by the length of time in which the change in speed occurred

$$a = \frac{v - u}{t_2 - t_1}$$

where a = acceleration, u = speed at time t_1 and v = speed at some later time t_2.

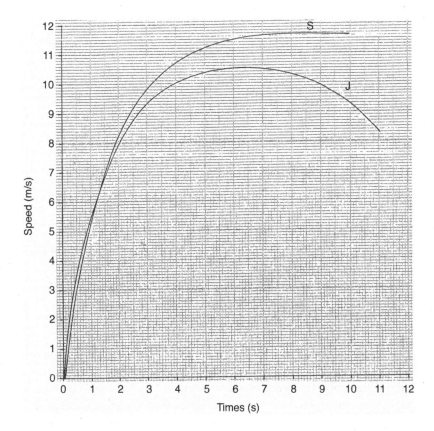

FIGURE 3.10 Speed-time graphs for a male junior international sprinter (J) and a male senior (S) elite sprinter in the 100 m sprint.

When the speed of a body increases during a particular period of time, the acceleration is positive. When the speed of a body decreases during a particular period of time, the acceleration is negative. Negative acceleration is usually referred to as deceleration.

The speed-time graph of the junior international sprinter shown in Figure 3.10 shows that his speed increased from zero at the start to a maximum speed of about 10.5 m/s in about 6.0 s. Consequently, his acceleration during this period is given by:

$$a = \frac{v-u}{t_2-t_1} = \frac{10.5\,\text{m/s}-0\,\text{m/s}}{6.0\,\text{s}-0\,\text{s}} = 1.75\,\text{m/s}^2 \text{ (metres per second per second)}$$

That is his speed increased by an average of 1.75 m/s for each second between the start and 6.0 s into the run. Figure 3.10 also shows that his speed decreased from a

TABLE 3.4 Comparison of performance of a male junior international (time = 11.12 s) with that of a senior elite sprinter (Carl Lewis, USA, final of the 1987 World Athletics Championships in Rome; time = 9.93 s) in the 100 m sprint

	Junior international	Senior elite
Time taken to achieve maximum speed (s)	6.4	7.5
Maximum speed (m/s)	10.5	11.7
Length of time that maximum speed was maintained (s)	0	2.4
Finishing speed (m/s)	8.2	11.7
Difference between maximum speed and speed at the finish (m/s)	−2.3	0

maximum speed of 10.5 m/s at about 6.5 s to about 8.2 m/s at the end of the run, which was completed in 11.12 s.

$$\text{i.e. } a = \frac{v - u}{t_2 - t_1} = \frac{8.2\,\text{m/s} - 10.5\,\text{m/s}}{11.12\,\text{s} - 6.5\,\text{s}} = \frac{-2.3\,\text{m/s}}{4.62\,\text{s}} = -0.50\,\text{m/s}^2$$

The negative sign indicates that the sprinter was decelerating during the period under consideration, i.e. his speed decreased at an average of 0.50 m/s for each second during the period 6.5 s to the end of the run.

Using the same method used to obtain distance–time data from the line of best fit distance–time graph, the speed of the junior international sprinter after each second of the run was obtained from the line of best fit speed–time graph in Figure 3.9. These data are shown in column 2 of Table 3.5. Column 3 of Table 3.5 shows the change in speed during each second of the run; the corresponding average acceleration of the sprinter in each one second interval is shown in column 4 of Table 3.5. The average acceleration–time data (plotted at the mid-points of the corresponding time intervals) and line of best fit acceleration–time graph are shown in Figure 3.11 together with the corresponding distance–time and speed–time graphs. The acceleration–time graph shows that the sprinter's acceleration was positive for about 6.4 s, i.e. his speed increased progressively during this period up to maximum speed of about 10.5 m/s. During the remainder of the sprint, the sprinter's acceleration was negative, resulting in a steady decrease in speed. Whereas it was not possible to estimate the acceleration of the sprinter just after the start, data reported by Baumann (1976) indicates that 0.2 s after the start, acceleration would be approximately 13 m/s² for this standard of sprinter (100 m time of 10.9 s–11.4 s). This is consistent with the acceleration–time data shown in Figure 3.11.

In Practical Worksheet 1, students collect distance–time data over a 15 m sprint and analyze the data to present the corresponding distance–time, speed–time and acceleration–time graphs.

TABLE 3.5 Cumulative time, cumulative speed, change in speed in each 1 s interval and average acceleration in each 1 s interval in a 100 m sprint by a male junior international athlete

Time (s)	Cumulative speed (m/s)	Change in speed (s)	Average acceleration in each second (m/s²)
1	5.35	5.35	5.35
2	7.80	2.45	2.45
3	9.25	1.45	1.45
4	10.00	0.75	0.75
5	10.38	0.38	0.38
6	10.50	0.12	0.12
7	10.50	0	0
8	10.30	−0.20	−0.20
9	9.90	−0.40	−0.40
10	9.30	−0.60	−0.60
11	8.25	−1.05	−1.05

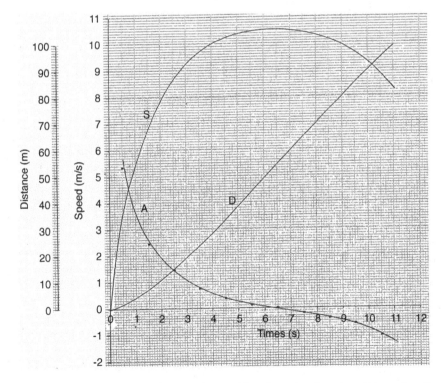

FIGURE 3.11 Distance–time (D), speed–time (S) and acceleration–time (A) graphs of a male junior international sprinter in the 100 m sprint.

Cycle length, cycle rate and speed of movement in human locomotion

Human locomotion refers to all forms of self-propelled transportation of the human body with or without the use of equipment. Human locomotion occurs mainly on land, such as walking, running and cycling, and in water, such as swimming, canoeing and rowing. All forms of human locomotion involve cycles of movement of the body in which each cycle of movement moves the body a certain distance. The distance achieved in each cycle of movement, referred to as cycle length, and the number of cycles per unit of time, referred to as the cycle rate, determine the speed of movement. For example, when cycle length is measured in m/cycle and cycle rate in Hz (cycles/s), speed is in m/s, i.e.

speed (m/s) = cycle length (m/cycle) × cycle rate (Hz)

Stride parameters and stride cycle in walking and running

In walking and running, cycle length and cycle rate are usually referred to as stride length and stride rate, respectively. Each cycle of movement from heel-strike to heel-strike of the same foot moves the body forward one stride (Figure 3.12a). One stride consists of two consecutive steps. The stride cycle refers to the movement of the body during a single stride. In walking, the stride cycle of the right leg begins with right heel-strike (contact of the ground with the right heel or, more often, the posterior-lateral part of the heel) which initiates the stance phase of the right leg, i.e. the period of the stride cycle when the right leg is in contact with the ground. The first part of the stance phase is a period of double support, i.e. when both feet are in contact with the ground (Figure 3.12b). This period of double support lasts for approximately 10% of the cycle, at which point the left foot leaves the ground (referred to as toe-off) and the left leg swings forward. During the swing phase of the left leg the right leg supports the body on its own; this period lasts for approximately 40% of the cycle and is referred to as the single-support phase of the right leg. At the end of the swing phase of the left leg, the left foot contacts the ground and another period of double support ensues. At approximately 60% of the cycle the right foot leaves the ground to begin its swing phase while the left leg experiences a period of single support. The cycle is completed by the heel-strike of the right foot. As the speed of walking increases, the duration of the periods of double support decreases until there is a sudden change from walking to running. The change is characterized by the absence of periods of double support and the presence of flight phases (when both feet are off the ground) between the single-support phases of each leg (Figure 3.12b, 3.12c).

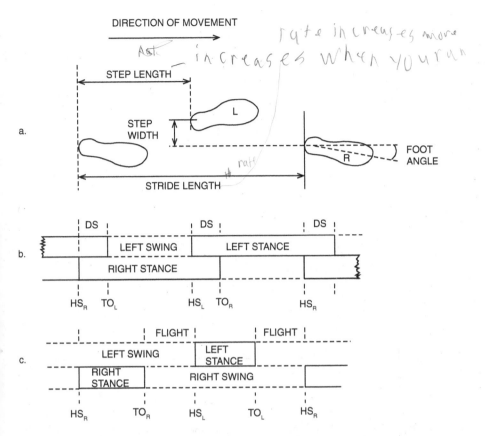

FIGURE 3.12   (a) Stride parameters and (b, c) stride cycle in walking (b) and running (c).

HS_L= heel-strike left, HS_R=heel-strike right
TO_L=toe-off left, TO_R=toe-off right

Effect of speed of walking and running on stride length and stride rate

Figure 3.13 shows the relationships between stride length (SL), stride rate (SR) and speed (S) of walking and running for a male student (Hay 2002). The SL-S and SR-S graphs are based on data obtained from 5 walking trials and 10 running trials. In the walking trials, the student was requested to walk at a constant speed in each trial, but at a slightly faster pace in each successive trial. All trials were recorded on video at 60 Hz and the stride length and stride rate in each trial (during a period of constant speed) were obtained by frame-by-frame playback using appropriate distance reference markers. A similar procedure was used in the running trials. Stride length and

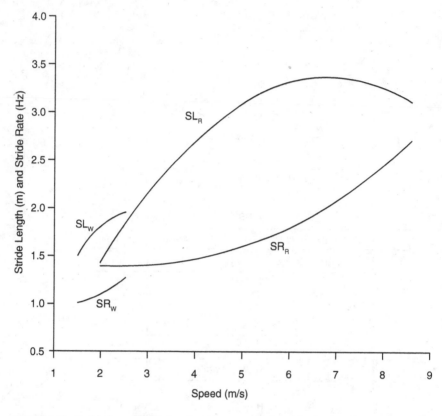

FIGURE 3.13 Stride length–speed and stride rate–speed graphs for a male student, walking and running. SL_W = stride length walking; SR_W = stride rate walking; SL_R = stride length running; SR_R = stride rate running.

stride rate data were obtained for five speeds of walking over the range 1.5 m/s to 2.6 m/s (moderate to fast pace) and 10 speeds of running over the range 2.1 m/s to 8.2 m/s (very slow to fast pace). The SL–S and SR–S graphs are the lines of best fit, reflecting the smooth changes in stride length and stride rate that normally occurs with increasing speed of walking and running for a given individual. Most people will naturally change from walking to running at about 2.3 m/s because it is more economic in terms of energy expenditure to do so (Alexander 1992). This change in form of locomotion is reflected in the distinct SL–S and SR–S graphs for walking and running. However, the shapes of the SL–S and SR–S graphs for walking and running are very similar. In particular, the SL–S graphs are concave downward and the SR–S graphs are concave upward. In addition, stride length makes the greatest contribution to increase in speed in the lower half of the speed range and stride rate makes the greatest contribution to increase in speed in the upper half of the speed range. Hay (2002) demonstrated that these relationships hold true for most forms of human locomotion, including walking, running, hopping, wheelchair racing, swimming, canoeing and kayaking.

Optimal stride length ⟨no principles for this⟩

Running economy, i.e. the rate of energy expenditure (oxygen uptake) for a given submaximal running speed, depends upon a number of biomechanical and physiological variables, but the interaction between the variables appears to be very complex (Williams and Cavanagh 1987; Kyrolainen *et al.* 2001). In any given situation, the stride length-stride rate combination adopted by a runner will depend upon the runner's personal anthropometric, anatomical and physiological characteristics and the environmental demands on the runner. For example, if the runner develops an injury, he is likely to alter his stride length and stride rate in order to minimize pain. Similarly, if the terrain is uneven or slippery, it is likely that the runner will adopt a stride length-stride rate combination that reduces the risk of falling. However, when there are no particular constraints, most runners naturally tend to adopt a stride length-stride rate combination that is optimal in terms of energy expenditure (Cavanagh and Williams 1982; Heinert *et al.* 1988). Figure 3.14 shows the relationship between oxygen uptake (energy expenditure) and stride length for a male distance runner running on a treadmill at 3.83 m/s (7 min/mile) at different stride length-stride rate combinations, including the runner's preferred combination. The graph indicates that the most economical stride length would be approximately 2.53 m, corresponding to a stride rate of 1.51 Hz. This was very close to the runner's preferred combination. Running at stride lengths longer or shorter than the optimal resulted in an increase in energy expenditure.

A number of researchers have investigated the relationship between stride length, height and leg length (Cavanagh *et al.* 1977; Elliot and Blanksby 1979). Figure 3.15

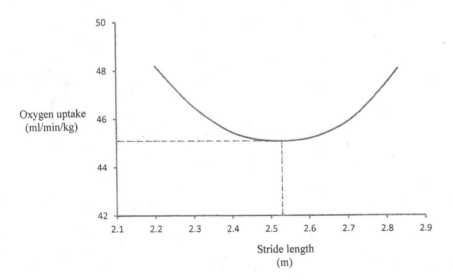

FIGURE 3.14 Relationship between stride length and oxygen uptake (energy expenditure) for a distance runner running on a treadmill at 3.83 m/s at different stride length-stride rate combinations. The most economical combination was a stride length of 2.53 m and a stride rate of 1.51 Hz.

shows the average stride length and average stride rate for 10 male and 10 female well-practised recreational runners running at 2.5 m/s, 3.5 m/s, 4.5 m/s and 5.5 m/s (Elliot and Blanksby 1979). The average heights and leg lengths of the men and women were 178.1 cm and 89.5 cm, 166.0 cm and 83.1 cm, respectively. At each speed, the women had a shorter average stride length and a higher average stride rate than the men. However, the average relative stride lengths (stride length divided by height and stride length divided by leg length) at each speed were very similar for both groups (Figure 3.16). This may reflect a subconscious optimization of personal

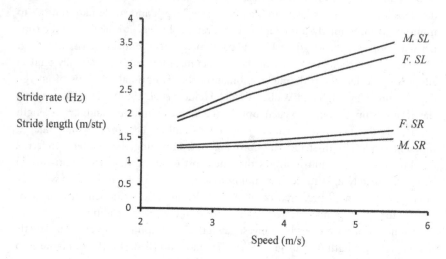

FIGURE 3.15 Average stride length and average stride rate for groups of male and female recreational runners running at 2.5 m/s, 3.5 m/s, 4.5 m/s and 5.5 m/s on a treadmill.

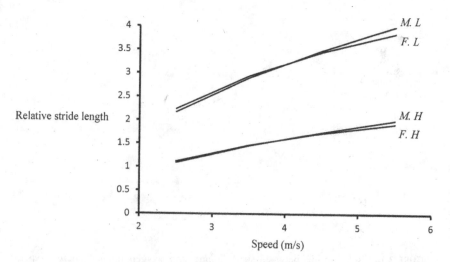

FIGURE 3.16 Relative stride length for groups of male (*M*) and female (*F*) recreational runners running at 2.5 m/s, 3.5 m/s, 4.5 m/s and 5.5 m/s on a treadmill. H = stride length divided by height; L = stride length divided by leg length.

and environmental constraints, common to men and women, that results in an optimum stride length-stride rate combination for constant speed running, especially in well-practised runners.

In Practical Worksheet 2, students use a treadmill to investigate the effect of increase in running speed on stride rate, stride length and relative stride length.

References

Alexander, R. M. (1992) *The human machine*. London: Natural History Museum.

Baumann, W. (1976) 'Kinematic and dynamic characteristics of the sprint start', in P. V. Komi (ed.) *Biomechanics VB*. Baltimore: University Park Press, pp. 194–199.

Cavanagh, P. R., Pollock, M. L. and Landa, J. (1977) 'A biomechanical comparison of elite and good distance runners', *Annals of New York Academy of Sciences* 301:328–345.

Cavanagh, P. R. and Williams, K. W. (1982) 'The effect of stride length variation on oxygen uptake in distance running', *Medicine and Science in Sports and Exercise* 14:30–35.

Daish, C. B. (1972) *The physics of ball games*. London: English University Press.

Elliot, B. C. and Blanksby, B. A. (1979) 'Optimal stride length considerations for male and female recreational runners', *British Journal of Sports Medicine* 13:15–18.

Hay, J. G. (2002) 'Cycle rate, length, and speed of progression in human locomotion', *Journal of Applied Biomechanics* 18:257–270.

Heinert, L. D., Serfass, R. C., Stull, G. A. (1988) 'Effect of stride length variation on oxygen uptake during level and positive grade treadmill running', *Research Quarterly for Exercise and Sport* 59:127–130.

Kyrolainen, H., Belli, A. and Komi, P. V. (2001) 'Biomechanical factors affecting running economy', *Medicine and Science in Sports and Exercise* 33(8):1330–1337.

Murase, Y., Hoshikawa, T., Yasuda, N. et al (1976) 'Analysis of changes in progressive speed during 100-meter dash', in P. V. Komi, (ed.) *Biomechanics VB*. Baltimore: University Park Press, p 200–207.

Wagner, G. (1998) 'The 100-meter dash: theory and experiment', *The Physics Teacher* 36(3):144–146.

Williams, K. R. and Cavanagh, P. R. (1987) 'Relationship between distance running mechanics, running economy, and performance', *Journal of Applied Physiology* 63(3):1236–1245.

Winter, D. A. (1990) *Biomechanics and motor control of human movement*, 2nd edn. New York: John Wiley.

4

LINEAR KINETICS

Kinematics is the branch of dynamics that describes the movement of bodies in relation to space and time. As described in Chapter 2, a linear kinematic analysis describes the movement of a body in terms of distance, speed and acceleration. Kinetics is the branch of dynamics that describes the forces acting on bodies, i.e. the cause of the observed kinematics. The human body, like any other body, will only begin to move or, if is already moving, change its speed or direction, when the resultant force acting on it (the resultant of all the external forces acting on it) becomes greater than zero. Furthermore, the amount of change in speed and/or direction that occurs will depend upon the magnitude and direction of the resultant force, i.e. there is a direct relationship between change of resultant force and change in movement. Isaac Newton (1642–1725) described this relationship in what has come to be known as Newton's laws of motion. In addition to the three laws of motion, Newton's law of gravitation describes the naturally occurring force of attraction that is always present between any two bodies. A body falls to the ground because of the gravitational attraction between the body and the earth and the planets are maintained in their orbits round the sun by the gravitational attraction between the planets and the sun. The purpose of this chapter is to introduce the fundamental mechanical concepts underlying linear kinetic analysis, i.e. analysis of the causes of changes in speed and direction. Practical Worksheets 3 to 10 are highlighted in the chapter. Ideally, each worksheet should be completed at the time that it is highlighted, before moving on to the next part of the chapter.

Objectives

After reading this chapter, you should be able to do the following:

1   Differentiate load, stress and strain.
2   Differentiate centre of gravity and stability.

3   Differentiate scalar and vector quantities.
4   Determine resultant force using the vector chain method and the method of trigonometry.
5   Differentiate mass and weight.
6   Describe the linear impulse–linear momentum relationship in relation to walking, running and jumping.

Centre of gravity

The human body consists of a number of segments linked by joints. Each segment contributes to the body's total weight (Figure 4.1a). Movement of the body segments relative to each other alters the weight distribution of the body. However, in any particular body posture the body behaves (in terms of the effect of body weight on the movement of the body) as if the total weight of the body is concentrated at a single point called the centre of gravity (also referred to as centre of mass) (Figure 4.1b). Body weight acts vertically downward from the centre of gravity along a line called the line of action of body weight. The concept of centre of gravity applies to all bodies, animate and inanimate.

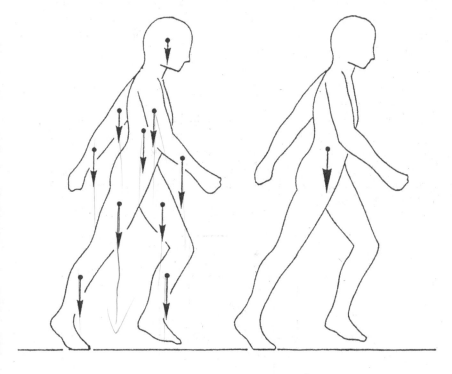

a.   b.

FIGURE 4.1   (a) Centres of gravity of body segments and lines of action of the weights of the segments. (b) Centre of gravity of the whole body and line of action of body weight.

BOX 4.1

The centre of gravity of an object is the point at which the whole weight of the object can be considered to act.

The position of an object's centre of gravity depends on the distribution of the weight of the object. For a regular-shaped object (of uniform density) such as a cube, oblong or sphere, the centre of gravity is located at the object's geometric centre (Figure 4.2).

For an irregular-shaped object, the centre of gravity may be inside or outside the object. The human body is an irregular shape. When standing upright, the centre of gravity of an adult is located inside the body close to the level of the navel (56.4 ± 2.8% of stature for women and 57.1 ± 2.3% of stature for men) and midway between the front and back of the body (Figure 4.3a) (Watkins 2000). Moving the arms forward to a horizontal position will move the centre of gravity slightly forward and upward (Figure 4.3b). Moving the arms from this position to over-head (Figure 4.3c) will move the centre of gravity slightly backward and upward. As the combined weight of both arms constitutes about 11% of body weight, any movement of the arms results in a fairly slight change in the position of the centre of gravity. However, movement of the trunk, which constitutes approximately 50% of body weight, will result in a relatively large change in the position of the centre of gravity. For example, full flexion of the trunk will result in the centre of gravity being located outside the body (Figure 4.3d). This position is similar to the posi-tion adopted by a pole vaulter when clearing the bar. The body's centre of gravity may also be located outside the body during postures involving full extension of the trunk, as in clearing the bar using the Fosbury flop technique in high jumping. Movements involving continuous change in the orientation of body segments to each other, such as walking and running, result in continuous change in the position of the body's centre of gravity.

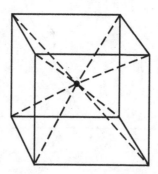

FIGURE 4.2 The centre of gravity of a regular shaped object, such as a cube, is located at the geometric centre of the object.

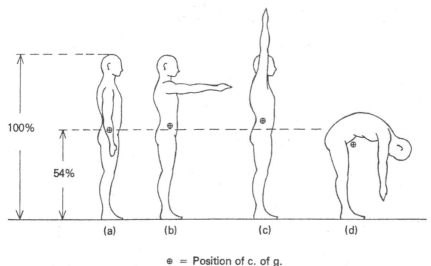

100%

54%

(a)   (b)   (c)   (d)

⊕ = Position of c. of g.

FIGURE 4.3 Movement of the location of the centre of gravity of the human body resulting from changes in the mass distribution of the body.

Stability

Figure 4.4 shows a regular cube-shaped block of wood resting on a horizontal surface. The centre of gravity of the block of wood is located at its geometric centre and the line of action of the weight of the wood intersects the base of support ABCD on which it is resting. If the block of wood is tilted over on any of the edges of the base of support, AB, BC, CD or AD, it will return to its original position provided that, at release, the line of action of its weight intersects the plane of the original base of support ABCD. This situation is shown in Figure 4.4c with respect to the edge BC. However, if, at release, the line of action of its weight does not intersect the original base of support, the block of wood will fall onto one of its other faces as shown in Figure 4.4d and 4.4e. With respect to a particular base of support, an object is stable when the line of action of its weight intersects the plane of the base of support and unstable when it does not. Consequently, the block of wood in Figure 4.4 is stable with respect to the base of support ABCD in the positions shown in Figure 4.4b and 4.4c, and unstable with respect to the base of support ABCD in the position shown in Figure 4.4d.

BOX 4.2

With respect to a particular base of support, an object is stable when the line of action of its weight intersects the plane of the base of support and unstable when it does not.

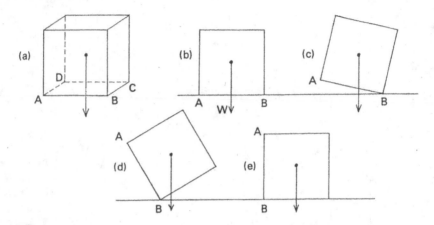

FIGURE 4.4 The line of action of the weight of a cube in relation to its base of support.

With regard to human movement, the terms stability and balance are often used synonymously. Maintaining stability of the human body is a fairly complex, albeit largely unconscious, process (Roberts, 1995). In upright standing the line of action of body weight intersects the base of support formed by the area beneath and between the feet (Figure 4.5a and b). The size of the base of support can be increased by moving the feet further apart. For example, moving one foot in front of the other increases anteroposterior stability, and moving one foot laterally increases side-to-side stability (Figure 4.5c and d). Combining these movements with a degree of flexion of the hips, knees, and ankles, as in certain movements in wrestling and box-ing, reduces the height of the centre of gravity and further increases stability.

In general, the lower the centre of gravity and the larger the area of the base of support, the greater stability is likely to be. For example, by moving from a stand-ing to a sitting position the body's centre of gravity is lowered and the area of the base of support is increased (Figure 4.6a, 4.6b and 4.6c). The recumbent position is one of the most stable positions of the human body since the area of the base of support is large and the centre of gravity is at its lowest (Figure 4.6d). Spreading the arms and legs on the floor would further increase stability. As the area of the base of support increases, the degree of muscular effort needed to maintain stability tends to decrease. For example, it is usually easier, in terms of muscular effort, to maintain stability when standing on both feet than when standing on one foot. Similarly, it is usually less tiring to sit than to stand, and less tiring to lie down than to sit. A person recovering from a leg injury may use crutches or a walking stick in order to relieve the load on the injured limb. The use of crutches also increases the area of the base of support and makes it easier for the user to maintain stability (Figure 4.5e and 4.5f).

As the area of the base of support decreases, the degree of tolerance in the movement of the line of action of body weight also decreases if stability is to be maintained. When the base of support becomes a knife-edge or something similar, such as a tightrope or very narrow beam, the amount of tolerance in the movement of the centre of gravity is zero in any direction other than along the line of support. Consequently, when an object is in a balanced position on a knife-edge support, the

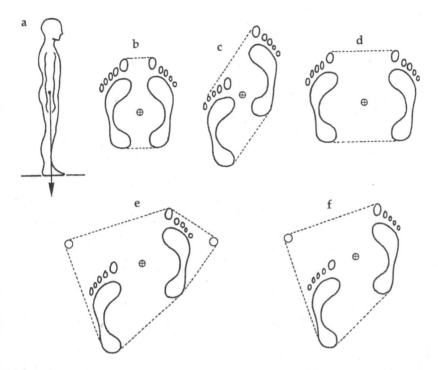

FIGURE 4.5 The line of action of body weight in relation to the base of support, (a, b) Standing upright, (c) Standing upright with the right foot in front of the left foot, (d) Standing upright with feet apart, side-by-side, (e) Standing with the aid of crutches or two walking sticks, (f) Standing with the aid of a walking stick in the left hand. The symbol ⊕ denotes the point of intersection of the line of body weight with the base of support.

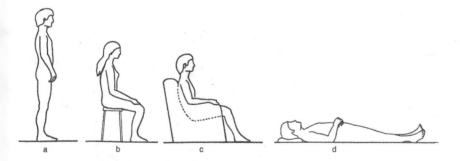

FIGURE 4.6 (a) Standing, (b, c) sitting and (d) lying postures.

centre of gravity of the object is located in the vertical plane through the line of support. By balancing an object in a number of different positions and noting the orientation of the vertical support plane to the object in each position, it may be possible to determine the position of the centre of gravity of the object which will be located at the point of intersection of the support planes.

Load, stress and strain

A load is any force or combination of forces that is applied to an object. There are three types of load: tension, compression and shear (Figure 4.7). Loads tend to deform the objects on which they act. Tension is a pulling (stretching) load that tends to make an object longer and thinner along the line of the force (Figure 4.7a, 4.7b). Compression is a pushing or pressing load that tends to make an object shorter and thicker along the line of the force (Figure 4.7a, 4.7c). A shear load comprises two equal (in magnitude), opposite (in direction), parallel forces that tend to displace one part of an object with respect to an adjacent part along a plane parallel to and between the lines of force (Figure 4.7a, 4.7d). The cutting load produced by scissors and garden shears is a shear load, while the cutting load produced by a

scissors = shear force

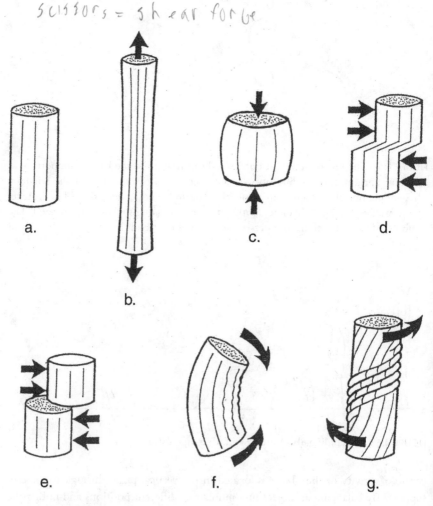

FIGURE 4.7 Types of load, (a) unloaded, (b) tension, (c) compression, (d) shear, (e) shear producing friction, (f) bending, (g) torsion.

knife is a compression load. It is also a shear load which forces one object to slide on another (Figure 4.7e). The sliding or tendency to slide is resisted by a force called friction which is exerted between and parallel to the two contacting surfaces.

The three types of load frequently occur in combination, especially in bending (Figure 4.7a, 4.7f) and torsion (Figure 4.7a, 4.7g). An object subjected to bending experiences tension on one side and compression on the other. An object subjected to torsion (twisting) simultaneously experiences tension, compression and shear. *+ torsion exp all 3 tension compression + shear*

In mechanics, the deformation of an object that occurs in response to a load is referred to as strain. For example, when a muscle contracts it exerts a tension load on the tendons at each end of the muscle and, consequently, the tendons experience tension strain, i.e. they are very slightly stretched. Similarly, an object subjected to a compression load experiences compression strain and an object subjected to a shear load experiences shear strain. Strain denotes deformation of the intermolecular bonds that comprise the structure of an object. When an object experiences strain, the intermolecular bonds exert forces that tend to restore the original (unloaded) size and shape of the object. The forces exerted by the intermolecular bonds of an object under strain are referred to as stress. Stress is the resistance of the intermolecular bonds to the strain caused by the load.

The stress on an object resulting from a particular load is distributed throughout the whole of the material sustaining the load. However, the level of stress in different regions of the material varies depending upon the amount of material sustaining the load in the different regions; the more material sustaining the load, the lower the stress. Consequently, stress is measured in terms of the average load on the plane of material sustaining the load at the point of interest.

strain deformation of object in response to load
stress resistance of intermolecular bonds of object to the strain caused by load

---

BOX 4.3

A load is any force or combination of forces applied to an object. Strain is the deformation of an object that occurs in response to a load. Stress is the resistance of the intermolecular bonds of an object to the strain caused by a load.

Tension stress

Figure 4.8a shows a person standing upright with the line of action of body weight slightly in front of the ankle joints. In this posture stability is maintained by isometric (static) contraction of the ankle plantar flexors as shown in the simple two-segment model in Figure 4.8b. If the force exerted by the ankle plantar flexors in each leg is 38 kgf (kgf = kilogram force; 1 kgf = the weight of a mass of 1 kg) and the cross sectional area of the Achilles tendon at P in Figure 4.8b, perpendicular to the

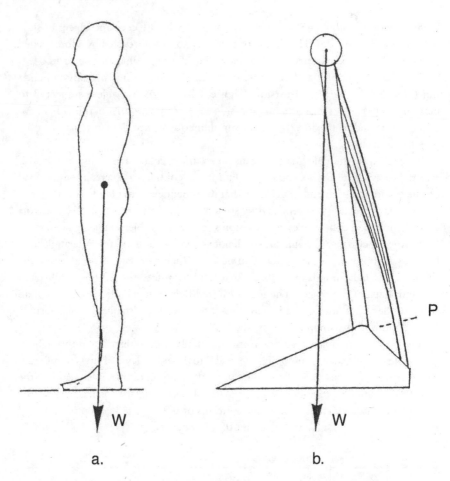

FIGURE 4.8 Tension load on the Achilles tendon.

tension load, is 1.8 cm² (square centimetres), then the tension stress on the tendon at P is 21.1 kgf/cm² (kilograms force per square centimetre), i.e.

$$\text{tension stress at } P = \frac{38 \text{ kgf}}{1.8 \text{ cm}^2}$$
$$= 21.1 \text{ kgf/cm}^2$$

Compression stress

When standing upright and barefoot, as in Figure 4.8a, the ground reaction force (the upward force exerted by the ground on the feet) exerts a compression load on the contact area of the feet (Figure 4.9a). In an adult the contact area is approximately 260 cm² (both feet) (Hennig *et al.* 1976). For a person weighing 70 kgf,

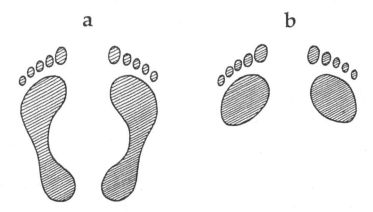

a   **b**

FIGURE 4.9 Supporting area of the feet, (a) Normal upright standing posture, (b) Standing upright with the heels off the floor.

the compression stress on the contact area of the feet (on a level floor, contact area perpendicular to the compression load) is 0.27 kgf/cm², i.e.

$$\text{compression stress} = \frac{70\,\text{kgf}}{260\,\text{cm}^2}$$
$$= 0.27 \ \text{kgf/cm}^2$$

By raising the heels off the ground, the contact area is approximately halved (Figure 4.9b). Since the compression load (body weight) is the same as before, it follows that the compression stress on the reduced contact area is approximately doubled. Compression stress is usually referred to as pressure.

Shear stress

Many of the joints, especially those in the lower back and pelvis, are subjected to shear load during normal everyday activities such as standing and walking. For example, in walking, there is a phase when one leg supports the body while the other leg swings forward (Figure 4.10a). In this situation the unsupported side of the body tends to move downward relative to the supported side, subjecting the pubic symphysis joint to shear load. In an adult male, the area of the pubic symphysis in the plane of the shear load is approximately 5 cm². If the shear load at the instant shown in Figure 4.10a is, for example, 2 kgf, then the shear stress on the joint is 0.4 kgf/cm², i.e.

$$\text{shear stress} = \frac{2\,\text{kgf}}{5\,\text{cm}^2}$$
$$= 0.4 \ \text{kgf/cm}^2$$

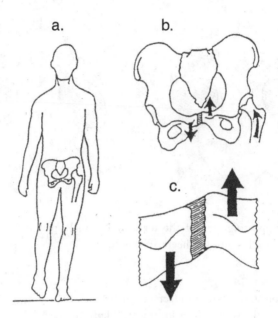

a.

b.

c.

FIGURE 4.10 Shear load on the pubic symphysis resulting from single leg support while walking.

[handwritten annotation: posture - orientation of body structures to each other usually applied to static or quasi static positions.]

Musculoskeletal system function

Posture refers to the orientation of the body segments to each other and is usually applied to static or quasi-static positions such as sitting and standing. When standing upright there are two forces acting on the body: body weight and the ground reaction force (Figure 4.11a). The combined effect of body weight and the ground reaction force is a compression load (experienced at the feet) that tends to collapse the body in a heap on the ground. This compression load increases with any additional weight carried by the body (Figure 4.11b). To prevent the body from collapsing while simultaneously bringing about desired movements, the movements of the various joints need to be carefully controlled by coordinated activity between the various muscle groups. For example, when standing upright the joints of the neck, trunk and legs must be stabilized by the muscles that control them, otherwise the body would collapse. Consequently, the weight of the whole body is transmitted to the floor by the feet, but the weight of individual body segments above the feet (head, arms, trunk and legs) is transmitted indirectly to the floor by the skeletal chain formed by the bones and joints of the neck, trunk and legs.

The transmission of body weight to the ground while maintaining an upright body posture illustrates the essential feature of musculoskeletal function, i.e. generation (by the muscles) and transmission (by the bones and joints) of forces that, in turn, enable us to exert forces on our physical environment so that we can maintain upright posture, transport the body and manipulate objects, often simultaneously.

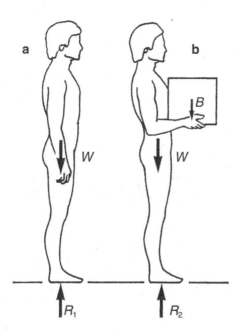

FIGURE 4.11 The forces acting on the body when standing, (a) standing upright and (b) standing upright with additional load. W = body weight, R_1 and R_2 = ground reaction forces, B = additional weight.

The forces generated and transmitted by the musculoskeletal system are referred to as internal forces. Forces that act on the body, such as body weight (the effect of gravity), ground reaction force, water resistance and air resistance, and forces that act on our hands (e.g. when holding or throwing a ball) and feet (e.g. kicking a ball) as we manipulate objects, are referred to as external forces.

forces that act on body   weight (gravity), ground reaction force,
water resistance air resistance

BOX 4.4

The musculoskeletal system generates and transmits internal forces to enable us to generate external forces to maintain upright posture, transport the body and manipulate objects, often simultaneously.

Friction

end the study for quiz here

When one object moves or tends to move across the surface of another, there will be a force parallel to the surfaces in contact which will oppose the movement or tendency to move. This force is called friction. Consider a block of wood resting

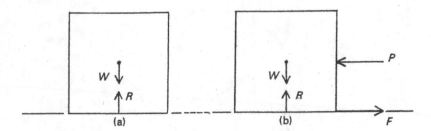

FIGURE 4.12 (a) The forces acting on a block of wood resting on a level table. (b) The forces acting on a block of wood resting on a level table, but tending to slide horizontally. W, weight of the block; R, normal reaction force; P, horizontal force applied to the side of the block; F, friction.

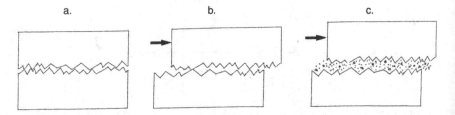

FIGURE 4.13 (a) Interdigitation of surface irregularities. (b) Slight separation of surfaces as a result of sliding. (c) Complete separation of surfaces as a result of lubrication.

on a level table (Figure 4.12). The only forces acting on the block are the weight of the block W and the force R exerted by the table on the block. Since the block is at rest, R is equal and opposite to W (Figure 4.12a). If an attempt is made to push the block along the surface of the table by applying a horizontal force P, the frictional force F between the contacting surfaces will begin to operate and oppose the tendency of the block to move (Figure 4.12b). As P increases, so does F until the block begins to move, i.e. F has a maximum value. This value is directly proportional to the degree of roughness of the two surfaces in contact and the force R. The three variables are related as follows:

$$F = \mu \cdot R \text{ Eq. } 4.1$$

where μ (Greek letter mu) is a measure of the roughness of the two surfaces in contact and is called the coefficient of friction between the two surfaces. The force R is referred to as the normal reaction force and is perpendicular to the plane of contact between the two surfaces.

The magnitude of μ depends upon the types of surface in contact and whether the surfaces are sliding on each other. Surfaces are never perfectly smooth, and the minor irregularities of the contacting surfaces interdigitate and resist sliding between the surfaces (Figure 4.13a). To initiate sliding, the minor irregularities have to be dragged over each other. In doing so, the surfaces tend to separate slightly which reduces the resistance to sliding, providing that the sliding is maintained (Figure 4.13b). Consequently, for any two surfaces in contact, μ (and therefore F) will be slightly less when the surfaces are sliding on each other than when the surfaces are not sliding on each other but tending to slide. Therefore, for any two surfaces, there is a coefficient of limiting (static) friction and a coefficient of sliding (dynamic) friction.

When no sliding occurs, the normal reaction force is distributed over those parts of the adjacent surfaces that are in contact; this will include the irregularities and some of the surfaces between the irregularities (Figure 4.13a). However, during sliding, the normal reaction force is exerted almost entirely by the irregularities (Figure 4.13b). Consequently, during sliding, the pressure exerted by the irregularities of one surface on the other surface is likely to be considerably increased and result in wear of the surface (similar to the effect of sandpaper on wood). The introduction of a fluid between the surfaces tends to separate not only the surfaces, but also the surface irregularities resulting in a considerable reduction in friction and wear. This is the principle of lubrication (Figure 4.13c).

In the absence of lubrication, μ is about 0.25–0.50 for wood on wood, 0.15–0.60 for metal on metal, 0.20–0.60 for wood on metal and 0.4–0.9 for wood on rubber (Serway and Jewett 2004). The difference between limiting and sliding friction between different pairs of materials can be easily demonstrated with a spring balance and a block of wood. For example, place a block of wood weighing about 1 kgf on a level wooden table. Apply a horizontal force to the block very gradually with a spring balance and note the maximum force recorded just before the block begins to move. The coefficient of limiting friction μ_L between the block and the table can then be estimated by using equation 4.1, i.e. $\mu_L = F_1/R$, where F_1 is the maximum force recorded on the spring balance just before the block begins to move and R is the weight of the block. Repeat the experiment and observe the force F_2 required to maintain sliding. The coefficient of sliding friction μ_S between the block and the table can then be estimated from $\mu_S = F_2/R$. Results similar to those shown in the first row of Table 4.1 will be obtained.

TABLE 4.1 Coefficient of limiting friction (μ_L) and sliding friction (μ_S) for a number of materials with wood

Support surface	Limiting friction		Sliding friction	
	F (kgf)	μ_L	F (kgf)	μ_S
polished wooden table	0.55	0.50	0.23	0.21
formica	0.33	0.30	0.18	0.16
resin floor tile	0.80	0.70	0.38	0.34
plain rubber mat	0.90	0.80	0.45	0.41

Normal reaction force = 1.1 kgf. F = horizontal force.

Different combinations of materials have different coefficients of friction and this can be demonstrated by varying the support surface in the preceding experiment. The second, third and fourth rows of Table 4.1 show the results obtained for μ_L and μ_S for the same block of wood and three other materials.

Equation 4.1 shows that the amount of friction, limiting and sliding between two surfaces is independent of the area of contact when the normal reaction force stays the same. The compression stress on the surfaces will vary with the area of contact, but the amount of friction will not change if the normal reaction force remains constant.

The development of adequate friction between the human body and the environment is essential for most actions of daily living, in particular, body transport (friction between the feet and the floor) and manipulation of objects (friction between the fingers and objects). The importance of the need for adequate friction in these types of actions is, perhaps, more obvious in sport where the quality of performance is likely to depend largely upon the ability of the players to create adequate friction between feet and playing surface and between hands and racket or other implement. In such cases, adequate friction is maintained by using materials that have appropriate coefficients of friction with the playing surface and with the hands. For example, in volleyball, basketball, squash and badminton, the soles of shoes are normally made of materials that will provide adequate friction with the playing surface. It follows that for most indoor sports, the playing surfaces should not be highly polished since this will reduce the coefficient of friction and increase the possibility of slipping. However, too much friction is likely to impair performance and result in injury, especially in sports that require rapid changes in speed and/or direction. Ideally, the sole of the shoe should turn as the player turns, but excessive friction may prevent the shoe turning and result in a twisting injury to the ankle or knee. This is also a potential problem in sports played on grass pitches where the players use studded boots. In these situations, the horizontal forces produced between boots and playing surface are largely shear forces on the studs rather than friction. However, if the studs are too long and sink fully into the pitch, the sole of the boot may not turn as the player turns which will increase the risk of injury.

There are many non-sporting situations in which it is important to ensure adequate friction in order to reduce the risk of injury. For example, an injured or aged person may rely heavily on walking sticks or crutches for support. It is very important that the sticks or crutches do not slip on the floor. Rubber has a high coefficient of friction with most materials and, consequently, rubber tips are usually fitted to the ends of the walking sticks and crutches to reduce the risk of slipping.

In some activities, skilful performance depends upon reducing friction between shoes and floor. For example, in ballroom dancing, good technique is largely dependent on the ability to slide and turn the feet on the floor with as little resistance as possible. Consequently, not only is the floor highly polished, but so are the soles of the dancer's shoes. Similarly, elite skiers wax the underside of their skis in order to reduce the amount of friction between the skis and the snow.

In Practical Worksheet 3, students determine the coefficients of limiting and sliding friction between shoe soles and playing surfaces.

Vector and scalar quantities

All quantities in the physical and life sciences can be categorized as either scalar or vector quantities. Quantities that can be completely specified by their magnitude (size) are called scalar quantities. These in include volume, area, time, temperature, mass, distance and speed. Quantities that require specification in both magnitude and direction are called vector quantities. These include displacement (distance in a given direction), velocity (speed in a given direction), acceleration and force. A vector quantity can be represented by a straight line with an arrowhead. The length of the line, with respect to an appropriate scale, corresponds to the magnitude of the quantity and the orientation of the line and arrowhead, with respect to an appropriate reference axis (usually horizontal or vertical) indicates the direction.

BOX 4.5

All quantities in the physical and life sciences can be categorized as either scalar or vector quantities. Quantities that can be completely specified by their magnitude (size) are called scalar quantities. Quantities that require specification in both magnitude and direction are called vector quantities.

Displacement vectors — *Distance covered Plus direction*

If a man runs 3 miles from a point A to a point B and then walks 2 miles from point B to a point C, it is clear that he has travelled a total distance of 5 miles. However, it is not possible to determine the position of C with respect to A since no information is given concerning the directions in which he ran and walked. However, if we are given the directions as well as the distances, we are then dealing with vector quantities, i.e. displacements and can, therefore, determine the position of C in relation to A. For example, if we are told that the man ran 3 miles due north from A to B and then walked 2 miles due east from B to C, the position of C in relation to A can be determined by considering the displacement vectors AB and BC. The displacements AB and BC are shown in Figure 4.14a. The position of C in relation to A is specified by the vector AC which is the vector sum of AB and BC, i.e. AC = AB + BC. The distance between A and C can be determined by measuring the line AC and converting this to miles using the distance scale. The direction of C in relation to A is specified by the angle θ. AC is referred to as the resultant vector of AB and BC, and AB and BC are referred to as component vectors. AC (3.6 miles N 33° E) is the resultant displacement of the man from the point A. Vector addition is clearly not the same as arithmetic (scalar) addition.

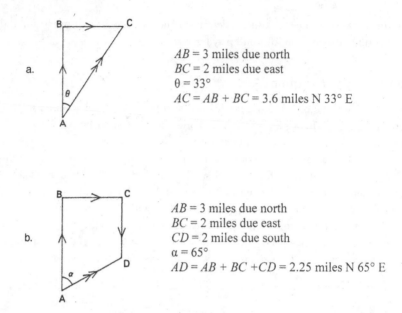

a.

$AB = 3$ miles due north
$BC = 2$ miles due east
$\theta = 33°$
$AC = AB + BC = 3.6$ miles N 33° E

b.

$AB = 3$ miles due north
$BC = 2$ miles due east
$CD = 2$ miles due south
$\alpha = 65°$
$AD = AB + BC + CD = 2.25$ miles N 65° E

FIGURE 4.14 Resultants of displacement vectors.

If the man walked 2 miles due south from C to a point D, the position of D in relation to A would be specified by the vector AD (Figure 4.14b). In this case, the resultant vector AD is the resultant of the three vectors AB, BC and CD. This example illustrates that irrespective of the number of component displacement vectors used to describe the movement of a body, the net result of all the component vectors can be specified by a single resultant displacement vector. This general principle applies to all vector quantities.

The method used in Figure 4.14 to determine the resultant of the component vectors is called the vector chain method, i.e. the component vectors are linked together in a chain (in any order) and the resultant vector runs from the starting point of the first component vector to the end point of the last component vector.

Velocity vectors

In addition to the vector chain method of determining the resultant of a number of component vectors, there is another method, the parallelogram of vectors, that is useful when there are only two component vectors, but somewhat laborious when there are three or more component vectors. In this method two component vectors extend from the same point to form adjacent sides of a parallelogram. The resultant of the two component vectors is given by the diagonal of the completed parallelogram. For example, if a ship without a keel starts to sail due north in a wind blowing S 60° W, the resultant velocity of the ship is specified by the resultant of the velocity V_1 of the ship resulting from the drive of the engines and the velocity V_2 of the ship

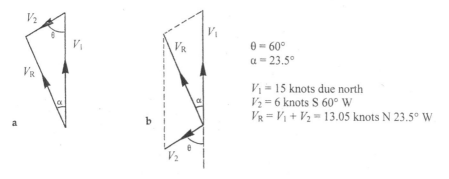

$\theta = 60°$
$\alpha = 23.5°$

$V_1 = 15$ knots due north
$V_2 = 6$ knots S 60° W
$V_R = V_1 + V_2 = 13.05$ knots N 23.5° W

FIGURE 4.15 Resultant velocity of a ship without a keel. (a) Vector chain method. (b) Parallelogram of vectors method.

resulting from the wind. The vector chain and parallelogram of vectors methods of determining the resultant velocity of the ship are shown in Figure 4.15. If $V_1 = 15$ knots due north and $V_2 = 6$ knots S 60° W, the resultant velocity of the ship $V_R = 13.05$ knots N 23.5° W.

When using the parallelogram of vectors method to determine the resultant of three or more component vectors, the first step is to find the resultant R_1 of any two component vectors. The resultant of R_1 and another component vector is then found and the process repeated until the resultant of all the component vectors is found.

Force vectors and resultant force

When standing upright, there are three forces acting on the human body: body weight W, the ground reaction force L on the left foot and the ground reaction force R on the right foot (Figure 4.16). The point of application of W in Figure 4.16 and subsequent figures is the centre of gravity of the body. In Figure 4.16, the resultant ground reaction force (resultant of L and R) is equal in magnitude but opposite in direction to W, i.e. the resultant force acting on the body is zero.

Figure 4.17 shows a sprinter in the set position of a sprint start, i.e. when the body is at rest and the resultant force acting on the body is zero. In this situation there are five forces acting on the body: body weight W, the forces L and R at the hands and the forces P and Q at the feet. The force vectors are shown in Figure 4.17a and the corresponding vector chain is shown in Figure 4.17b. Since the resultant force acting on the sprinter is zero, the vector chain is a closed loop, i.e. irrespective of the order of the force vectors in the chain, the end of the last vector coincides with the start of the first vector. Figure 4.18a shows the sprinter just after the start as he accelerates forward under the action of the resultant force acting on his body, i.e. the resultant of his body weight and the forces acting on his feet. Figure 4.18b shows the corresponding vector chain and resultant force.

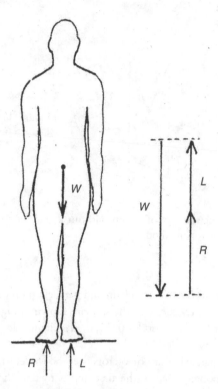

FIGURE 4.16 The forces acting on the human body when standing upright and the corresponding vector chain: W, body weight; L, force on the left foot; R, force on the and right foot.

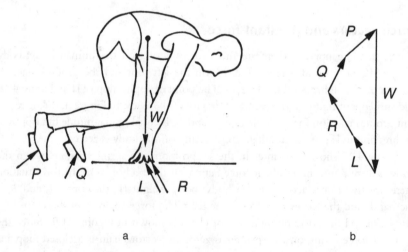

a   b

FIGURE 4.17 (a) The forces acting on a sprinter in the set position of a sprint start, (b) The corresponding vector chain. W, body weight = 70 kgf; P, force on the right foot = 21.5 kgf at 40.6° to the horizontal; Q, force on the left foot = 18.5 kgf at 63.1° to the horizontal; L, force on the left hand = 23.3 kgf at 58.0° to the horizontal; R, force on the right hand = 23.3 kgf at 58.0° to the horizontal; scale, 1 cm = 10 kgf.

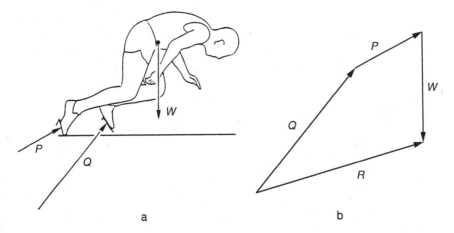

a

b

FIGURE 4.18 (a) The forces acting on a sprinter just after the start of a race, (b) Corresponding vector chain. W, body weight = 70 kgf; P, force on the right foot = 48 kgf at 28° to the horizontal; Q, force on the left foot = 102 kgf at 51° to the horizontal; R = 11.1 cm = 111 kgf at ≈ 16.5° to the horizontal; scale, 1 cm = 10 kgf.

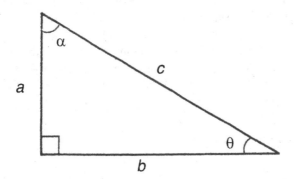

FIGURE 4.19 Definition of sine, cosine and tangent in a right-angled triangle.

Trigonometry of a right-angled triangle

Whereas the vector chain and parallelogram of vectors methods of determining the resultant of a number of component vectors are very useful, it is often more practical to use trigonometry, especially when there are a large number of vectors. Trigonometry is the branch of mathematics that deals with the relationships between the lengths of the sides and the sizes of the angles in a triangle. Figure 4.19 shows a right-angled triangle in which one angle (between sides a and b) is 90°. The angles between sides a and c, and sides b and c, are α (Greek lower case letter alpha) and θ (Greek lower case letter theta), respectively.

In a right-angled triangle, the two angles less than 90° (α and θ in Figure 4.19), can be specified by the ratio between the lengths of any two sides of the triangle.

The three most common ratios are sine, cosine and tangent, and they are defined in relation to the particular angle under consideration. For example, in relation to angle θ in Figure 4.19, side a is referred to as the opposite side, side b is referred to as the adjacent side and side c is the hypotenuse, the side of the triangle opposite the right angle.

The sine of θ is defined as the ratio of the opposite side to the hypotenuse, i.e.

$$\text{sine}\,\theta = \frac{\text{opposite side}}{\text{hypotenuse}} = \frac{a}{c}$$

The cosine of θ is defined as the ratio of the adjacent side to the hypotenuse, i.e.

$$\text{cosine}\,\theta = \frac{\text{adjacent side}}{\text{hypotenuse}} = \frac{b}{c}$$

The tangent of θ is defined as the ratio of the opposite side to the adjacent side, i.e.

$$\text{tangent}\,\theta = \frac{\text{opposite side}}{\text{adjacent side}} = \frac{a}{b}$$

Most electronic calculators provide a range of trigonometric ratios including sine (sin), cosine (cos) and tangent (tan). Alternatively, tables of sine, cosine and tangent (for angles between 0° and 90°) can be obtained in publications such as Castle (1969). The lengths of sides and sizes of angles in right-angled triangles can be calculated using sine, cosine and tangent functions provided that two sides or one side and one other angle are known. With reference to Figure 4.19, for example, if $c = 10$ cm and $\theta = 30°$, the lengths of sides a and b and the size of angle α can be determined as follows.

Calculation of the length of side a

$$\frac{a}{c} = \sin\theta$$
$a = c \cdot \sin\theta$ (i.e. c multiplied by $\sin\theta$)
$a = c \cdot \sin 30°$

From sine tables, $\sin 30° = 0.5$ (i.e., the ratio of the length of side a to the length of side c is 0.5). Since $c = 10$ cm and $\sin 30° = 0.5$, it follows that

$a = 10$ cm $\times$ 0.5
$a = 5$ cm

Calculation of the length of side b

$b = c \cdot \cos\theta$
$b = c \cdot \cos\theta$ (i.e. c multiplied by $\cos\theta$)
$b = c \cdot \cos 30°$

From cosine tables, cos 30° = 0.866 (i.e., the ratio of the length of side b to the length of side c is 0.866). Since $c = 10$ cm and cos 30° = 0.866, it follows that

$$b = 10 \text{ cm} \times 0.866$$
$$b = 8.66 \text{ cm}$$

Calculation of angle α

Angle α can be determined a number of ways:

1 The sum of the three angles in any triangle (with or without a right angle) is 180°. As the sum of θ and the right angle is 120°, it follows that $\alpha = 180° - 120° \doteq 60°$.

2 The lengths of all three sides of the triangle are known: $a = 5$ cm, $b = 8.66$ cm and $c = 10$ cm. Consequently, α can be determined by calculating the sine, cosine or tangent of the angle:

$$\sin \alpha = \frac{b}{c} = \frac{8.66 \text{ cm}}{10 \text{ cm}} = 0.866,$$
$$\alpha = 60°$$

$$\cos \alpha = \frac{a}{c} = \frac{5 \text{ cm}}{10 \text{ cm}} = 0.5,$$
$$\alpha = 60°$$

$$\tan \alpha = \frac{b}{a} = \frac{8.66 \text{ cm}}{5 \text{ cm}} = 1.732,$$
$$\alpha = 60°$$

Pythagoras's theorem

Pythagoras, a Greek mathematician (572–497 BC), showed that in a right-angled triangle the square of the hypotenuse is equal to the sum of the squares of the other two sides. Therefore, with respect to Figure 4.19,

$$\vec{c}^2 = a^2 + b^2$$
$$c = \sqrt{(a^2 + b^2)}$$

This can be demonstrated with the data from the preceding example, where $a = 5$ cm, $b = 8.66$ cm and $c = 10$ cm: $a^2 = 25$, $b^2 = 75$ and $c^2 = 100$.

Resolution of a vector into component vectors

Just as the resultant of any number of component vectors can be determined, any single vector can be replaced by any number of component vectors that have the same effect as the single vector. The process of replacing a vector by two or more component vectors is referred to as the resolution of a vector. In analyzing human movement, displacement, velocity and force vectors are frequently resolved into vertical and horizontal components using trigonometry. The example of the sprinter in Figure 4.18 will be used to illustrate how the resolution of forces by trigonometry is used to determine the resultant force acting on the sprinter. There are three steps in the process.

1 Resolve all of the forces into their vertical and horizontal components

Figure 4.20a shows the forces acting on the sprinter: body weight W, the force P on the right foot and the force Q on the left foot. In Figure 4.20b, P and Q have been replaced by their vertical (P_V and Q_V) and horizontal (P_H and Q_H) components.

P_V = vertical component of P

P_H = horizontal component of P

$\dfrac{P_V}{P} = \sin 28°$

$P_V = P \times \sin 28° = 48 \text{ kgf} \times 0.4695 = 22.5 \text{ kgf}$

$\dfrac{P_H}{P} = \cos 28°$

$P_H = P \times \cos 28° = 48 \text{ kgf} \times 0.8829 = 42.4 \text{ kgf}$

Q_V = vertical component of Q

Q_H = horizontal component of Q

$\dfrac{Q_V}{Q} = \sin 51°$

$Q_V = Q \times \sin 51° = 102 \text{ kgf} \times 0.7771 = 79.3 \text{ kgf}$

$\dfrac{Q_H}{Q} = \cos 51°$

$Q_H = Q \times \cos 51° = 102 \text{ kgf} \times 0.6293 = 64.2 \text{ kgf}$

2 Calculate the vertical component R_V and horizontal component R_H of the resultant force R acting on the sprinter

$R_V = P_V + Q_V - W$

$R_V = 22.5 \text{ kgf} + 79.3 \text{ kgf} - 70 \text{ kgf} = 31.8 \text{ kgf}$

$R_H = P_H + Q_H$

$R_H = 42.4 \text{ kgf} + 64.2 \text{ kgf} = 106.6 \text{ kgf}$

3 Calculate R and the angle θ of R with respect to the horizontal

R, R_V and R_H are shown in Figure 4.21. From Pythagoras's theorem,

$R^2 = R_V{}^2 + R_H{}^2$

$R^2 = 12\,374.8$

$R = 111.2 \text{ kgf}$

$\tan\theta = \dfrac{R_V}{R_H} = 0.2983$

$\theta = 16.6°$

As expected, R and θ are the same as in the vector chain solution in Figure 4.18.

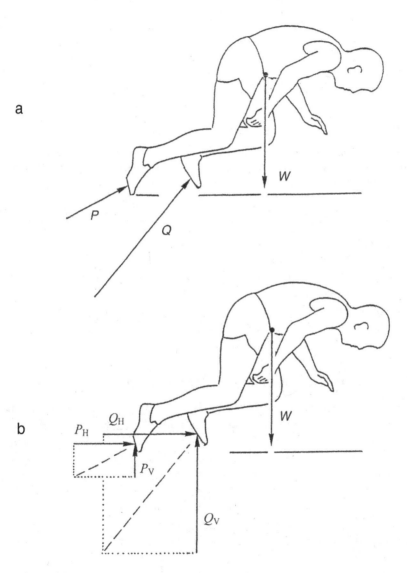

FIGURE 4.20 (a) The forces acting on a sprinter just after the start of a race and (b) the vertical and horizontal components of the forces. $W = 70$ kgf; $P = 48$ kgf at 28° to the horizontal; $Q = 102$ kgf at 51° to the horizontal.

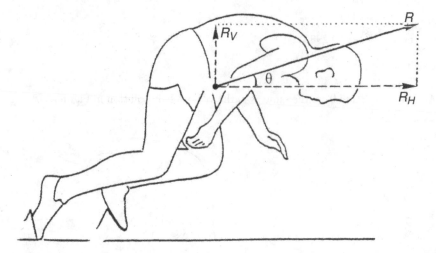

FIGURE 4.21 Resultant force acting on a sprinter just after the start of a race: R = resultant force; R_V = vertical component of R; R_H = horizontal component of R; R and θ are calculated in the text.

BOX 4.6

Any single vector can be replaced by any number of component vectors that have the same effect as the single vector. The process of replacing a vector by two or more component vectors is referred to as the resolution of a vector.

Trajectory of the centre of gravity in walking

During walking, the movement of the body as a whole is reflected in the movement of the whole body centre of gravity which normally follows a fairly smooth up-down side-to-side trajectory. When viewed from the side (median plane view), as shown in Figure 4.22, the centre of gravity moves up and down twice during each stride with the low points of the trajectory occurring close to the mid-points of the double-support phases and the high points of the trajectory occurring close to the mid-points of the single-support phases. When viewed from overhead (horizontal plane view), as shown in Figure 4.22, the trajectory of the centre of gravity follows the support phases, moving right during the period from the mid-point of single support of the left leg to the mid-point of single support of the right leg and moving left during the period from the mid-point of single support of the right leg to the mid-point of single support of the left leg. The vertical excursion (up-down range of motion) of the centre of gravity during walking increases with increasing

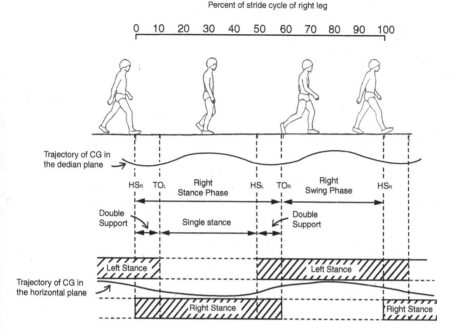

Percent of stride cycle of right leg

FIGURE 4.22 The stride cycle in walking: CG, centre of gravity; HS_L, heel-strike left, HS_R; heel-strike right; TO_L, toe-off left; TO_R, toe-off right.

walking speed and ranges from approximately 2.7 cm at 0.7 m/s (slow walking speed: 1.57 mph) to approximately 4.8 cm at 1.6 m/s (moderate walking speed: 3.58 mph) (Dagg 1977; Orendurff et al. 2004). In contrast, the mediolateral excursion (side-to-side range of motion) of the centre of gravity during walking decreases with increasing walking speed and ranges from approximately 7.0 cm at 0.7 m/s to approximately 3.8 cm at 1.6 m/s.

Ground reaction force in walking

The trajectory of the whole body centre of gravity during walking (as in any movement) is determined by the resultant force acting on the body. During a period of single support, as in Figure 4.23, the resultant force acting on the body is determined by body weight and the ground reaction force exerted on the grounded foot. During a period of double support, the resultant force acting on the body is determined by body weight and the ground reaction forces exerted on both feet. As body weight is constant (magnitude and direction), the movement of the centre of gravity reflects the magnitude and direction of the ground reaction forces, i.e. a change in the movement of the centre of gravity is the result of a change in the magnitude and/or direction of the ground reaction forces.

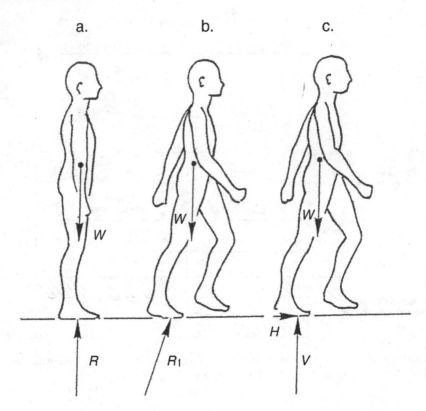

FIGURE 4.23 The ground reaction force in standing and walking, (a) Standing upright, (b, c) Push-off in walking. W, body weight; R, ground reaction force while standing; R_1, ground reaction during push-off; H, horizontal component of R_1; V, vertical component of R_1.

When standing upright, the ground reaction force is equal in magnitude but opposite in direction to body weight, i.e. the resultant force acting on the body is zero (Figure 4.23a). To start walking or running (or to move horizontally by any other type of movement such as jumping or hopping), the body must push or pull against something to provide the necessary resultant force to move it in the required direction. In walking and running, forward movement is achieved by pushing obliquely downward and backward against the ground. Provided that the foot does not slip, the leg thrust results in a ground reaction force, equal in magnitude and opposite in direction to that of the leg thrust, directed obliquely upward and forward which moves the body forward while maintaining an upright posture (Figure 4.23b). To understand the effect of the ground reaction forces, it is useful to resolve them into their vertical and horizontal components. In Figure 4.23c, the ground reaction force on the right foot has been resolved into its horizontal and vertical components. The vertical component counteracts body weight, i.e. the resultant vertical force acting on the body remains close to zero, and the horizontal component (resultant horizontal force) results in forward movement.

Components of the ground reaction force

Figure 4.24 shows the ground reaction force (F) and the anteroposterior (F_X), vertical (F_Y) and mediolateral (F_Z) components of the ground reaction force at one point in the single-support phase of the right leg in walking. Figure 4.25 shows the F_X, F_Y and F_Z components of the ground reaction force (force–time curves) exerted on each leg during one walking stride of the right leg (heel-strike of the right foot to the next heel-strike of the right foot).

The vertical component of the ground reaction force exerted on each leg is characteristically dominated by two smooth peaks, with the rise and fall of each peak taking up about half of the stance phase (Figure 4.25). The rise and fall of the

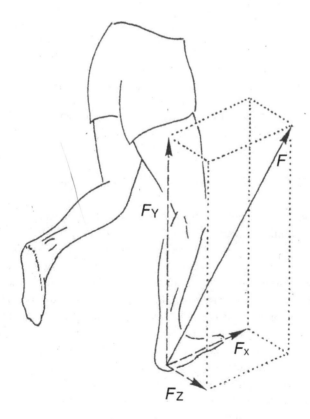

FIGURE 4.24 Anteroposterior (F_X), vertical (F_Y) and mediolateral (F_Z) components of the ground reaction force F.

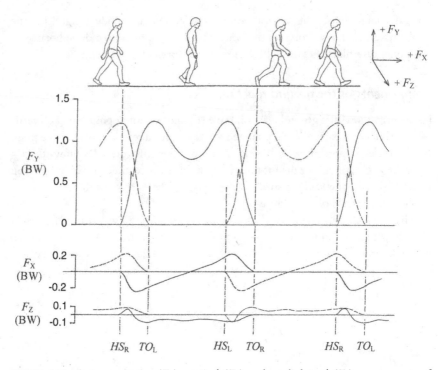

FIGURE 4.25 Anteroposterior (F_X), vertical (F_Y) and mediolateral (F_Z) components of the ground reaction force during the walking stride cycle of the right leg. BW, body weight; HS_L, heel-strike left; HS_R, heel-strike right; TO_L, toe-off left; TO_R, toe-off right; solid line, right leg; dotted line, left leg.

first peak roughly corresponds to the period from heel-strike to heel-off and the rise and fall of the second peak roughly corresponds to the period from heel-off to toe-off.

Like the vertical component, the anteroposterior component is normally characteristically dominated by two smooth peaks whose rise and fall correspond to the rise and fall of the two peaks of the vertical component. The resultant anteroposterior component of force acts backward from the mid-point of double support to heel-off (a braking force), indicating deceleration of the centre of gravity, i.e. the forward speed of the body is decreased. In the heel-off to toe-off period the resultant anteroposterior component acts forward, indicating forward acceleration of the centre of gravity, i.e. the forward speed of the body is increased.

The resultant mediolateral component of force acts medially during single stance and changes direction during double support, i.e. from medial on right foot to medial on left foot during the left heel-strike to right toe-off period (Figure 4.25). When walking straight forward, the mediolateral component is normally very small resulting in little side-to-side movement of the body.

In addition to the characteristic smooth phases of the vertical, anteroposterior and mediolateral components of the ground reaction force, all three components are often characterized by a single or multiple transient spikes soon after heel-strike which reflect the impact of the heel with the ground (see F_Y in Figure 4.25). Shock–absorbing footwear will reduce or eliminate these transient spikes (Czerniecki 1988).

Centre of pressure

The ground reaction force is distributed across the whole of the area of contact between the feet and the floor. Figure 4.26a shows the contact area when standing barefoot on both feet; the contact area is much smaller than the area of the base of support. Figure 4.26b shows the contact area when standing on one foot and Figure 4.26c shows the contact area when standing on one foot with the heel raised off the ground. In Figure 4.26b and 4.26c, the contact area is very similar to the base of support. Whereas the ground reaction force is distributed across the whole of the contact area, the effect of the ground reaction force on the movement of the body is as if the ground reaction force acts at a single point, which is referred to as the centre of pressure (just as the whole weight of the body appears to act at the whole body centre of gravity in terms of the effect of body weight on the movement of the body). With respect to Figure 4.26, the centre of pressure is at the point of intersection of the line of action of body weight with the base of support.

BOX 4.7

The effect of the ground reaction force on the movement of the body is as if the ground reaction force acts at a single point, which is referred to as the centre of pressure.

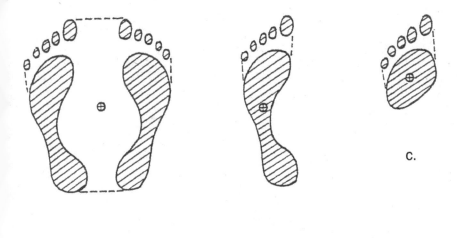

a.　　　　　　　　　　　b.

FIGURE 4.26 Location of the centre of pressure when (a) standing upright on both feet, (b) standing on the left foot and (c) standing on the left foot with the heel off the floor.

In Practical Worksheet 4, students use a force platform to record and then analyze the anteroposterior and vertical components of the ground reaction force acting on a subject while walking.

Trajectory of the centre of gravity in running

As in walking, the movement of the whole body centre of gravity in running normally follows a fairly smooth up-down side-to-side trajectory. When viewed from the side (median plane view), as shown in Figure 4.27, the centre of gravity moves up and down twice during each stride with the low points of the trajectory occurring close to the mid-points of the stance phases and the high points of the trajectory occurring close to the mid-points of the flight phases. When viewed from overhead (horizontal plane view), as shown in Figure 4.27, the trajectory of the centre of gravity follows the stance phases, moving left during the period from the mid-point of stance of the right leg to the mid-point of stance of the left leg and moving right during the period from the mid-point of stance of the left leg to the mid-point of stance of the right leg. Most adults naturally make the transition from walking to running at about 2.3 m/s (Alexander 1992). The vertical excursion (up-down range of motion) of the centre of gravity during running increases from approximately 6 cm at 2.3 m/s to approximately 9 cm at 5.0 m/s followed by a decrease to approximately 6 cm over the 6 m/s to top speed ($\approx$ 11.5 m/s) range (Weyand *et al.* 2000; Weyand *et al.* 2010). Mediolateral excursion (side-to-side range of motion) of the centre of gravity during running is approximately 3 cm to 4 cm over the 2.3 m/s to top speed range (Cavanagh and Lafortune 1980).

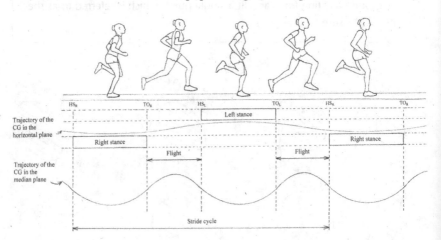

FIGURE 4.27   Stride cycle in running: CG, centre of gravity; HS_R, heel-strike right; HS_L, heel-strike left; TO_R, toe-off right; TO_L, toe-off left.

z- movement is medial lateral Excursion

old & self-reported

Ground reaction force in running

Approximately 80% of runners and joggers are rear-foot strikers, i.e. they contact the ground initially with the posterior-lateral aspect of the shoe (Kerr *et al.* 1983). The remaining 20% of runners and joggers contact the ground initially with either the middle of the foot (mid-foot strikers) or the front part of the foot (forefoot strikers). Figure 4.28 shows the anteroposterior, vertical and mediolateral components of the ground reaction force acting on the right foot of a well-practised rear-foot striker while running at about 4.5 m/s. Contact time is 205 ms. The graphs are typical of well-practised middle-distance and long-distance rear-foot strikers over the middle-distance to long-distance speed range (Cavanagh and Lafortune 1980). The anteroposterior component F_X is responsible for changes in forward velocity. The anteroposterior component exhibits two distinct phases, with each phase taking up about half of contact time. In the first phase (48% of contact time), F_X is negative with a single smooth peak of 0.41 body weight (BW) after 45 ms (22% of contact). Consequently, forward velocity decreases during this negative phase. In the second part of contact (52% of contact time), F_X is positive with a single smooth peak of 0.47 BW after 142 ms (69% of contact). Consequently, forward velocity increases during this positive phase. The negative phase is referred to as the absorption (braking) phase and the positive phase is referred to as the propulsion (acceleration) phase. In constant speed running at 4.5 m/s, forward velocity decreases about 0.2 m/s in the absorption phase and increases about 0.2 m/s in the propulsion phase (Cavanagh and Lafortune 1980).

The vertical component F_Y is responsible for changes in vertical velocity. The downward vertical velocity of the body at foot-strike is reduced to zero during the absorption phase. In the propulsion phase, upward velocity progressively increases. F_Y exhibits two peaks, with the first peak of 2.2 BW occurring after 32 ms (16% of contact time). A second peak, of 2.9 BW after 93 ms (45% of contact time), indicates maximum vertical compression of the leg (as vertical velocity is reversed) and corresponds closely with the end of the absorption phase. In constant speed running at 4.5 m/s, vertical velocity decreases about 1.6 m/s in the absorption phase and increases about 1.6 m/s in the propulsion phase (Cavanagh and Lafortune 1980). The change in vertical velocity of the body during contact time is reflected in the vertical displacement of the centre of gravity (down during absorption, up during propulsion) as shown in the picture sequence in Figure 4.28.

The mediolateral component F_Z is responsible for changes in mediolateral velocity. The mediolateral component is very small (maximum of 0.1 BW) relative to the anteroposterior and vertical components. It is negative for most of contact time, indicating a small medially directed force.

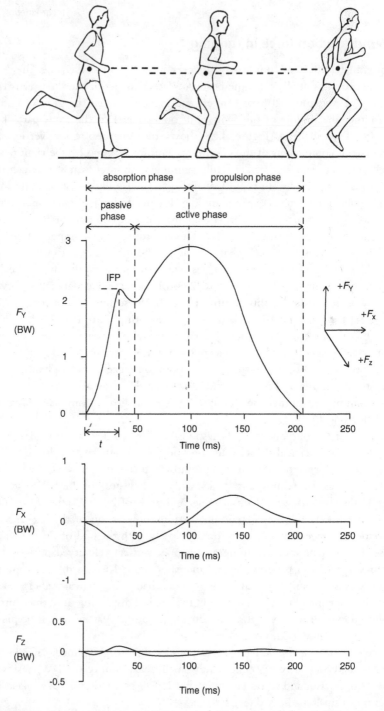

FIGURE 4.28 The anteroposterior (F_X), vertical (F_Y) and mediolateral (F_Z) components of the ground reaction force acting on the right foot of a well-practised rear-foot striker while running at about 4.5 m/s. BW, body weight; IFP, impact force peak; t, time to impact force peak.

Active and passive loading

In most activities of everyday life, the magnitude and direction of the ground reaction force is determined by muscular activity under conscious control. In these circumstances, when the ground reaction force, or any other external load (apart from body weight), is completely controlled by conscious muscular activity, the load is called an active load. Because they are under conscious control, active loads are unlikely to be harmful under normal circumstances. In everyday situations the muscles respond to changes in external loading to ensure that the body is not subjected to harmful loads.

However, it takes a finite time for muscles to fully respond (in terms of appropriate changes in the magnitude and direction of muscle forces) to changes in external loading; this time lag is referred to as muscle latency. Muscle latency varies between approximately 30 ms and 75 ms in adults (Nigg *et al.* 1984; Watt and Jones 1971). Consequently, muscles cannot fully respond to changes in external loading that occur in less than the latency period of the muscles. In these circumstances the body is forced to respond passively (by passive deformation) to the external load; this type of load is a passive load. The body is unable to control passive loads and is vulnerable to injury from high passive loads.

The body is subjected to passive loading during the period of muscle latency following heel-strike in walking and running. Consequently, during the absorption phase the ground reaction force is initially a passive load and then an active load (Figure 4.28). The period of muscle latency following heel-strike is referred to as the passive phase of ground contact and roughly corresponds to the period between heel-strike and foot-flat (when the forefoot contacts the floor). During the remainder of ground contact, i.e. from foot-flat to toe-off, the ground reaction force is an active load and this period is referred to as the active phase of ground contact (Figure 4.28).

The passive phase of ground contact in walking and running is characterized by a rapid rise in the vertical component of the ground reaction force, resulting in a relatively sharp peak, referred to as the impact force peak, within the first 30 ms–50 ms after impact (Figures 4.25 and 4.28). The force then declines slightly before rising again at the start of the active phase of ground contact.

The slope of the vertical component of the ground reaction force during the passive phase reflects the rate of loading (impact force peak divided by the time to impact force peak); the steeper the slope, the higher rate of loading. The higher the rate of loading, the higher the strain on the system of materials subjected to the passive load, i.e. the support surface, the shoe (including insole and sock) and the human body, especially the ankle and foot. The higher the strain, the greater the risk of damage or injury. The rate of loading depends upon the stiffness of the system; the greater the stiffness, the higher the rate of loading. Stiffness refers to the resistance of a material (or combination of materials) to deformation; the greater the resistance, the stiffer the material.

BOX 4.8

Muscles cannot fully respond to changes in external loading that occur in less than the latency period of the muscles. In these circumstances the body responds passively and is vulnerable to injury from high passive loads.

In Practical Worksheet 5, students use a force platform to record and then analyze the anteroposterior and vertical components of the ground reaction force acting on a subject while running.

Linear momentum *dependent on velocity*

In terms of linear motion, the inertia of a body at rest, i.e. its reluctance to move, depends entirely on its mass; the larger the mass, the greater the inertia and the greater the force that is needed to move it. The inertia of a moving body, i.e. the reluctance of the body to change its speed or direction of movement, depends upon its mass and linear velocity. The product of a body's mass and linear velocity is referred to as the linear momentum of the body. A cricket ball of mass 0.156 kg moving with a linear velocity of 40 m/s (about 90 mph) has a linear momentum of 6.27 kg·m/s, i.e.

> linear momentum of ball = 0.156 kg × 40 m/s = 6.27 kg·m/s (kilogram metres per second)

Anyone who has ever been hit by a rapidly moving cricket ball or hockey ball will appreciate that the ball exhibited a great reluctance to change its speed and direction; this is reflected in the force exerted by the ball on impact.

In sports, the mass of a player during a game is fairly constant, if the loss of mass due to the exercise is discounted. Consequently the linear momentum of a player will vary directly with his or her linear velocity; the greater the linear velocity, the greater the linear momentum and the greater the force that will be needed to change speed and direction. In rugby, a well-used ploy is to set up a situation in which the ball can be passed to a player who is moving rapidly forward close to the opposition goal line. The greater the linear momentum of the player when he receives the ball, the more difficult it will be for opposition to stop him going over the goal line. For example, a player of mass 70 kg moving with a linear velocity of 5 m/s has a linear momentum of 350 kg·m/s, i.e.

> linear momentum of player = 70 kg × 5 m/s = 350 kg·m/s

In order to stop the player dead in his tracks, the defending team would have to tackle the player with a linear momentum of the same magnitude, but opposite in direction. This would be difficult to achieve due to the difference in speed of movement of the attacking player and the tacklers.

Further reference to velocity and momentum in this chapter, unless specified, will refer to linear velocity and linear momentum. Angular velocity and angular momentum are covered in Chapter 6.

Newton's laws of motion and gravitation

Irrespective of the number of forces acting on a body, the resultant force acting on a body at rest is zero. A body at rest will only begin to move when the resultant force acting on it becomes greater than zero. Similarly, the resultant force acting on a body that is moving with uniform linear velocity, i.e. in a straight line with constant speed, is also zero. It will only change direction, accelerate or decelerate when the resultant force acting on it becomes greater than zero. Furthermore, the amount of change in speed or direction that occurs will depend upon the magnitude and direction of the resultant force, i.e. there is a direct relationship between change of resultant force and change in movement. Isaac Newton described this relationship in what has come to be known as Newton's laws of motion. There are three laws of motion, sometimes referred as the law of inertia (first law), law of momentum (second law) and law of interaction (third law). In addition to the three laws of motion, Newton's law of gravitation (law of attraction) describes the naturally occurring force of attraction that is always present between any two bodies. A body falls to the ground because of the gravitational attraction between the body and the earth, and the planets are maintained in their orbits round the sun by the gravitational attraction between the planets and the sun.

Newton's first law of motion

The first law of motion incorporates the fundamental principle that a change in resultant force is necessary to bring about a change in movement. The law may be expressed as follows:

> The resultant force acting on a body at rest or moving with uniform linear velocity is zero and the body will remain at rest or continue to move with uniform linear velocity unless the resultant force acting on it becomes greater than zero.

For example, at the start of a soccer match, a player kicks the ball (changes the resultant force acting on the ball) in order to get the ball moving. Similarly, the speed of a passenger travelling on a bus will be the same as that of the bus. If the speed of the bus is suddenly reduced by braking or a collision, the passenger, unless suitably restrained, will be thrown forward as she will tend to move forward with the speed that she possessed before the bus braked. Seat belts are usually worn by passengers in motor vehicles in order to reduce the risk of injury due to sudden changes in speed.

Not all forces produce or bring about a change in movement. Whether a particular force has any effect on the movement of a body depends upon the size of the force in relation to the inertia of the body. For example, in order to lift a barbell, the lifter must exert an upward force that is greater than the weight of the barbell, otherwise the barbell will not move.

Newton's law of gravitation: gravity and weight

It is alleged that Newton was sitting under an apple tree one day when he saw an apple fall from the tree and that this observation led to the formulation of Newton's law of gravitation. The truth of the allegation cannot be confirmed, but the phenomenon of the natural force of attraction between bodies is a fundamental characteristic of the physical world. The law of gravitation may be expressed as follows:

> Every body attracts every other body with a force which varies directly with the product of the masses of the two bodies and inversely with the square of the distance between them.

Thus, the force of attraction F between two objects of masses m_1 and m_2 at a distance d apart is given by

$$F = \frac{G \cdot m_1 \times m_2}{d^2}$$

Eq. 4.2

where G is a constant referred to as the Gravitational Constant and d is the distance between the centres of mass of the two bodies. The law of gravitation means that the force of attraction between any two bodies will be greater the larger the masses of the bodies and the closer they are together. It is, perhaps, hard to appreciate that a force of attraction exists between any two bodies. However, the force of attraction between bodies is normally minute and has no effect on the movement of the bodies. For example, the force of attraction between two men, each of mass 70 kg, standing 0.5 m apart is approximately one ten-millionth of a kilogram force (10^{-7} kgf). This force of attraction becomes even smaller the further apart the men move.

There is, however, one body that results in a significant force of attraction between itself and other bodies, i.e. the earth. In relation to the law of gravitation, the earth is simply a massive body (radius 6.37×10^3 km; Elert 2000) with a huge mass (5.98×10^{24} kg; Elert 2000). Even though the distance between the centre of the earth (assumed to be the centre of mass of the earth) and any body on the surface of the earth (or in space close to the surface of the earth) is extremely large, the force of attraction between the earth and any other body is much larger than that which exists between any two bodies on or close to the earth's surface. This is due to the huge mass of the earth. The force of attraction between the earth and any other body is not large enough to have any effect on the movement of the earth, but it is certainly large enough to pull any body towards the earth. For example, consider two light bulbs hanging from separate flexes a few feet apart on the same ceiling. By the law of gravitation there will be a force of attraction exerted between each light bulb and the earth, such that each light bulb and flex hangs vertically. There will also be a force of attraction exerted between the two light bulbs. However, the magnitude of this force is insignificant and the light bulbs continue to hang vertically rather than angled toward each other.

The force of attraction between the earth and any body is referred to as the weight of the body. This is the force of attraction that keeps us in contact with the earth or brings us back to the surface of the earth very quickly should we momentarily leave it as, for example, when jumping off the ground. By the law of gravitation, the weight W of an object B may be expressed as,

$$W = \frac{G \cdot m_B \cdot m_e}{d_e^2}$$
Eq. 4.3

where G = Gravitational Constant = $6.673 \times 10^{-11} \cdot m^3 \cdot kg^{-1} \cdot s^{-2}$ (Elert 2000)

m_B = mass of the object

m_e = mass of the earth = 5.98×10^{24} kg

d_e = radius of the earth = 6.37×10^3 km

Since G and m_e are constants, the term $G \cdot m_e/d_e^2$ is constant for any point on the earth's surface, i.e.

$$W = m_B \cdot g$$
Eq. 4.4

where $g = \dfrac{G \cdot m_e}{d_e^2}$
Eq. 4.5

and g, not to be confused with G, is gravity. The earth is not a perfect sphere, d being slightly greater at the equator than at the poles. Since g varies inversely with the square of d, g is slightly greater at the poles than at the equator. It follows that the weight of an object will be slightly greater at the poles than at the equator. The law of gravitation applies to all bodies, including all of the planets. As the masses and radii of the planets differ from each other, it follows that the weight of an object on a particular planet (the force of attraction between the object and a particular planet) will be different from its weight on every other planet. For example, the mass of the moon ($0.073\,483 \times 10^{24}$ kg; Elert 2000) is approximately 1/81 of that of the earth and the radius of the moon (1.74×10^3 km; Elert 2000) is approximately

7/25 of that of the earth. Consequently, the weight of the object B on the moon can be expressed as

$$W_m = \frac{G \cdot m_B \cdot m_m}{d_m{}^2}$$

Eq. 4.6

where W_m = weight of the object on the moon

$\quad G$ = Gravitational constant

$\quad m_B$ = mass of the object

$\quad m_m$ = mass of the moon = 0.073 483 × 10²⁴ kg

$\quad d_m$ = radius of the moon = 1.74 × 10³ km

As $m_m = 0.0123m_e$ and $d_m = 0.2731d_e$, substitution for m_m and d_m in equation 4.6 results in

$$W_m = \frac{0.0123G \cdot m_B \cdot m_e}{0.0746d_e{}^2} = \frac{0.1649G \cdot m_B \cdot m_e}{d_e{}^2} \approx \frac{G \cdot m_B \cdot m_e}{6d_e{}^2}$$

Eq. 4.7

Since $W_e = \dfrac{G \cdot m_B \cdot m_e}{d_e{}^2}$

Eq. 4.8

where W_e = weight of the object on earth, it follows from equations 4.7 and 4.8 that

$$W_m \approx \frac{W_e}{6}$$

i.e. the weight of the object on the moon is approximately one-sixth of its weight on earth.

Since the mass of the object is constant, it follows that the moon's gravity is approximately one-sixth of the earth's gravity. This can be clearly demonstrated by manipulating equation 4.7, i.e.

$$W_m = m_B \cdot \frac{G \cdot m_e}{6d_e{}^2} = m_B \cdot g_m$$

where g_m = the moon's gravity = $\dfrac{G \cdot m_e}{6d_e{}^2}$

Eq. 4.9

From equations 4.5 and 4.9, it follows that $g_m = g/6$, where g is the earth's gravity.

The reduced gravity on the moon has two main effects on the movement of astronauts on the surface of the moon. First, the strength of a particular astronaut on the moon would be the same as on earth, but his weight on the moon would be approximately one-sixth of his weight on earth. Therefore, he would be able project himself off the surface of the moon far more easily than he could on earth.

Second, the astronaut would be attracted back to the surface of the moon by a force of approximately one-sixth of the attraction force on earth. Consequently, he would appear to float down to the surface of the moon rather than fall rapidly as on earth.

Newton's second law of motion: the impulse of a force

From Newton's first law of motion, the resultant force acting on a body must be greater than zero in order to alter the motion of the body. A change in the velocity of a body will result in a simultaneous change in the momentum of the body (momentum = mass × velocity). When the resultant force acting on a body is greater than zero, the change in momentum, increase or decrease, experienced by the body depends upon the magnitude and direction of the resultant force and the length of time that the resultant force acts on the body. It was this realization that led Newton to formulate his second law of motion. The law may be expressed as follows:

> When a force (resultant force greater than zero) acts on a body, the change in momentum experienced by the body takes place in the direction of the force and is directly proportional to the magnitude of the force and the length of time that the force acts.

The law can be expressed algebraically as follows:

$$F{\cdot}t \propto m{\cdot}v - m{\cdot}u \qquad\qquad \text{Eq. 4.10}$$

where
F = magnitude of the resultant force
t = duration of force application
m = mass of the object
u = velocity of the object at the start of force application
v = velocity of the object at the end of force application

The term $F{\cdot}t$ (the product of the force F and duration of force application t), is referred to as the impulse of the force. The term $m{\cdot}v - m{\cdot}u$ is the change in momentum experienced by the object as a result of the impulse of the force. When v is greater than u, i.e. an increase in momentum, F is an accelerating force. When v is less than u, i.e. a decrease in momentum, F is a decelerating or braking force.

From equation 4.10,

$$F \propto \frac{m \cdot v - m \cdot u}{t} \qquad\qquad \text{Eq. 4.11}$$

The right side of the equation indicates the rate of change of momentum. The second law is often expressed in terms of equation 4.11, i.e.

> When a force (resultant force greater than zero) acts on a body, the rate of change of momentum experienced by the body is directly proportional to the magnitude of the force and takes place in the direction of the force.

From equation 4.11,

$$F \propto \frac{m(v-u)}{t} \qquad \text{Eq. 4.12}$$

As $a = \frac{(v-u)}{t}$, where a = the average acceleration of the body during time t, it follows from equation 4.12 that

$$F \propto m \cdot a \qquad \text{Eq. 4.13}$$

The second law is often expressed in terms of equation 4.13, i.e.

> When a force (resultant force greater than zero) acts on a body, the acceleration experienced by the body is directly proportional to the magnitude of the force and takes place in the direction of the force.

Since mass is constant, it is clear from equation 4.13 that there is a direct relationship between F and a, i.e. the constant of proportionality between F and a is 1. Consequently,

$$F = m \cdot a \qquad \text{Eq. 4.14}$$

Newton's second law of motion is often expressed as equation 4.14, but the impulse-momentum expression is more widely used in the context of sport, i.e.

$$F \cdot t = m \cdot v - m \cdot u \qquad \text{Eq. 4.15}$$

Newton's second law of motion is sometimes referred to as the impulse-momentum relationship or impulse-momentum principle. It has wide application in sport, as performance in many sports is concerned with increasing and decreasing speed of movement (and, therefore, changes in momentum) of the human body or associated implements such as bats and balls (Watkins 2014). The principle has directly or indirectly led to the development or modification of some sports techniques. For example, in the shot put, the velocity of the shot as it leaves the thrower's hand is determined by the impulse of the force exerted on it by the thrower. The force exerted by the thrower depends largely on his strength; in general, the stronger the thrower, the greater the amount of force that he will be able to apply to the shot. The length of time that the thrower can apply force to the shot depends upon his/her technique, i.e. the movement pattern (the way the body segments move in relation to each other) during the whole putting action.

Originally, shot put technique consisted largely of a standing put (Figure 4.29e–g). In a standing put, the thrower stands sideways to the intended direction of the shot with the left foot (for a right-handed thrower) against the stop-board and the right foot close to the centre of the 2.135 m (7 ft) diameter shot put circle. The thrower then rotates the trunk and flexes the right leg to obtain a position (Figure 4.29e) from which a powerful thrusting action can be made (Figure 4.29e–g). Development of the technique resulted from attempts to utilize the rear part of the circle in order to apply force to the shot for a longer period of time (and over a greater distance, see Chapter 7) and, thereby, increase the impulse applied to the shot. The greater the impulse, the greater the release velocity of the shot, and other things being equal, such as the height and angle of release, the greater the distance achieved. At the 1952 Olympic Games in Helsinki, the winner of the men's shot put (Parry O'Brien, USA) demonstrated a new technique which is still the most popular technique. In the O'Brien or glide technique, as it is called, the thrower takes up a starting position in the rear of the circle, facing in the opposite direction to that of the intended direction of the shot, with the toe of the right foot (for a right-handed thrower) against the inner side of the circle. The thrower then flexes his hips and knees such that the shot may actually be outside the circle (Figure 4.29a). From this position the movement across the circle is initiated by an explosive extension

(a)   (b)   (c)   (d)

(e)   (f)   (g)

FIGURE 4.29 Glide (O'Brien) shot put technique.

of the left leg closely followed by and in association with extension of the right leg (Figure 4.29b). The purpose of this movement is to generate velocity of the shot in the direction of the put. Prior to landing with the left foot close to the stop-board, the thrower flexes the right knee and moves the right foot underneath his body such that it lands about halfway across the circle (Figure 4.29c–d). At this stage the thrower is close to a position from which the final thrusting movement, basically a standing put, can be made (Figure 4.29d–g). The advantage of the O'Brien technique is that as a result of the impulse of the force applied to the shot during the movement across the circle, the shot will already be moving in the direction of the put before the final putting action is initiated. Consequently, the total impulse applied to the shot during the complete sequence of movements will be greater than that applied in a standing put, resulting in a greater release velocity.

The technique of discus throwing originally consisted of a standing throw, i.e. half a turn that was made from the front of the 2.5 m (8 ft 2 1/2 in) diameter discus circle (Figure 4.30f–i). The most popular technique now involves one and three-quarter turns from a starting position in the back of the circle with the thrower facing the opposite direction to that of the throw. The (right-handed) thrower starts the turning movement from a position with the shoulders turned as far as possible to the right (Figure 4.30a). The thrower then turns to the left and performs a fast rotating-stepping movement across the circle into a position from which the final slinging action can be initiated. The impulse of the force applied to the discus using the one and three-quarter turns technique is greater than that in a half turn standing throw and, consequently, results in a greater release velocity. Some shot putters use a one and three-quarter turns technique (rotation shot put technique) similar to that used in discus.

FIGURE 4.30 One and three-quarter turn discus throw technique.

BOX 4.9

Newton's second law of motion is sometimes referred to as the impulse-momentum relationship or impulse-momentum principle. It has wide application in sport, as performance in many sports is concerned with increasing and decreasing speed of movement of the human body or associated implements such as bats and balls.

Units of force

From Newton's second law of motion, the relationship between the acceleration a experienced by a mass m when acted upon by a resultant force F is given by equation 4.14, i.e. $F = m \cdot a$. In the SI system, the unit of force is the newton (N). In accordance with equation 4.14, a newton is defined as the force acting on a mass of 1 kg that accelerates it at 1 m/s², i.e.

$$1 \text{ N} = 1 \text{ kg} \times 1 \text{ m/s}^2 \text{ (i.e. } 1 \text{ N} = 1 \text{ kg·m/s}^2) \text{ Eq. } 4.16$$

From Newton's law of gravitation,

$$W = m \cdot g \text{ Eq. } 4.17$$

where W = weight of the mass m and g = gravity. It follows from equations 4.14 and 4.17 that gravity is an acceleration. The magnitude of gravity varies slightly at different points on the earth's surface (see earlier section on Newton's law of gravitation) with an average value of 9.81 m/s², i.e. in the absence of air resistance, an object falling freely close to the earth's surface will accelerate at 9.81 m/s² (and decelerate at 9.81 m/s² if thrown vertically upward). From equation 4.17, the weight of a mass of 1 kg, referred to as 1 kgf (kilogram force, see Table 1.1) is 9.81 N, i.e.

$$1 \text{ kgf} = 1 \text{ kg} \times 9.81 \text{ m/s}^2 = 9.81 \text{ N}$$

The kgf is referred to as a gravitational unit of force. Most weighing machines in everyday use, such as kitchen scales and bathroom scales, are graduated in kgf or lbf (pounds force). Thus the weight of a man of mass 70 kg can be expressed as 70 kgf or 686.7 N, i.e.

$$70 \text{ kgf} = 70 \text{ kg} \times 9.81 \text{ m/s}^2 = 686.7 \text{ N}$$

In calculations using SI units, the unit of force is the newton and all forces, including weights, must be expressed in newtons. For example, consider the sprinter in Figure 4.21. If the resultant force acting on the sprinter is 111.2 kgf and his mass is 70 kg, it follows from equation 4.14 that the acceleration a of the sprinter in the direction of the resultant force at the instant shown in the figure is given by

$$a = \frac{F}{m}$$

where $F = 111.2$ kgf and $m = 70$ kg. To complete the calculation, F (equivalent to the weight of a mass of 111.2 kg) must be expressed in newtons, i.e.

$$F = 111.2 \text{ kgf} = 111.2 \text{ kg} \times 9.81 \text{ m/s}^2 = 1090.9 \text{ N}$$

Therefore $a = \dfrac{1090.9\,\text{N}}{70\,\text{kg}} = 15.58\,\text{m/s}^2$

Average force on a soccer ball during a place kick

Consider the average force exerted on a soccer ball of mass 0.45 kg during a kick. Assume that the ball is initially at rest. If the time of contact between the player's boot and the ball is 0.05 s and the velocity of the ball following the kick is 30 m/s (67.1 mph), the average force F exerted on the ball during the kick can be determined by using the impulse–momentum form of Newton's second law of motion (equation 4.15), i.e.

$$F{\cdot}t = m{\cdot}v - m{\cdot}u$$
$$\text{and } F = \frac{m(v - u)}{t}$$

where $t = 0.05$ s, $m = 0.45$ kg, $u = 0$ and $v = 30$ m/s.

Therefore,

$$F = \frac{0.45\,\text{kg}(30\,\text{m/s} - 0\,\text{m/s})}{0.05\,\text{s}}$$

$$F = \frac{13.5\,\text{kg}{\cdot}\text{m/s}}{0.05\,\text{s}} = 270\,\text{N}$$

As 1 kgf = 9.81 N

then $F = \dfrac{270\,\text{kgf}}{9.81} = 27.52\,\text{kgf}$

In this example, the change in momentum of the ball as a result of the kick was 13.5 kg·m/s, i.e.

$$\text{Change in momentum} = m{\cdot}v - m{\cdot}u$$
$$= 0.45 \text{ kg} \times 30 \text{ m/s} - 0.45 \text{ kg} \times 0$$
$$= 13.5 \text{ kg·m/s}$$

The change in momentum of the ball was produced by the impulse of a force of 270 N (average force) acting on the ball for a period of 0.05 s, i.e.

Impulse of force $= F \cdot t$
$$= 270 \text{ N} \times 0.05 \text{ s} = 13.5 \text{ N·s}$$

It follows that the unit of measurement of impulse, newton seconds (N·s), and the unit of measurement of momentum, kilogram metres per second (kg·m/s), are equivalent. This can be demonstrated as follows:

From equation 4.16, $1 \text{ N} = 1 \text{ kg·m/s}^2$
i.e. $\text{N·s} = \text{kg·m/s}^2 \times \text{s} = \text{kg·m/s}$

Average force on a golf ball during a drive

The average force exerted on a golf ball during a drive can be calculated in the same way as in the preceding example. For example, if F is the average force exerted on the ball, the mass of the ball $m = 0.046$ kg (1.62 ounces), $u = 0$, $v = 70$ m/s (156.6 mph) and t (time of contact between club-head and ball) $= 0.0005$ s, then

$$F = \frac{m(v - u)}{t}$$
$$F = \frac{0.046 \, \text{kg}(70 \, \text{m/s} - 0 \, \text{m/s})}{0.0005 \, \text{s}} = 6440 \, \text{N} = 656 \, \text{kgf}$$

Since 1 tonf $= 1016$ kgf, then $F = 0.64$ tonf.

Free body diagram

A diagram showing, in vector form, all of the forces acting on a body as if isolated from its surroundings is called a free body diagram. The forces represented may be contact forces such as pulls, pushes, support forces, wind resistance and buoyancy forces, or attraction forces such as weight. The only forces acting on the man in Figure 4.31a are his weight W and the ground reaction force R. In a free body diagram, the point of application of a force may be indicated by either the tail end or the arrow tip of the vector. In Figure 4.31a the point of application of R is indicated by the tail of the vector and in Figure 4.31b the point of application of R is indicated by the arrow tip of the vector. In Figure 4.31a and 4.31b the point of application of W is the whole body centre of mass. When only the linear effect of the forces acting on a body are considered (rather than linear and angular), the free body diagram may be simplified by representing the body as a point from which the forces arise, as in Figure 4.31c.

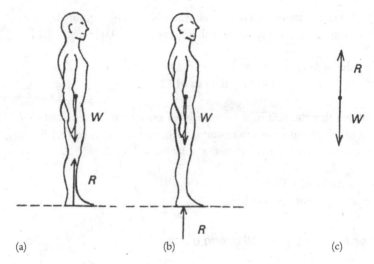

FIGURE 4.31 The forces acting on a man standing upright. W = body weight, R = ground reaction force.

In Practical Worksheet 6, students use a force platform to record and then analyze the impulses of the anteroposterior and vertical components of the ground reaction force acting on a subject while running.

In Practical Worksheet 7, students use a force platform to record and then analyze the impulse of the vertical component of the ground reaction force acting on a subject in a countermovement vertical jump.

In Practical Worksheet 8, students use a force platform to record and then analyze the impulses of the vertical components of the ground reaction forces acting on a subject in a countermovement vertical jump with an arm swing and in a countermovement vertical jump without an arm swing.

In Practical Worksheet 9, students use a force platform to record and then analyze the impulses of the anteroposterior and vertical components of the ground reaction force acting on a subject in a standing long jump.

Newton's third law of motion

When a soccer player kicks a ball, there is a period of time in which the ball and the player's boot are in contact. During contact, the player exerts a force on the ball and simultaneously experiences a force exerted by the ball on his foot (Figure 4.32). Furthermore, the greater the force exerted by the player on the ball, the greater the force exerted by the ball on his foot. Similarly, the greater the force exerted by a shot putter on the shot, the greater the force exerted by the shot on the putter's hand. These examples indicate that whenever one body A exerts a force on another body B, then body B will simultaneously exert a force on body A. What is not so evident is that the forces are equal in magnitude and opposite in direction.

FIGURE 4.32 The force A exerted by a soccer player on a ball when kicking the ball and the simultaneous equal and opposite force R exerted by the ball on the kicker's foot.

This phenomenon is the basis of Newton's third law of motion. The law may be expressed as follows:

> Whenever one body A exerts a force on another body B, body B simultaneously exerts an equal and opposite force on body A.

In Practical Worksheet 10, students use a force platform to determine the reactive strength index of subjects in rebound jumping.

References

Alexander, R. M. (1992) *The human machine.* London: Natural History Museum.

Castle, F. (1969) *Five-figure logarithmic and other tables.* London: Macmillan.

Cavanagh, P. R. and Lafortune, M. A. (1980) 'Ground reaction forces in distance running', *Journal of Biomechanics* 13:397–406.

Czerniecki, J. M. (1988) 'Foot and ankle biomechanics in walking and running: A review', *American Journal of Physical Medicine and Rehabilitation* 67(6):246–252.

Dagg, A. I. (1977) *Running, walking and jumping: The science of locomotion.* London: Wykeham.

Elert, G. (ed.) *The physics factbook.* Online. Available: http://hypertextbook.com/facts/2000/KatherineMalfucci.shtml

Hennig, E. M., Staats, A. and Rosenbaum, D. (1994) 'Plantar pressure distribution patterns of young children in comparison to adults', *Foot and Ankle* 15:35–40.

Kerr, B. A., Beauchamp, L. and Fisher, B. (1983) 'Foot-strike patterns in distance running', in B. M. Nigg and B. A. Kerr (eds.) *Biomechanical aspects of sports shoes and playing surfaces.* Calgary: University Printing, pp. 34–45.

Nigg, B. M., Denoth, J., Kerr, B., Luethi, S., Smith, D. and Stacoff, A. (1984) 'Load, sports shoes and playing surfaces', in E. C. Frederick (ed.) *Sport shoes and playing surfaces.* Champaign, IL: Human Kinetics, pp. 1–23.

Orendurff, M. S., Segal, A. D., Klute, G. K., Berge, J. S., Rohr, E. S. and Kadel, N. J. (2004) 'The effect of walking speed on center of mass displacement', *Journal of Rehabilitation Research & Development* 41(6A):829–834.

Serway, R. A. and Jewett, J. W. (2004) *Physics for scientists and engineers.* Fort Worth: Harcourt College.

Watkins, J. (2000) 'The effect of body configuration on the locus of the whole-body centre of gravity', *Journal of Sports Sciences* 18(1):10.

Watkins, J. (2014) *Fundamental biomechanics of sport and exercise.* London: Routledge.

Watt, D.G.D. and Jones, G. M. (1971) 'Muscular control of loading from unexpected falls in man', *Journal of Physiology* 219:729–737.

Weyand, P. G., Sandell, R. F., Prime, D.N.L. and Bundle, M. W. (2010) 'The biological limits to running speed are imposed from the ground up', *Journal of Applied Physiology* 108:950–961.

Weyand, P. G., Sternlight, D. B., Bellizzi, M. J. and Wright, S. (2000) 'Faster top running speeds are achieved with greater ground reaction forces not more rapid leg movements', *Journal of Applied Physiology* 89:1991–1999.

5

ANGULAR KINEMATICS

The purpose of this chapter is to introduce the fundamental mechanical concepts underlying angular kinematic analysis, in particular, angular displacement, angular velocity and angular acceleration. Practical Worksheet 11 should be completed after reading the chapter.

Objectives

After reading this chapter, you should be able to do the following:

1 Differentiate angular distance, angular displacement, angular speed, angular velocity and angular acceleration.
2 Differentiate degrees and radians.
3 Describe the relationship between linear velocity and angular velocity.
4 Describe the relationship between linear acceleration and angular acceleration.

Angular displacement, angular velocity and angular acceleration

Figure 5.1 shows a man performing a single leg raise from a lying position. In raising his left leg from position 1 to position 2, the centre of gravity of his leg moves a linear distance s, i.e. the arc of a circle of radius r about the mediolateral axis a_H through the left hip joint. Simultaneously, his leg rotates an angular distance θ about a_H.

In trigonometry, angular distance is usually measured in degrees. There are 360 degrees in one complete revolution. Figure 5.2a shows a gymnast performing a giant circle on a horizontal bar. By rotating about the bar, i.e. about the axis a_B, from position A to position D the gymnast will rotate an angular distance of 180° and an angular displacement (angular distance in a clockwise direction) of 180°. By rotating from

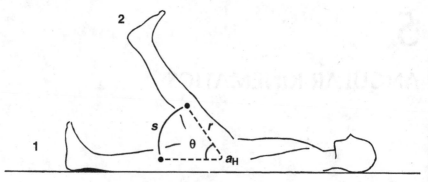

FIGURE 5.1 Linear movement (*s*) of the centre of gravity of the leg and angular movement (θ) of one leg in a single-leg raise. a_H, mediolateral axis through the hip joint; *r*, distance between a_H and the centre of gravity of the leg.

position A back to position A the gymnast will have travelled an angular distance of 360°, i.e. one revolution. Angular displacement must reflect the number of revolutions between the initial and final positions of the object following a period of rotation.

In mechanics, angular distance is usually measured in radians (rad). One radian is the angle subtended at the centre of a circle by an arc of the circle that is the same length as the radius of the circle (Figure 5.3). The circumference of a circle $= 2\pi \cdot r$ where *r* is the radius of the circle, i.e.

$$360° = \frac{2\pi r}{r} \text{rad}$$
$$= 2\pi \text{ rad}$$
$$= 6.2832 \text{ rad (as } \pi = 3.1416)$$

Therefore,

$$1° = 0.017\ 45 \text{ rad } (6.2832/360)$$
$$1 \text{ rad} = 57.3° \ (360/6.2832)$$

Angular speed is the rate of change of angular distance. In mechanics, angular speed is usually measured in rad/s (radians per second). When the direction of rotation is specified, the term angular velocity is used rather than angular speed. The symbol for angular velocity is ω (Greek lower case letter omega). Figure 5.2b shows the movement of the gymnast between positions B and C. The average angular velocity of the gymnast between positions B and C is given by

$$\omega = \frac{\theta_C - \theta_B}{t_C - t_B}$$

Eq. 5.1

where

θ_B = angular displacement of position B relative to position A

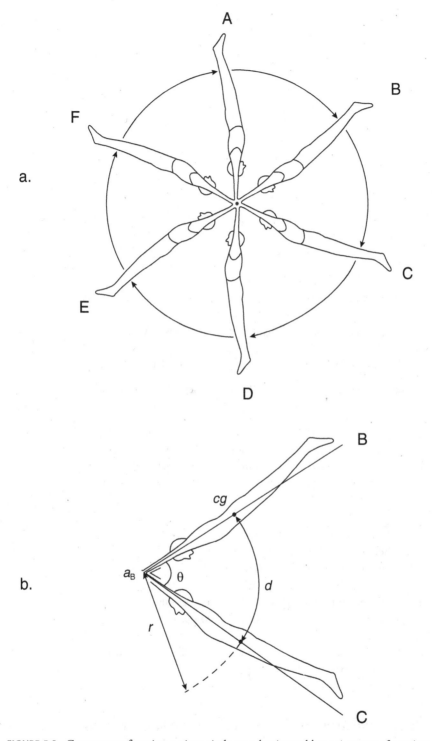

FIGURE 5.2 Gymnast performing a giant circle on a horizontal bar. *cg*, center of gravity; a_B, horizontal axis along the center of the bar; r, distance between a_B and *cg* = radius of the circle followed by the *cg*; *d*, linear distance travelled by *cg*; θ = angular distance travelled by the body.

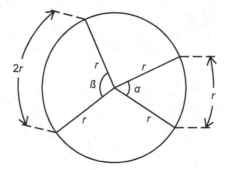

FIGURE 5.3 A radian is the angle subtended at the centre of a circle by an arc on the circumference of the circle that is the same length as the radius of the circle. r, radius of the circle; $\alpha = 1$ radian; $\beta = 2$ radians.

θ_C = angular displacement of position C relative to position A
t_B = time at position B with respect to position A
t_C = time at position C with respect to position A

If $\theta_B = 60°$, $\theta_C = 125°$, $t_B = 1.43$ s, $t_C = 1.69$ s, then

$$\omega = \frac{125° - 60°}{1.69\,s - 1.43\,s} = 250°/s\,(degrees\,per\,second) = 4.36\,rad/s$$

Angular acceleration is the rate of change of angular velocity. In mechanics, angular acceleration is usually measured in rad/s² (radians per second per second). The symbol for angular acceleration is α (Greek lower case letter alpha). The average angular acceleration of the gymnast between positions B and C is given by

$$\alpha = \frac{\omega_C - \omega_B}{t_C - t_B} \qquad\qquad Eq.\ 5.2$$

where
ω_B = angular velocity at position B
ω_C = angular velocity at position C
t_B = time at position B with respect to position A
t_C = time at position C with respect to position A

If $\omega_B = 3.13$ rad/s, $\omega_C = 5.55$ rad/s, $t_B = 1.43$ s, $t_C = 1.69$ s, then

$$\alpha = \frac{5.55\,rad/s - 3.13\,rad/s}{1.69\,s - 1.43\,s} = 9.31\,rad/s^2$$

Relationship between linear velocity and angular velocity

In Figure 5.2b, if the orientation of the gymnast's body segments to each other remains the same between positions B and C, i.e. if the centre of gravity moves along the arc d of a circle of radius r in a time t, then the average linear velocity v of the centre of gravity during this period is given by

$$v = \frac{d}{t}$$

Eq. 5.3

If the body rotates through an angle θ during the same period, then the average angular velocity of the body is given by

$$\omega = \frac{\theta}{t}$$

Eq. 5.4

As θ degrees $= d/r$ radians, then

$$d = r\theta$$

Eq. 5.5

By substitution of d from equation 5.5 into equation 5.3,

$$v = \frac{r \cdot \theta}{t}$$

Eq. 5.6

By substitution of θ/t from equation 5.4 into equation 5.6,

$$v = r\omega$$

Eq. 5.7

That is, the linear velocity of the centre of gravity is equal to the product of the radius of the circle (distance from the axis of rotation to the centre of gravity) and the angular velocity of the body. The radian is a dimensionless variable, i.e. it has no unit because it is the ratio of two distances (the arc of the circle and the radius of the circle). Consequently, the product $r\omega$ is in m/s (where r is in metres and ω is in rad/s). For example, in Figure 5.2b, if $r = 1$ m and $\omega = 3.13$ rad/s at position B, then v at B $= 3.13$ m/s.

Relationship between linear acceleration and angular acceleration

From equation 5.7, it follows that $v_B = r\omega_B$ and $v_C = r\omega_C$ where v_B, v_C and ω_B, ω_C are the linear and angular velocities of the centre of gravity of the gymnast at positions B and C in Figure 5.2. Consequently, the average linear acceleration a (Roman lower case letter a) of the centre of gravity between positions B and C is given by

$$a = \frac{v_C - v_B}{t} = r\frac{(\omega_C - \omega_B)}{t}$$

As $\dfrac{(\omega_C - \omega_B)}{t} = \alpha =$ angular acceleration (Eq. 5.2), it follows that

$$a = r\alpha$$

Eq. 5.8

That is, the linear acceleration of the centre of gravity in the direction of v is equal to the product of the radius of the circle (distance from the axis of rotation to the centre of gravity) and the angular acceleration of the body. As the direction of a is perpendicular to r, i.e. tangent to the circle, a is referred to as tangential acceleration and sometimes denoted a_T. In Figure 5.2b, if $r = 1$ m and $\alpha = 9.31$ rad/s^2 at position C, then a_T at C $= 9.31$ m/s^2.

Kinematic analysis

A kinematic analysis of the movement of the body as a whole in a particular activity would involve a description of the linear displacement, linear velocity and linear acceleration of the whole-body centre of gravity during the movement. The linear kinematic analysis of a 100 m sprint in Chapter 3 and the linear kinematic analysis of a 15 m sprint in Practical Worksheet 1 are examples of this type of analysis. In the analysis of the 100 m sprint, the distance-time data was obtained by replaying the video and measuring the time to complete successive 10 m intervals by counting the number of frames at 50 Hz. In Practical Worksheet 1, the distance-time data was obtained by measuring the 5 m split times in a 15 m sprint with photocells. To obtain kinematic information on the movement of the whole-body centre of gravity in movements other than straight line walking and running, it is usually necessary to record the movement on film or video and carry out a frame-by-frame analysis of the movement of individual body segments. The film or video is projected one frame at a time and the positions of the body segments are recorded in terms of the x and y coordinates of various points on the body with respect to an appropriate reference origin. Reference distances in the X and Y directions are also recorded so that distances on the image can be converted to actual distances for the purpose of calculating velocity and acceleration data. Other reference points may also be recorded, such as the positions of the reuther board and vaulting horse when analyzing the performance of a vault in gymnastics. The points recorded for each frame of video constitute the spatial model and the number of points in the spatial model is determined prior to analysis. The points in the spatial model that define the body segments are usually the main joint centres. The process of recording the x and y coordinates of the points in the spatial model in computer-based video analysis systems is referred to as digitization. The x-y coordinate data can be used in a variety of ways, in particular, representation of the movement of the body in the form of a stick figure and the calculation of linear kinematics (e.g. the movement of whole-body centre of gravity) and angular kinematics (e.g. angular movement of particular body segments).

Stick-figure sequence

Figure 5.4 shows a stick-figure sequence of a standing flic-flac presented on a fixed frame of reference, i.e. with respect to the same origin. This method produces a set of overlapping images which may be difficult to interpret if too many images are

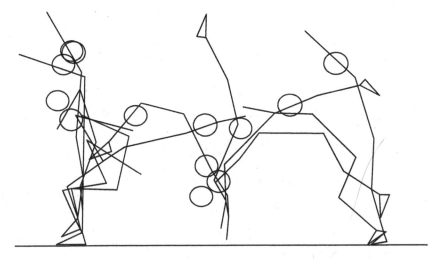

FIGURE 5.4 Stick-figure sequence of a standing flic-flac on a fixed frame of reference.

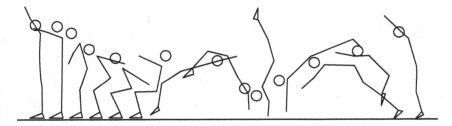

FIGURE 5.5 Stick-figure sequence of a standing flic-flac on a displaced frame of reference.

presented. This problem can be overcome by presenting the images on a displaced frame of reference, i.e. the images are displaced horizontally by a fixed amount to produce one or more rows of images so that the change in body position between images can be more clearly seen. Figure 5.5 shows the same sequence as in Figure 5.4 presented on a displaced frame of reference.

Whole-body centre of gravity

As will be shown in Chapter 6, the position of the whole-body centre of gravity can be determined from the positions of the body segments. Figure 5.6 shows the change in the position of the whole body centre of gravity during the hand-ground contact phase of the flic-flac shown in Figures 5.4 and 5.5. The vertical displacement of the centre of gravity is minimal and similar to the movement of the axle of a wheel rolling along the ground. This indicates minimal work done in lowering and lifting the centre of gravity during the ground contact phase and, therefore, good technique. Poor technique would be characterized by the centre of gravity

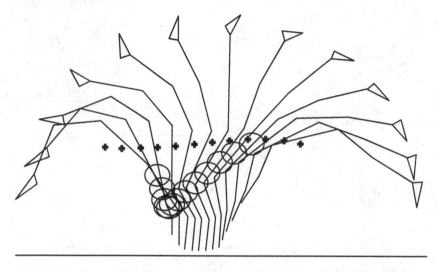

FIGURE 5.6 Change in the position of the whole-body centre of gravity during the hand-ground contact phase of a standing flic-flac on a displaced frame of reference.

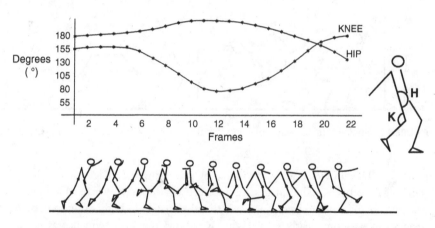

FIGURE 5.7 Hip and knee angular displacement-time graphs of the kicking leg in a place kick in rugby.

moving downward during the first part of ground contact (shoulder, elbow and wrist flexion) and upward (shoulder, elbow and wrist extension) during the second part of ground contact.

Angular kinematics

Figure 5.7 shows a stick-figure sequence of a right-footed player performing a place kick in rugby. The stick-figure sequence is presented on a displaced frame of reference together with the corresponding hip joint angle-time and knee joint angle-time graphs of the kicking leg. The graphs show two distinct phases, the backswing of the leg (frames 5 to 12) which involves simultaneous hip extension and knee flexion, followed by the kicking action (frames 12 to 22) which involves simultaneous hip flexion and knee extension.

In Practical Worksheet 11, students video a subject performing a penalty kick in rugby and analyze the video to produce angular displacement-time and angular velocity-time graphs of the hip and knee joints of the kicking leg.

6

ANGULAR KINETICS

Newton's laws of motion apply to angular motion as well as linear motion. The purpose of this chapter is to describe the fundamental mechanical concepts underlying the study of angular kinetics, in particular, the turning effect of a force, angular impulse and angular momentum. Practical Worksheets 12 to 15 are highlighted in the chapter. Ideally, each worksheet should be completed at the time that it is highlighted, before moving on to the next part of the chapter.

Objectives

After reading this chapter, you should be able to do the following:

1 Differentiate angular kinematics and angular kinetics.
2 Describe the various methods of determining the location of the centre of gravity of the human body.
3 Differentiate concentric force, eccentric force and couple.
4 Describe the relationship between angular impulse and angular momentum.

Moment of a force

Consider a rectangular block of wood resting on a table, as shown in Figure 6.1a. The centre of gravity of the block of wood is located at its geometric centre and the line of action of its weight intersects the base of support ABCD. If the block is tilted over onto one of the edges of the base of support, such as the edge BC, as in Figure 6.1b, the weight of the block W will tend to rotate the block about the supporting edge back to its original resting position in Figure 6.1a. The tendency to restore the block to its original position is the result of the moment (or turning moment) of W about the axis of rotation BC. The magnitude of the moment of

a.   b.

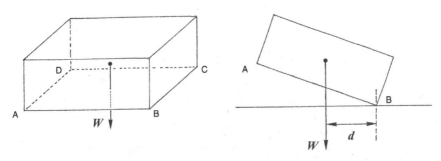

FIGURE 6.1 The turning moment of a force, (a) Block of wood at rest on base of support ABCD. (b) Turning moment $W{\cdot}d$ of the weight of the block W, tending to restore the block to its original resting position after being tilted over on edge BC: d, moment arm of W about edge BC.

W about the axis BC is equal to the product of W and the perpendicular distance d between the axis BC and the line of action of W (Figure 6.1b), i.e.

> moment of W about axis AB $= W{\cdot}d$ (W multiplied by d)
> If $W = 2$ kgf and $d = 0.1$ m, then
> moment of W about axis AB $= 2\text{kgf} \times 0.1$ m $= 0.2$ kgf·m
> As 2 kgf $= 19.62$ N, then
> moment of W about axis AB $= 19.62$ N $\times 0.1$ m $= 1.962$ N·m

The N·m (newton metre) is the unit of moment of force in the SI system (Table 1.1).

In general, when a force F acting on an object rotates or tends to rotate the object about some specified axis, the moment of F is defined as the product of F and the perpendicular distance d between the axis of rotation and the line of action of F, i.e. moment of $F = F{\cdot}d$. The axis of rotation is often referred to as the fulcrum and the perpendicular distance between the line of action of the force and the axis of rotation is usually referred to as the moment arm of the force. The moment of a force is sometimes referred to as torque. For a given moment of force, the greater the force, the smaller the moment arm of the force and vice versa. For example, in trying to push open a heavy door, much less force will be required if the force is applied to the side of the door furthest away from the hinges, i.e. a large moment arm, than if the force is applied to the door close to the hinges, i.e. a small moment arm.

BOX 6.1

The moment of a force is the product of the magnitude of the force and the perpendicular distance between the line of action of the force and the axis of rotation.

Clockwise and anticlockwise moments

When an object is acted upon by two or more forces which tend to rotate the object, the actual amount and speed of rotation that occurs will depend upon the resultant moment acting on the object, i.e. the resultant of all the individual moments. For example, consider two boys A and B sitting on a see-saw S as shown in Figure 6.2. A see-saw is normally constructed so that its centre of gravity coincides with the fulcrum, i.e. in any position, the line of action of its weight will pass through the fulcrum and, therefore, the weight of the see-saw will not exert a turning moment on the see-saw since the moment arm of its weight about the fulcrum will be zero. Consequently, in Figure 6.2 the only moments tending to rotate the see-saw will be those exerted by the weights of the two boys. The weight of A will exert an anticlockwise moment $W_A \times d_A$ and the weight of B will exert a clockwise moment $W_B \times d_B$. When $W_A \times d_A$ is greater than $W_B \times d_B$, there will be a resultant anticlockwise moment acting on the see-saw such that boy B will be lifted as boy A descends. When $W_A \times d_A$ is equal to $W_B \times d_B$, i.e. when the clockwise moment is equal to the anticlockwise moment, the resultant moment acting on the see-saw will be zero and the see-saw will not rotate in either direction, but remain perfectly still in a balanced position. Consequently, if the weight of one of the boys is known, the weight of the other boy can be found by balancing the see-saw with one boy on each side of the fulcrum with both boys off the floor and then equating the clockwise and anticlockwise moments. For example, if $W_A = 40$ kgf and in the balanced position $d_A = 1.5$ m and $d_B = 2.0$ m, then by equating moments about the fulcrum,

anticlockwise moments (ACM) = clockwise moments (CM)
$$40 \text{ kgf} \times 1.5 \text{ m} = W_B \times 2.0 \text{ m}$$

$$W_B = \frac{40\,\text{kgf} \times 1.5\,\text{m}}{2.0\,\text{m}} = 30\,\text{kgf}$$

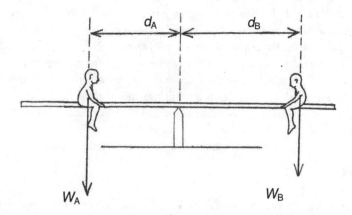

FIGURE 6.2 Two boys sitting on a see-saw. W_A, weight of boy A; W_B, weight of boy B; d_A, moment arm of W_A; d_B, moment arm of W_B.

BOX 6.2

When an object is acted upon by two or more forces which tend to rotate the object, the amount and speed of rotation that occurs will depend upon the resultant moment.

In this example, it was not necessary to involve the weight of the see-saw in the calculations, as it had no moment about the fulcrum. However, provided that both the weight of the see-saw and the position of its centre of gravity are known, the weight of boy B could be found by balancing the see-saw, with one boy each side of the fulcrum, about any point on its length and then equating the clockwise and anticlockwise moments as before. For example, Figure 6.3 shows the see-saw in a balanced position with the centre of gravity of the see-saw located a distance of 0.25 m to the right of the fulcrum. By equating the anticlockwise and clockwise moments,

$$W_A \times d_A = (W_S \times d_S) + (W_B \times d_B)$$

where W_S = weight of the see-saw = 20 kgf
and d_S = moment arm of W_S about the fulcrum = 0.25 m

If $W_A = 40$ kgf, $d_A = 1.25$ m and $d_B = 1.5$ m, then
40 kgf × 1.25 m = (20 kgf × 0.25 m) + (W_B × 1.5 m)
50 kgf·m = 5 kgf·m + (1.5 × W_B) kgf·m

$$W_B = \frac{45\,\text{kgf.m}}{1.5\,\text{m}} = 30\ \text{kgf}$$

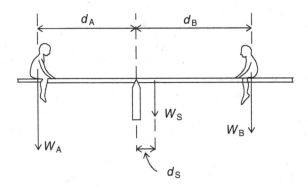

FIGURE 6.3 Two boys sitting on a see-saw in a balanced position with the centre of gravity of the see-saw located a distance to the right of the fulcrum: W_A, weight of boy A = 40 kgf; d_A, moment arm of W_A =1.25 m; W_S, weight of see-saw = 20 kgf; d_S, moment arm of W_S = 0.25 m; W_B, weight of boy B; d_B, moment arm of W_B = 1.5 m.

BOX 6.3

The moment of the resultant of any number of forces about any axis is equal to the algebraic sum of the moments of the individual forces about the same axis. This is referred to as the principle of moments.

Location of the centre of gravity of the human body

In all movements, the movement of the whole body centre of gravity (CG) and, therefore, the movement of the body as a whole, is determined by the impulse of the resultant force acting on the body during the movement. For example, in a long jump, take-off velocity is determined by the velocity of the CG generated in the run-up and the impulse of the resultant force acting on the CG during the period from touchdown to take-off (Figure 6.4). Provided that the velocity of the jumper at the instance of touchdown is known and the components of the ground reaction force are recorded from touchdown to take-off, the take-off velocity of the jumper can be determined from the impulse of the resultant force acting on the jumper from touchdown to take-off. However, force platforms are not usually available. Furthermore, the position of the CG at take-off, as well as take-off velocity would be needed to describe the trajectory of the CG during flight. In this situation, the position of the CG at take-off and the velocity of the CG at take-off can be estimated by video analysis of the movement. In the video analysis, the position of the CG in the median plane in each frame of video of the movement (as in Figure 6.4) is determined by application of the principle of moments; this results in a set of horizontal displacement-time data (the x coordinate data) and a set of vertical displacement-time data (the y coordinate data). If one of the frames corresponds with take-off, the corresponding x-y coordinates will correspond to the position of the CG at take-off. If one of the frames does not correspond with take-off (which will depend upon the frame rate), the position of the CG at take-off will need to be estimated from the horizontal displacement-time and vertical displacement-time data. The horizontal velocity of the CG at take-off can be determined from the horizontal displacement-time data by the process described in the section on linear kinematics of a 100 m sprint in Chapter 3. The vertical velocity of the CG at take-off can be determined by the same process. Take-off velocity (magnitude and direction) can be determined from the horizontal velocity and vertical velocity at take-off.

There are two approaches to determining the position of the whole body centre of gravity, the direct (whole body) approach, in which the body is considered as a whole and the indirect (segmental) approach, in which the body is considered to consist of a number of segments (Hay 1973). In both approaches, the three-dimensional position of the centre of gravity is determined from the intersection of three non-parallel planes that contain the centre of gravity.

FIGURE 6.4 Position and velocity of the whole body centre of gravity of a female long jumper at touchdown and take-off: Velocity vectors based on mean data in Lees *et al.* (1993).

Direct approach

The position of the centre of gravity of the human body may be estimated by equating the moment of body weight while resting on a plane wooden board supported by two parallel knife edge supports. This method is referred to as the reaction board method. Figure 6.5a shows a plane wooden board (approximately 2.5 m × 0.5 m) supported in a horizontal position by two parallel knife edge supports, one of which rests on a set of weighing scales. Figure 6.5b shows a free body diagram of the board. The weight of the board can be measured by simply weighing it. By taking moments about knife edge support A,

$$CM = ACM$$
$$W_B \times d_1 = S_1 \times l$$
$$\text{i.e. } d_1 = \frac{S_1 \times l}{W_B}$$

where
W_B = weight of the board,
l = distance between the knife edge supports,
S_1 = vertical force exerted by the scales on knife edge support B,
d_1 = horizontal distance between knife edge support A and the vertical plane containing the centre of gravity of the board.

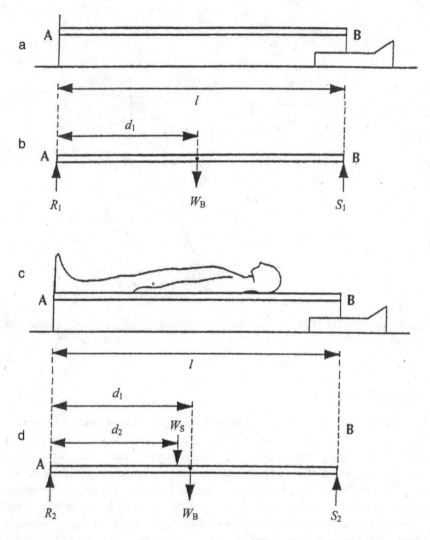

FIGURE 6.5 Reaction board method of determining the position of the centre of gravity of the human body, (a) A plane wooden board supported in a horizontal position by two parallel knife edge supports A and B, with edge B resting on a set of weighing scales, (b) A free body diagram of the board, (c) A man lying on the board with the soles of his feet coincident with the vertical plane through knife edge support A. (d) A free body diagram of the board with the man lying on it: W_B, weight of the board; W_s, weight of the man; l, distance the knife edge supports; R_1, vertical force exerted by edge A on the board without the man; R_1, vertical force exerted by edge A on the board without the man lying on it; W_B, vertical force exerted by the scales on knife edge support B without the man; R_2, vertical force exerted by the scales on knife edge support B with the man lying on it; d_1 = horizontal distance between knife edge support A and the vertical plane containing the centre of gravity of the board; d_2, horizontal distance between knife edge support A and the vertical plane containing the centre of gravity of the man.

Figure 6.5c shows a man lying on the board with the soles of his feet coincident with the vertical plane through knife edge support A. Figure 6.5d shows a free body diagram of the board with the man lying on it. W_B, l and d_1 will be the same as before the man lay on the board, but the vertical force exerted by the scales on the board will increase due to the weight of the man. By taking moments about knife edge support A,

$$CM = ACM$$
$$(W_B \times d_1) + (W_S \times d_2) = S_2 \times l$$

where
W_S = weight of the man,
S_2 = vertical force exerted by the scales on knife edge support B,
d_2 = horizontal distance between knife edge support A and the vertical plane containing the centre of gravity of the man.

i.e. $W_S \times d_2 = (S_2 \times l) - (W_B \times d_1)$
$W_S \times d_2 = (S_2 \times l) - (S_1 \times l)$ (as $W_B \times d_1 = S_1 \times l$)
$$d_2 = \frac{l \times (S_2 - S_1)}{Ws}$$

For example, if

$S_1 = 10$ kgf
$S_2 = 39.5$ kgf
$W_S = 72$ kgf
$l = 2.5$ m
then $d_2 = \dfrac{2.5 \text{ m} \times (39.5 \text{ kgf} - 10 \text{ kgf})}{72 \text{ kgf}}$
$d_2 = 1.024$ m

Therefore, the vertical plane containing the centre of gravity of the man will be at a distance of 1.024 m from knife edge support A. If the height of the man is 1.83 m (6 ft), his centre of gravity will be located in the transverse plane at 55.9% of his stature (1.024 m/1.83 m $\times$ 100% = 55.9%) when standing upright. By repeating the procedure with the body in two other orientations, the position of the centre of gravity of the body can be estimated by finding the point of intersection of the three planes.

This method is referred to as the one-dimension reaction board method, since the orientation of the body has to be changed to locate the position of the centre of gravity in each separate plane.

In Practical Worksheet 12, students use a one-dimension reaction board to examine the effect of changes in body position on the position of the whole body centre of gravity.

Indirect approach

In the indirect approach, the human body is considered to consist of a number of segments linked by joints. Each segment has its own weight and centre of gravity. Provided that the weight of each segment and the position of the centre of gravity of each segment can be determined, the position of the whole body centre of gravity can be determined by application of the principle of moments, i.e. the sum of the moments of the weights of the segments about any particular axis is equal to the moment of the total weight. Figure 6.6 shows a female long jumper just before take-off with her body divided into nine segments: combined trunk, head and neck; left upper arm; combined left forearm and hand; right upper arm; combined right forearm and hand; left thigh; combined left shank (lower leg) and foot; right thigh; combined right shank and foot. The position of the centre of gravity of each segment is shown together with the position of the whole body centre of gravity. The coordinate of the whole body centre of gravity with respect to any axis of rotation and any dimension can be determined by applying the principle of moments as shown in Figure 6.6.

The method is fairly straightforward and has been incorporated into a range of commercially available video motion analysis software. However, the accuracy of the method depends largely on the accuracy with which the weights of the segments and the positions of their centres of gravity can be determined. A number of studies have been undertaken to provide this data. The main studies may be classified as cadaver studies, immersion studies and anthropomorphic models (Hay 1973, Sprigings *et al.* 1987).

Cadaver studies

The earliest reported cadaver study appears to be that of Harless in 1860 (Hay 1973), who dissected two adult male cadavers. In 1889, Braune and Fischer (Hay 1973) dissected four adult male cadavers. Each cadaver was frozen solid with the joints of the upper and lower limbs in mid-range position. The segments were then separated by sawing through each joint in a plane that bisected the angle between the segments. Each segment was then weighed and the position of its centre of gravity determined by balancing or suspension. The most comprehensive and most frequently cited cadaver studies are those of Dempster (1955) and Clauser *et al.* (1969), who used very similar methods to those of Braune and Fischer. Dempster dissected eight white male cadavers (age range 52–83 years) and presented individual and average data on segmental weight (percentage of total weight), segmental centre of gravity position (as a proportion of the distance between defined segmental end points) and segment density. Loss of weight due to dismemberment, especially unknown quantities of body fluids, resulted in the sum of the average segment weights and, therefore, the sum of the average segmental percentages (97.2%) being less than the corresponding whole body data (which were recorded prior to dissection). Dempster indicated that the weight loss was proportional to the weight of the segments. In the average segmental weight data presented in Table 6.1, the 2.8% weight

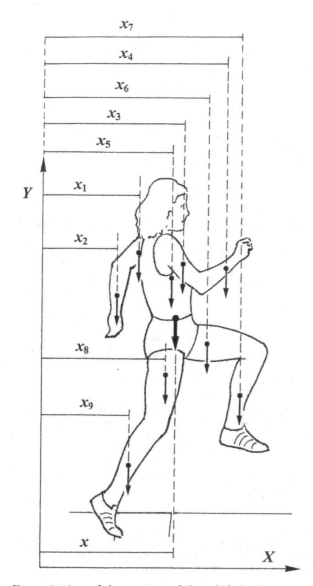

FIGURE 6.6 Determination of the position of the whole body centre of gravity by application of the principle of moments. By taking moments about the Z axis in the X dimension, $W \cdot x = W_1 \cdot x_1 + W_2 \cdot x_2 + W_3 \cdot x_3 + W_4 \cdot x_4 + W_5 \cdot x_5 + W_6 \cdot x_6 + W_7 \cdot x_7 + W_8 \cdot x_8 + W_9 \cdot x_9$ where W = total weight of the body; x = moment arm of W = X coordinate of the whole body centre of gravity; W_1 = weight of the left upper arm; x_1 = moment arm of W_1; W_2 = weight of combined left forearm and hand; x_2 = moment arm of W_2; W_3 = weight of the right upper arm; x_3 = moment arm of W_3; W_4 = weight of combined right forearm and hand; x_4 = moment arm of W_4; W_5 = combined weight of trunk, head and neck; x_5 = moment arm of W_5; W_6 = weight of the left thigh; x_6 = moment arm of W_6; W_7 = weight of combined left shank and foot; x_7 = moment arm of W_7; W_8 = weight of the right thigh; x_8 = moment arm of W_8; W_9 = weight of combined right shank and foot; x_9 = moment arm of W_9, i.e.

$$x = \frac{W_1 \cdot x_1 + W_2 \cdot x_2 + W_3 \cdot x_3 + W_4 \cdot x_4 + W_5 \cdot x_5 + W_6 \cdot x_6 + W_7 \cdot x_7 + W_8 \cdot x_8 + W_9 \cdot x_9}{W}.$$

TABLE 6.1 Mean segment weights (percentage of total weight) and centre of gravity locations (proportion of segment length in direction indicated) for adult men (Dempster 1955; Clauser *et al.* 1969; Plagenhoef *et al.* 1983)

Segment[*]	Dempster[1]		Clauser et al.[2]		Plagenhoef et al.[3]	
	Weight	CG locus	Weight	CG locus	Weight CG	Locus
Upper arm	2.73	0.436[a]	2.6	0.513[a]	3.25	0.436[a]
Forearm	1.59	0.430[b]	1.6	0.390[b]	1.87	0.430[b]
Hand	0.62	0.506[c]	0.7	0.480[c]	0.65	0.468[c]
Forearm & hand	2.21	0.677[d]	2.3	0.626[d]	2.52	0.671[d]
Whole upper limb	4.94	0.512[e]	4.9	0.413[e]	5.77	0.50[e]
Thigh	9.93	0.433[f]	10.3	0.372[f]	10.50	0.433[f]
Shank	4.63	0.433[g]	4.3	0.371[g]	4.75	0.434[g]
Foot	1.44	0.429[h]	1.5	0.449[h]	1.43	0.50[h]
Shank & foot	6.07	0.434[i]	5.8	0.475[i]	6.18	0.605[i]
Whole lower limb	16.00	0.434[j]	16.1	0.382[j]	16.68	0.436
Trunk, head & neck	58.13	0.604[k]	58.0	0.604[m]	55.10	0.566[k]
Trunk, head & neck	58.13	0.346[n]	58.0	0.346[p]	55.10	0.370[n]
Head & neck	8.13	0.433[q]	7.3	0.433[r]	8.26	0.45[q]
Head	7.00[s]	0.545[t]	7.0[s]	0.545[t]	7.0[s]	0.545[t]
Trunk	50.00	0.620[v]	50.7	0.620[w]	46.48	0.630[v]

[*] segments in the anatomical position (Figure 3.4)
[a] shoulder axis to elbow axis
[b] elbow axis to wrist axis
[c] wrist axis to first interphalangeal joint of the second finger
[d] elbow axis to styloid process of the ulna
[e] shoulder axis to styloid process of the ulna
[f] hip axis to knee axis
[g] knee axis to ankle axis
[h] intersection of the line joining the ankle axis and the ball of the foot and the vertical line perpendicular with the sole of the foot that divides the foot in the ratio 0.429 to 0.571 from heel to toe
[i] knee axis to medial malleolus
[j] hip axis to ankle axis
[k] top of head to hip axis with head, neck and trunk in normal upright posture
[m] top of head to hip axis with head, neck and trunk in normal upright posture (Dempster 1955)
[n] shoulder axis to hip axis with trunk in normal upright posture
[p] shoulder axis to hip axis with trunk in normal upright posture (Dempster 1955)
[q] top of head to centre of body of 7th cervical vertebra
[r] top of head to centre of body of 7th cervical vertebra (Dempster 1955)
[s] data from Braune and Fischer (1889), reported by Hay (1973)
[t] top of head to occipital-atlas joint, from Braune and Fischer (1889), reported by Hay (1973)
[v] shoulder axis to hip axis
[w] shoulder axis to hip axis (Dempster 1955)
[1] Mean data from 8 white male cadavers (age range 52–83 years)
[2] Mean data from 13 white male cadavers (age range 28–74 years)
[3] Mean weight data from 35 living college-age men using water immersion method and density data from Dempster (1955) and mean CG locus data from seven living college-age men using water immersion method

discrepancy has been distributed in proportion to the segmental percentages so that the total percentage is 100% rather than 97.2%. For example, the percentage weight of each upper arm is given as 2.73%, which is equal to 2.65/97.2 × 100, where 2.65% is the average percentage weight of the upper arm reported by Dempster.

Clauser *et al.* (1969) dissected 13 adult male cadavers (age range 28–74 years), selected to closely approximate a wide range of body types. Care was taken to minimize tissue loss during dismemberment. The average data for segmental weight and segmental centre of gravity locus from the Clauser *et al.* study is shown in Table 6.1.

There do not appear to be any reported data on segment weights and segment centre of gravity loci in female cadavers.

Immersion studies

As mass is the product of volume and density, a number of studies have estimated segmental masses by measuring the volume of the segments by water displacement (carefully immersing each segment or segments in a tank of water and measuring the volume of water displaced) and multiplying the volume of the segment by the corresponding average segmental density reported by Dempster (1955). The most comprehensive immersion study carried out on living subjects would appear to be that of Plagenhoef *et al.* (1983). Segmental volumes of 135 college-age athletes (100 women and 35 men) were measured. The corresponding average segmental weights are shown in Table 6.1 for men and Table 6.2 for women. Segmental centre of gravity loci were estimated using seven men and nine women (from the group of 135 subjects) using the immersion method described by Clauser *et al.* (1969); this involves immersing the segment to a proportion of its volume (using average data presented by Clauser *et al.*) that corresponds to the plane of the segmental centre of gravity. The average segmental centre of gravity loci from the Plagenhoef *et al.* study are shown in Table 6.1 for men and Table 6.2 for women. The studies referred to in Tables 6.1 and 6.2 did not all report data for the same segments. Consequently, to complete the data sets in Tables 6.1 and 6.2, data has been included from other studies as indicated.

Anthropomorphic models

To personalize the determination of segment weights and segment centre of gravity positions for a particular subject, a number of anthropomorphic models have been developed; these include Whitsett (1963), Hanavan (1964), Hatze (1980) and Yeadon (1990). All of the models are based on anthropometric measurements taken directly from the subject. The measurements are used to construct geometric representations of the body segments. The masses of segments are estimated from segment volume and average density and the positions of segmental centres of gravity are estimated by mathematical methods on the basis of the geometry of the segment shapes. The main disadvantages of anthropomorphic models are that anthropometric measurements have to be taken directly from the subject and the time required

TABLE 6.2 Mean segment weights (percentage of total weight) and centre of gravity locations (proportion of segment length in direction indicated) for adult women (Plagenhoef et al. 1983)[†]

Segment[*]	Weight	CG Locus
Upper arm	2.90	0.458[a]
Forearm	1.57	0.434[b]
Hand	0.50	0.468[c]
Forearm & hand	2.07	0.657[d]
Whole upper limb	4.97	0.486[e]
Thigh	11.75	0.428[f]
Shank	5.35	0.419[g]
Foot	1.33	0.50[h]
Shank & foot	6.68	0.568[i]
Whole lower limb	18.43	0.420[j]
Trunk, head & neck	53.20	0.603[k]
Trunk, head & neck	53.20	0.450[m]
Head & neck	8.20	0.45[n]
Head	7.00[p]	0.545[q]
Trunk	45.00	0.569[m]

[*] segments in the anatomical position (Figure 3.4)
[a] shoulder axis to elbow axis
[b] elbow axis to wrist axis
[c] wrist axis to first interphalangeal joint of the second finger
[d] elbow axis to styloid process of the ulna
[e] shoulder axis to styloid process of the ulna
[f] hip axis to knee axis
[g] knee axis to ankle axis
[h] intersection of the line joining the ankle axis and the ball of the foot and the vertical line perpendicular with the sole of the foot that divides the foot in the ratio 0.429 to 0.571 from heel to toe
[i] knee axis to medial malleolus
[j] hip axis to ankle axis
[k] vertex (top of head) to hip axis with head, neck and trunk in normal upright posture
[m] shoulder axis to hip axis with trunk in normal upright posture
[n] vertex (top of head) to centre of body of 7th cervical vertebra
[p] from Braune and Fischer (1889), reported by Hay (1973)
[q] top of head to occipital-atlas joint, from Braune and Fischer (1889), reported by Hay (1973)
[†] Mean weight data from 100 living college-age women using water immersion method and density data from Dempster (1955) and mean CG locus data from nine living college-age women using water immersion method.

to take all the measurements may be considerable. For example, the time required to take the 242 measurements required for applying the Hatze (1980) model is about 80 minutes per subject (Sprigings et al. 1987).

It is reasonable to expect that a personalized model would be more accurate than the application of average percentage data from cadaver and immersion studies.

However, the comparative data currently available is meagre (Sprigings *et al.* 1987) and seems to indicate that the difference in the results of the different methods (in the estimated position of the whole body centre of gravity) is unlikely to be significant in the analysis of whole body movement.

The major advantage of using percentage data for segment weight and segment centre of gravity position is that the position of the whole body centre of gravity of the subject can be determined from a video image without the need for any anthropometric information about the subject. Not surprisingly, the application of percentage data for segment weight and segment centre of gravity position is the preferred method in most biomechanical analyses, especially those based on video analysis.

Determination of the whole body centre of gravity by the application of the principle of moments

In undertaking segmental analysis, the analyst has to decide the number of segments that will constitute the segmental model. The more segments in the model, the greater the number of segmental end points and, therefore, the greater the time needed to digitize each frame of video. Digitization refers to the process of identifying and recording the coordinates of each point in the segmental model as well as reference points for the origin and axes of the reference axis system upon which the analysis will be based (Figure 6.7). The number of segments in the model will largely depend on the purpose of the analysis. For example, if the description of ankle movement is an important objective, it will be necessary to have separate shank and foot segments for each leg. However, the weight of each foot is small relative to total body weight and the effect of movement of the foot relative to the shank on the position of the whole body centre of gravity is likely to be insignificant. Consequently, if the main objective of the analysis is the movement of the whole body centre of gravity, the analyst may decide to regard the shank and foot as a single segment. Similarly, the forearm and hand may be regarded as a single segment. In detailed biomechanical analyses of elite long jumpers, researchers have used a number of segmental models ranging from an 11-segment model (Lees *et al.* 1993) to a 16-segment model (Linthorne *et al.* 2005).

Figure 6.7 shows the image of a female long jumper just before take-off taken from a video frame and superimposed, for the purpose of analysis, onto a one-centimetre grid. The segment end points defining a 9-segment model (defined in Figure 6.6) are shown. The first two columns of Table 6.3 show the x and y coordinates of the segment end points. Column 6 of Table 6.3 shows the corresponding x and y coordinates of the segment centres of gravity. These points are shown in Figure 6.7. Table 6.4 shows the coordinates of the segment centres of gravity and the coordinates of the whole body centre of gravity, determined by application of the principle of moments. In applying the principle of moments, it is not necessary to know the actual body weight of the subject. Use of the segment weight proportions rather than the segment weights in the calculation of segment and body

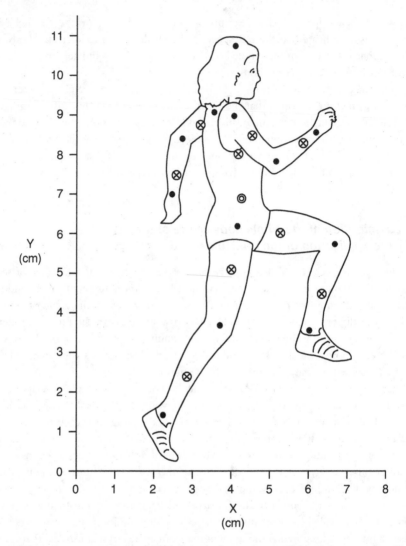

FIGURE 6.7 Segment end points (•) defining a 9-segment model and the corresponding positions of the segment centres of gravity (⊗) and whole body centre of gravity (◎).

weight moments will give the same result. However, as proportion has no unit (it is simply a number because it is the ratio of two weights), the units of the calculated moments will be cm rather than N·cm. This may be confusing to some students and so a nominal body weight of 63 kgf (618 N) has been used in the illustration in Table 6.4.

In Practical Worksheet 13, students use a one-dimension reaction board to compare the direct and indirect (segmental) methods of determining the position of the whole body centre of gravity of the human body. In Practical Worksheet 14,

TABLE 6.3 Coordinates of the segment end points and segment centres of gravity of the female long jumper shown in Figure 6.7

Segment	Coordinates[1] (cm)		Length[2] (cm)	CGP[3]	CGS[4] (cm)	CGO[5] (cm)
	a	b	c			
Right upper arm	Shoulder	Elbow				
x	3.8	4.9	1.1	0.458	0.50	4.30
y	9.0	7.9	−1.1	0.458	−0.50	8.50
Right forearm & hand	Elbow	Wrist				
x	4.9	5.9	1.0	0.657	0.66	5.56
y	7.9	8.6	0.7	0.657	0.46	8.36
Left upper arm	Shoulder	Elbow				
x	3.3	2.5	−0.8	0.458	−0.37	2.93
y	9.1	8.4	−0.7	0.458	−0.32	8.78
Left forearm & hand	Elbow	Wrist				
x	2.5	2.3	−0.2	0.657	−0.13	2.37
y	8.4	7.0	−1.4	0.657	−0.92	7.48
Trunk, head & neck	Vertex	Right Hip*				
x	3.8	4.0	0.2	0.603	−0.12	3.92
y	10.8	6.2	−4.6	0.603	−2.77	8.03
Right thigh	Hip	Knee				
x	4.0	3.6	−0.4	0.428	−0.17	3.83
y	6.2	3.7	−2.5	0.428	−1.07	5.13
Right shank & foot	Knee	Ankle				
x	3.6	2.2	−1.4	0.568	−0.79	2.81
y	3.7	1.4	−2.3	0.568	−1.31	2.39
Left thigh	Hip	Knee				
x	4.0	6.5	2.5	0.428	1.07	5.07
y	6.2	5.8	−0.4	0.428	−0.17	6.03
Left shank & foot	Knee	Ankle				
x	6.5	5.9	−0.6	0.568	−0.34	6.16
y	5.8	3.6	−2.2	0.568	−1.25	4.55

[1] x and y coordinates of segment end points a and b
[2] length of segment in the dimension = b − a
[3] position of segmental centre of gravity as a proportion of segment length in direction a to b (from Table 6.2)
[4] position of segmental centre of gravity in the dimension in relation to a
[5] coordinates of the position of the centre of gravity of the segment = a + c
*In this example, the coordinates of the left hip joint and right hip joint are the same. If the coordinates of the left hip and right hip had been different from each other, it would have been necessary to find the midpoint of the line linking the two joints as the hip reference point for determining the position of the centre of gravity of the trunk, head and neck segment.

TABLE 6.4 Coordinates of the segment centres of gravity and whole body centre of gravity (determined by the principle of moments) of the female long jumper shown in Figure 6.7

Segment	Coordinates[1]		Weight[2]	Weight[3]	Moment X[4]	Moment Y[5]
	(cm)			(N)	(N·cm)	(N·cm)
	x	y				
Right upper arm	4.30	8.50	0.0290	17.92	77.06	152.32
Right forearm and hand	5.56	8.36	0.0207	12.79	71.13	106.92
Left upper arm	2.93	8.78	0.0290	17.92	37.47	157.34
Left forearm & hand	2.37	7.48	0.0207	12.79	30.31	95.67
Trunk, head & neck	3.92	8.03	0.5320	328.78	1288.80	2640.07
Right thigh	3.83	5.13	0.1175	72.61	278.11	372.51
Right shank & foot	2.81	2.39	0.0668	41.28	116.00	98.66
Left thigh	5.07	6.03	0.1175	72.61	368.13	437.84
Left shank & foot	6.16	4.55	0.0668	41.28	254.28	187.82
Totals				618.00	2521.29	4249.15
Coordinates of CG [6]	4.08	6.87				

[1] x and y coordinates of the segmental centres of gravity from Table 6.3 (cm)
[2] Weight of segments as a proportion of total body weight (from Table 6.2)
[3] Weight of segments in newtons (total body weight = 63 kgf = 618 N)
[4] Moments of the segmental weights about Z axis with respect to X dimension (N·cm)
[5] Moments of the segmental weights about Z axis with respect to Y dimension (N·cm)
[6] Moment of body weight = sum of moments of segments,

  i.e. $W \cdot x_G$ = sum of Moment X
  where W = body weight = 618 N and x_G = X coordinate of CG
  i.e. $x_G = \dfrac{\text{sum of Moment X}}{W} = \dfrac{2521.29\,\text{N·cm}}{618\,\text{N}} = 4.08\,\text{cm}$

Similarly,

  $y_G = \dfrac{\text{sum of Moment Y}}{W} = \dfrac{4249.15\,\text{N·cm}}{618\,\text{N}} = 6.87\,\text{cm}$

  where y_G = Y coordinate of CG

students record a video of a standing long jump and analyze the video to determine take-off distance, flight distance and landing distance.

BOX 6.4

There are two approaches to determining the position of the centre of gravity of the human body: the direct (whole body) approach and the indirect (segmental) approach.

Concentric force, eccentric force and couple

A see-saw is constrained to rotate about the fixed horizontal axis through its fulcrum and a door is constrained to rotate about the fixed vertical axis through its hinges. When an object is free to rotate within a particular plane, i.e. it is not constrained to rotate about any particular axis, and a force acts on the object that causes or tends to cause the object to rotate, the rotation will occur about an axis that passes through the centre of gravity of the object. For example, Figure 6.8a shows an overhead view of a curling stone resting on a perfectly flat horizontal ice rink. The stone is acted on by a horizontal force F which is concentric, i.e. the line of action of F passes through the centre of gravity of the stone. A concentric force produces or tends to produce rectilinear translation. Assuming that the friction between the stone and the ice is negligible, the only horizontal force acting on the stone is the concentric force F. Consequently, the stone will experience or tend to experience rectilinear translation, i.e. move in a straight line in the direction of F (Figure 6.8a, 6.8b). In a vertical jump, i.e. when the purpose of the movement is simply to raise the centre of gravity as high as possible off the ground without rotation or horizontal movement, the ground reaction force will be concentric (Figure 6.9).

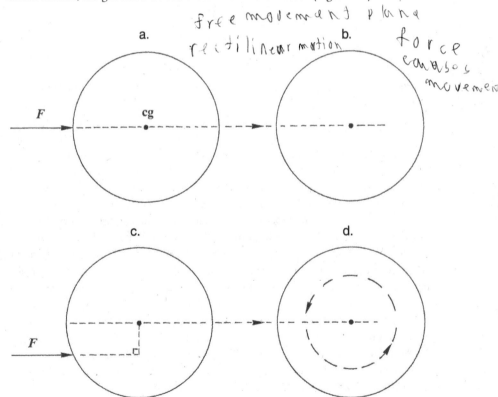

FIGURE 6.8 Overhead view of a curling stone, (a) Concentric force, (b) Eccentric force, cg, centre of gravity of the stone.

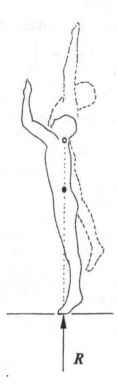

FIGURE 6.9 Concentric ground reaction force R in a vertical jump without rotation or horizontal movement.

In Figure 6.8c, the horizontal force F is eccentric, i.e. its line of action does not pass through the centre of gravity of the stone. An eccentric force produces or tends to produce simultaneous rectilinear translation and rotation of an object about an axis that passes through the centre of gravity of the object and is perpendicular to the eccentric force. Consequently, in response to the eccentric force F, the stone will experience or tend to experience simultaneous rectilinear translation and rotation about the vertical axis passing through its centre of gravity (Figure 6.8c, 6.8d).

Most movements in sport that involve rotation of the whole body during flight are preceded by a ground contact phase prior to take-off in which the ground reaction force is eccentric to the performer's centre of gravity. For example, Figure 6.10 shows a gymnast performing a front somersault following a run-up. Prior to take-off, the line of action of the ground reaction force R passes behind the gymnast's centre of gravity. The effect of the eccentric ground reaction force will be to move the centre of gravity in the direction of R (mainly upward, but also slightly forward in Figure 6.10) and simultaneously to help to generate forward rotation of the body about the mediolateral axis through the centre of gravity.

Figure 6.11 shows an overhead view of a child's roundabout, which is designed to rotate about a fixed vertical axis through its point of support. In response to an eccentric horizontal force F applied to one of the handrails of the roundabout, the

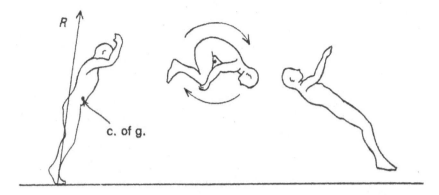

FIGURE 6.10 Eccentric ground reaction force *R* during take-off in a forward somersault.

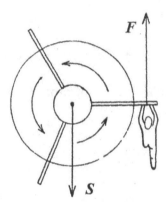

FIGURE 6.11 Overhead view of a child's roundabout: *F*, eccentric force exerted on one of the handrails; S, horizontal force, equal and opposite to *F*, exerted by the vertical support on the roundabout. *F* and S form a couple resulting in rotation with no translation.

vertical support exerts an equal and opposite force S on the roundabout. The tendencies of *F* and S to translate the roundabout (*F* upward and S downward with respect to Figure 6.11) cancel each other out, but the turning effect of *F* rotates the roundabout, i.e. the roundabout rotates, but does not translate. The force system produced by *F* and S is called a couple, i.e. a system of two parallel, equal and opposite forces, one concentric and one eccentric (as in Figure 6.11) or both eccentric, that tend to rotate an object in the same direction about a particular axis. A couple produces or tends to produce rotation without translation. Rotation of any object about a fixed axis is the result of a couple. The magnitude of a couple is the product of one of the forces and the perpendicular distance between the two forces. The larger the couple, the greater the angular acceleration and, therefore, the greater the angular velocity.

The systems of forces that result in translation, rotation or simultaneous translation and rotation may be summarized as follows. Consider an object that is free to translate and rotate within a particular plane, i.e. it is not constrained to translate in any particular direction or to rotate about any particular axis:

- *Concentric force system*: If the line of action of the resultant force acting on the object is parallel to the plane of movement and acts through the centre of gravity of the object, the object will experience or tend to experience rectilinear translation, but will not rotate. This is a concentric force system.
- *Eccentric force system*: If the line of action of the resultant force acting on the object is parallel to the plane of movement, but does not act through the centre of gravity of the object, the object will experience or tend to experience simultaneous rectilinear translation and rotation about an axis perpendicular to the plane of movement that passes through the centre of gravity of the object. This is an eccentric force system.
- *Couple*: If the resultant of the forces acting on the object rotate or tend to rotate the object about an axis which does not move (translate) in the plane of movement, the force system is a couple.

Rotation and Newton's first law of motion

From the previous section, an object at rest will only begin to rotate about a particular axis when the resultant force acting on the object is an eccentric force or couple. Newton's laws of motion apply to linear motion and angular motion. With regard to angular motion, the first law of motion may be expressed as follows:

> The resultant moment acting on a body at rest or rotating about a particular axis with constant angular velocity (assuming no change in the shape of the object while rotating) is zero and the body will remain at rest or continue to rotate with constant angular velocity unless acted upon by an unbalanced eccentric force or couple.

For example, consider a bicycle turned upside down so that it rests on its handlebars and saddle (Figure 6.12). Each wheel will remain at rest until an eccentric force or couple is applied to it with respect to the horizontal axis a_S through the spindle of the wheel. When the pedals are turned clockwise with respect to Figure 6.12a, the chain will exert an eccentric force on the rear wheel such that the wheel will start to rotate in a clockwise direction about a_S (Figure 6.12b). When the pedals are brought to rest (provided that the wheel is not a fixed wheel that rotates clockwise and anticlockwise in direct response to corresponding rotation of the pedals), the wheel will continue to rotate even though there is no couple or eccentric force acting on it. Furthermore, the wheel is likely to rotate for some considerable time unless a counterrotation eccentric force, in the form of a brake, is applied to the wheel. If a brake is not applied to the wheel, the duration of rotation of the wheel will depend

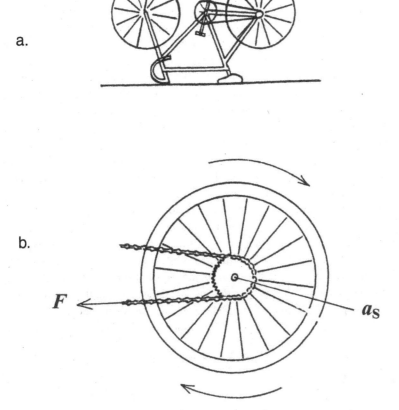

FIGURE 6.12 Application of an unbalanced eccentric force to the rear wheel of a bicycle by the chain as a result of rotation of the pedals: F, force exerted by the chain; a_S, axis through the spindle of the wheel.

entirely on the amount of friction between the wheel and its spindle. The friction exerts a counterrotation couple on the wheel and eventually brings it to rest; the greater the friction, the sooner the wheel is brought to rest. If the friction could be eliminated, the wheel would continue to rotate forever with constant angular velocity.

In such movements as somersaults (Figure 6.10), in which the human body rotates freely in space during the flight phase of the movement, the rotation of the body will take place about an axis that passes through the centre of gravity of the body. Furthermore, the angular velocity of the body about the axis of rotation will remain constant, provided that the orientation of the body segments to each other does not change. The rotation of the body in such movements is ultimately reduced to zero by the action of the ground reaction force on landing (which exerts an unbalanced counterrotation eccentric force).

Moment of inertia

The resistance of an object to an attempt to change its linear motion (resistance to start moving if it is at rest and resistance to change its speed and/or direction if it is moving) is referred to as its inertia. The inertia of an object is directly proportional to its mass; the larger the mass, the greater the inertia. The resistance of an object to an attempt to change its angular motion (resistance to start rotating about a particular axis if it is at rest and resistance to change its angular speed and/or direction if it is rotating) is referred to as its moment of inertia. The moment of inertia of an object about a particular axis depends not only on the mass of the object, but also on the distribution of the mass of the object about the axis of rotation. The closer the mass of the object to the axis of rotation or the more concentrated the mass of the object around the axis of rotation, the smaller will be the moment of inertia of the object and the easier it will be (the smaller the moment of force) to start the object rotating or to keep it rotating if is already rotating.

The moment of inertia of an object about a particular axis of rotation is obtained by multiplying the mass of each particle of the object by the square of its distance from the axis of rotation and summing for the whole object. In the SI system, the unit of moment of inertia is kilogram metres squared ($kg \cdot m^2$). As the distribution of the mass of an object about a particular axis changes, so will the distance of some or all of the particles of mass from the axis of rotation. Consequently, the moment of inertia of the object about the axis of rotation will also change.

BOX 6.5

The moment of inertia of an object about a particular axis of rotation is the resistance of the object to an attempt to change its angular motion.

Figure 6.13 shows three positions of a gymnast rotating about a horizontal bar. In position 1, the mass of the gymnast is distributed as far away as possible from the axis of rotation. Consequently, the moment of inertia of the gymnast about the axis of rotation will be highest in this position. In position 2, the legs are much closer to the bar than in position 1 such that the moment of inertia of the gymnast about the bar will be smaller in position 2 than in position 1. In position 3, the trunk and legs are much closer to the bar than in positions 1 and 2, and the moment of inertia of the gymnast about the bar will be smaller in position 3 than in positions 1 and 2.

The mass distribution of an object about a particular axis is reflected in the radius of gyration of the object about the axis. The moment of inertia I of an object about a particular axis is equivalent to that of a mass m, equal to the mass of the object, rotating about the axis at a distance k from the axis, where k is the radius gyration, i.e.

$$I = m \cdot k^2$$

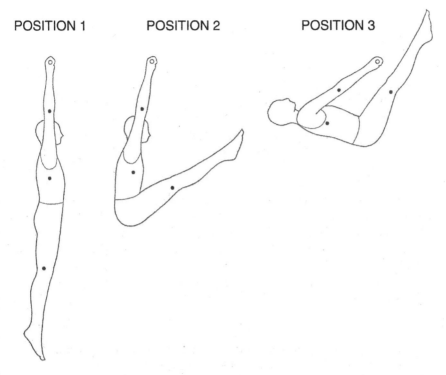

POSITION 1   **POSITION 2**   **POSITION 3**

FIGURE 6.13   Three positions of a gymnast rotating about a horizontal bar. The dots indicate the centres of gravity of the arm, the leg and the combined trunk, head and neck.

For comparative purposes, the moment of inertia of an object about a particular axis is often expressed in terms of $m \cdot k^2$. For a given object, m is constant, but k and, therefore, the moment of inertia of the object, depend upon the distribution of the mass of the object about the axis of rotation.

In Practical Worksheet 15, students use a turntable to determine the moment of inertia and radius of gyration of the human body about a vertical axis while in a seated position.

Angular momentum

Just as an object of mass m (kg) moving with linear velocity v (m/s) has linear momentum $m \cdot v$ (kg·m/s), an object rotating about a particular axis has angular momentum $I \cdot \omega$ (kg·m²/s), where I (kg·m²) is the moment of inertia of the object about the axis and ω (rad/s) is the angular velocity of the object about the axis. Whereas the mass of an object is constant (unless part of the mass is removed or more mass is added), the moment of inertia of a rotating object can be changed by simply redistributing the mass about the axis of rotation. From Newton's first law of motion, the angular momentum of an object about a particular axis of rotation will remain constant until the object is acted upon by an unbalanced eccentric force or couple. Therefore, if the moment of inertia of an object rotating freely about a particular axis is changed, there will be a simultaneous change in the angular velocity of the object so that the angular momentum of the object remains unchanged. This principle is referred to as the conservation of angular momentum and it has great significance in movements of the human body that involve rotation during flight.

Figure 6.14 shows the successive positions of a gymnast during the performance of a front somersault following a run-up. During the flight phase (positions 2–9) the gymnast rotates in the median plane about the mediolateral axis a_Z through his centre of gravity. Since there are no unbalanced turning moments acting on the gymnast during flight, the angular momentum of the gymnast about a_Z will be conserved, i.e. remain constant. To land on his feet, the gymnast must complete the forward somersault very quickly. By tucking his body (positions 2–5), the gymnast reduces the moment of inertia of his body about a_Z which simultaneously results in an increase in his angular velocity about a_Z. Suppose that the moment of inertia of his body about a_Z in position 5 is half that in position 2. Since his angular momentum about a_Z is the same in both positions, it follows that

$$I_2 \cdot \omega_2 = I_5 \cdot \omega_5$$

where I_2, I_5 and ω_2, ω_5 are the moments of inertia and angular velocities of the gymnast about a_Z in positions 2 and 5, respectively. As $I_5 = I_2/2$, then,

$$I_2 \cdot \omega_2 = \frac{I_2}{2} \omega_5$$

i.e. $\omega_5 = 2\omega_2$

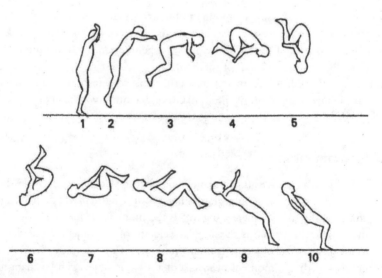

FIGURE 6.14 Successive positions of a gymnast during the performance of a front somersault following a run-up.

By halving the moment of inertia, the angular velocity is doubled. The increased angular velocity will enable the gymnast to complete the forward somersault in half the time that it would have taken if he had not tucked his body. In the second part of the flight phase (positions 6–9), the gymnast extends his body which increases his moment of inertia and decreases his angular velocity about a_z in preparation for landing.

BOX 6.6

The angular momentum of an object about a particular axis is the product of its moment of inertia and angular velocity about the axis.

Rotation and Newton's second law of motion

When a resultant moment M acts on an object about a particular axis of rotation, the angular acceleration α experienced by the object about the axis of rotation is directly proportional to the moment of inertia I of the object about the axis of rotation, i.e. $M = I \cdot \alpha$. This equation (directly analogous to $F = m \cdot a$; see equation 4.14) represents Newton's second law of motion in relation to rotation.

As $M = I \cdot \alpha$, then $M = I(\omega_2 - \omega_1)/t$ (from equation 5.2) and

$$M \cdot t = I \cdot \omega_2 - I \cdot \omega_1 \text{ Eq. 6.1}$$

where t is the duration of the moment M and ω_1 and ω_2 are the angular velocities of the object at t_1 and t_2 where $t = t_2 - t_1$.

Newton's second law of motion in relation to rotation is often expressed in terms of equation 6.1 (directly analogous to $F \cdot t = m \cdot v - m \cdot u$; see equation 4.15) as follows:

When a resultant moment greater than zero acts on an object about a particular axis of rotation, the change in angular momentum experienced by the object takes place in the direction of the moment and is directly proportional to the magnitude of the moment and the duration of the moment.

When the amount of force and size of the moment arm that constitute a particular moment are not specified, for example, in describing the turning effect on part of a machine, the term torque is used rather than moment.

From equation 6.1, it is clear that to maximize the angular momentum of an object about a particular axis, it is necessary to apply as much moment as possible for as long as possible. The product $M \cdot t$ of the moment M and duration t of the moment is called the impulse of the moment, i.e. the angular impulse. The angular impulse–angular momentum principle is widely used in sports,

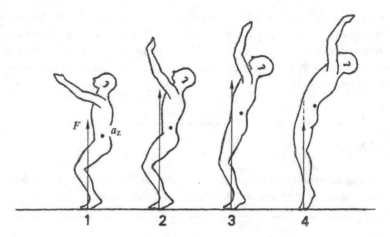

FIGURE 6.15 Eccentric ground reaction force F prior to take-off in a standing back somersault. The linear impulse of F generates linear momentum of the whole body centre of gravity in the direction of F and the angular impulse of F about a_Z generates backward angular momentum of the body about a_Z.

especially those involving rotation of the whole body, such as gymnastics and diving (Watkins 2014).

Figure 6.15 shows four successive positions of a gymnast prior to take-off during the performance of a standing back somersault. Prior to take-off, the gymnast needs to generate sufficient upward linear momentum and sufficient backward angular momentum about the mediolateral axis a_Z through his centre of gravity to perform the somersault and land on his feet. These requirements are met by a vertical eccentric ground reaction force, which passes in front of a_Z (Figure 6.15).

BOX 6.7

To maximize the change in angular momentum of an object about a particular axis of rotation, it is necessary to maximize the angular impulse applied to the object.

Rotation and Newton's third law of motion

From Newton's first law of motion, when an object is rotating about a particular axis with constant angular momentum, the resultant moment acting on the object is zero. Internal forces may alter the moment of inertia of the object about the axis of rotation, but angular momentum will be conserved. When internal forces change the moment of inertia of an object about a particular axis, there is a simultaneous change in the angular momentum of each part of the object. For example, in a

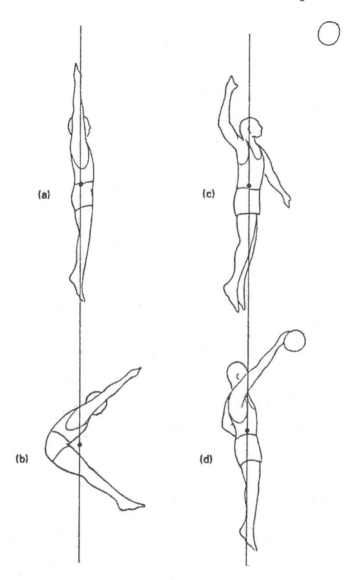

FIGURE 6.16 (a, b) Pike jump. (c, d) Volleyball spike.

pike jump (Figure 6.16a–6.16b), the pike is achieved by flexion of the hips which simultaneously increases the angular momentum of the upper body in a clockwise direction with respect to Figure 6.16a and increases the angular momentum of the legs in an anticlockwise direction with respect to Figure 6.16a so that angular momentum is conserved. When the hip flexors contract to produce the pike position, they pull equally on both of their attachments, the upper body and the legs. Therefore, the angular impulse of the hip flexors on the upper body is exactly the same in magnitude, but opposite in direction to that exerted on the legs so that the angular momentum of the body about the mediolateral axis through the hip joints is unchanged, i.e. it remains zero.

The action of the hip flexors in piking the body in a pike jump is an example of the operation of Newton's third law of motion in relation to rotation. The law may be expressed as follows:

> When an object A exerts a moment on another object B, there will be an equal and opposite moment exerted by object B on object A.

The effect of Newton's third law in relation to rotation is most clearly seen in movements that occur during flight when the body has little, if any, angular momentum as, for example, in a pike jump (Figure 6.16a, 6.16b) and spiking a volleyball (Figure 6.16c–6.16d).

References

Clauser, C., McConnville, C. and Young, J. (1969) 'Weight, volume and centre of mass segments of the human body', AMRL-TR-69–70. Wright-Patterson Air Force Base, Ohio.

Dempster, W. T. (1955) 'Space requirements of the seated operator', WADC Technical Report 55–159. Wright-Patterson Air Force Base, Ohio.

Hanavan, E. P. (1964) 'A mathematical model of the human body', AMRL Technical Report 64–102, Wright-Patterson Air Force Base, Ohio.

Hatze, H. (1980) 'A mathematical model for the computational determination of parameter values of anthropomorphic segments', *Journal of Biomechanics* 13:833–843.

Hay, J.G. (1973) 'The center of gravity of the human body', In *Kinesiology III: American Alliance for Health, Physical Education and Recreation*, Washington DC, pp. 2–44.

Lees, A., Fowler, N. and Derby, D. (1993) 'A biomechanical analysis of the last stride, touchdown and take-off characteristics of the women's long jump', *Journal of Sports Sciences* 11:303–314.

Linthorne, N. P., Guzman, M. S. and Bridgett, L. A. (2005) 'Optimal take-off angle in the long jump', *Journal of Sports Sciences* 23(7):703–712.

Plagenhoef, S., Evans, F. G. and Abdelnour, T. (1983) 'Anatomical data for analysing human motion', *Research Quarterly for Exercise and Sport* 54(2):169–178.

Sprigings, E. J., Burko, D. B., Watson, G. and Laverty, W. H. (1987) 'An evaluation of three segmental methods used to predict the location of the total body CG for human airborne movements', *Journal of Human Movement Studies* 13:57–68.

Watkins, J. (2014) *Fundamental biomechanics of sport and exercise*. London: Routledge.

Whitsett, C. E. (1963) 'Some dynamic response characteristics of weightless man', AMRL Technical Report 63–18, Wright-Patterson Air Force Base, Ohio.

Yeadon, M.R. (1990) 'The simulation of aerial movement: II. A mathematical inertia model of the human body', *Journal of Biomechanics* 23:67–74.

7

WORK, ENERGY AND POWER

There are a number of different forms of energy including heat, light, sound, electricity, chemical and mechanical. The total amount of energy in the universe is constant; it cannot be created or destroyed, it can only be transformed from one form to another. All interactions in nature are the result of transformation of energy from one form to another. For example, the combustion of oil, gas or coal produces heat that can be used to produce electricity that can be used to produce heat in a toaster; heat and light in a light bulb; heat, light and sound in a television; or mechanical energy in the form of movement in a model train. Living organisms consume nutrients in order to produce chemical energy to maintain all of the life processes. The majority of the energy produced from nutrients is used to produce mechanical energy in the form of movement of the body segments. Transformation of energy into mechanical energy is referred to as work. All forms of energy are equivalent in their capacity to do work, i.e. bring about the transfer of energy from one body to another through the action of a force or forces that deform or change the position or speed of movement of the bodies. Power is the rate of transformation of energy from one form to another. Mechanical power is the rate at which energy is transformed in the form of work. The purpose of this chapter is to describe the relationships between work, mechanical energy and mechanical power in human movement. Practical Worksheets 16 to 19 are highlighted at the end of the chapter.

Objectives

After reading this chapter, you should be able to do the following:

1   Differentiate the work of a force and the work of the moment of a force.
2   Differentiate average power and instantaneous power.

3 Describe the components of mechanical energy.
4 With respect to human movement, differentiate internal work and external work.

Work and kinetic energy

Newton's second law of motion expresses the relationship between impulse and momentum. With regard to linear motion,

$$F{\cdot}t = m{\cdot}v - m{\cdot}u \text{ (equation 4.15)}$$

where
F = resultant force (greater than zero) acting on an object of mass m
t = duration of the resultant force
u = velocity of the object at the start of force application
v = velocity of the object at the end of force application

If F is a constant force, resulting in constant acceleration, the average velocity v_a of the object during the period t is given by

$$v_a = \frac{u+v}{2} \qquad\qquad \text{Eq. 7.1}$$

If $u = 0$, then

$$F{\cdot}t = m{\cdot}v \qquad\qquad \text{Eq. 7.2}$$

and

$$v_a = \frac{v}{2} \qquad\qquad \text{Eq. 7.3}$$

If d is the distance moved by the object during the period t, then

$$v_a = \frac{d}{t} \qquad\qquad \text{Eq. 7.4}$$

It follows from equations 7.3 and 7.4 that

$$t = \frac{2d}{v} \qquad\qquad \text{Eq. 7.5}$$

By substitution of t from equation 7.5 into equation 7.2,

$$F{\cdot}d = \frac{m{\cdot}v^2}{2} \qquad\qquad \text{Eq. 7.6}$$

The quantity $F \cdot d$ is the work done by the force on the mass m. A force does work when it moves its point of application in the direction of the force, and the amount of work done is defined as the product of the force and the distance moved by the point of application of the force. The quantity $m \cdot v^2/2$ is the change in translational (linear) kinetic energy of the mass m resulting from the work done on it. The translational kinetic energy of an object is the energy possessed by the object due to its linear velocity. An object of mass m moving with linear velocity v has translational kinetic energy equal to $m \cdot v^2/2$. A stationary object has no translational kinetic energy as $v = 0$. Energy is the capacity to do work. A body can do work if it has energy. There are a number of different forms of energy including heat, light, sound, electricity, chemical and mechanical. Translational kinetic energy is a form of mechanical energy and work is the transformation of any form of energy into mechanical energy. Equation 7.6 is referred to as the work-energy equation in relation to the work of a force; it expresses the relationship between the work done on an object by a force and the resulting change in the translational kinetic energy of the object (Watkins 2014). As will be described shortly, the moment of a force can also do work.

When a body A does work on another body B, energy is transferred from A to B. In this process, body B is moved or its type of movement is changed, i.e. it experiences acceleration or deceleration, usually combined with deformation. Figure 7.1 shows the movement of a soccer ball from the instant of contact with the kicker's foot to the instant of separation of foot and ball. If the ball is at rest before the kick, the velocity of the ball after the kick can be determined by applying equation 7.6. For example, if

$F = 607.5$ N $=$ the average force exerted on the ball during the kick,
$d = 0.27$ m $=$ contact distance (distance moved by the ball in the direction of F while in contact with the kicker's foot)
$m = 0.45$ kg $=$ the mass of the ball

then the work done W on the ball by the kicker is given by

$$W = F \cdot d = 607.5 \text{ N} \times 0.27 \text{ m} = 164 \text{ J}$$

In the SI system, the unit of work is the joule (J) (after James Joule 1818–1889). One joule is the work done by a force of 1 newton (N) when it moves its point of application a distance of 1 metre (m) in the direction of the force. The units of work, energy and moment of a force consist of the same combination of base units, $kg \cdot m^2/s^2$. To distinguish these quantities, the unit for work and energy is the joule (J) and the unit for moment of a force is the newton metre (N·m). From equation 7.6, the velocity v of the ball after the kick is given by

$$v = \sqrt{(2F \cdot d / m)} = 27.0 \text{ m/s} \ (60.4 \text{ mph})$$

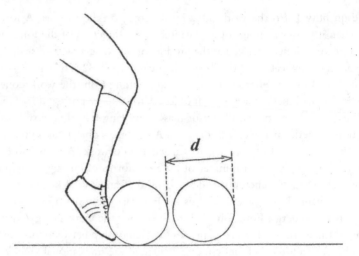

FIGURE 7.1 Distance *d* moved by a soccer ball while in contact with the kicker's foot when kicked from rest.

BOX 7.1

All interactions in nature are the result of transformation of energy from one form to another. Transformation of energy into mechanical energy is referred to as work. In the SI system, the unit of work is the joule.

Strain energy

In drawing a bow, the archer does work on the bow by pulling on the arrow which, in turn, pulls on the bowstring (Figure 7.2a). Figure 7.2b shows the corresponding load-deformation curve of the force exerted on the bow. As the bow is drawn, the work done on the bow, represented by the area under the load-deformation curve, is stored in the bow which deforms like a spring. The work done on the bow is stored in the bow as strain energy, i.e. energy that can be used to do work on the arrow (propel the arrow forward via the bowstring) when the bowstring is released. Strain energy is a form of mechanical energy, i.e. energy that can do work. The amount of work done by the archer on the bow, i.e. the amount of strain energy stored in the bow, is $F \cdot d$ where F is the average force exerted on the bowstring and d is the distance that the bow is drawn back. When the arrow is released, the bow recoils and the strain energy stored in the bow is transformed into work on the arrow via the bowstring. The arrow separates from the bowstring with kinetic energy equivalent to the strain energy stored in the drawn bow, i.e. $F \cdot d = m \cdot v^2/2$, where F = average force exerted on the arrow by the bowstring, d = distance over which F is applied, m = mass of arrow and v = release speed of the arrow.

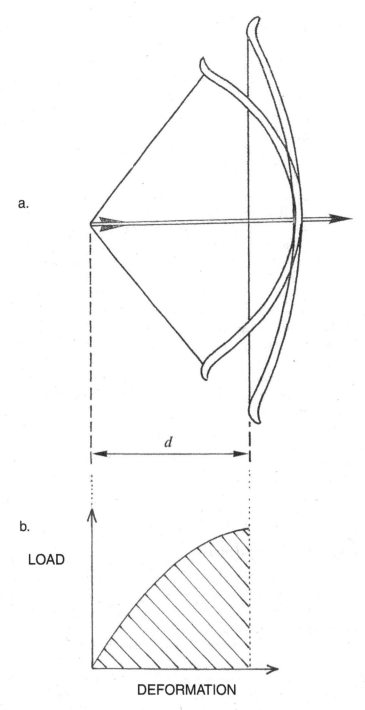

FIGURE 7.2 Storage of strain energy in a bow. (a) Deformation of a bow through a distance *d*. (b) Load-deformation curve of the force exerted on the bow and the corresponding deformation of the bow. The work done on the bow, i.e. the strain energy stored in the bow, is represented by the shaded area under the load-deformation curve.

Many materials store strain energy in response to loading, for example, a stretched elastic band, a trampoline, a springboard in diving, a beat board in vaulting and a pole in pole vaulting. Strain energy is a form of potential energy, i.e. stored energy, that, given appropriate conditions, may be used to do work.

Gravitational potential energy

If an object is held above ground level and then released, it will fall to the ground due to the force of its own weight. The work done on the object by the force of its own weight W when it falls a distance h is given by $W \cdot h$. Consequently, when an object of weight W is held a distance h above the ground, it possesses gravitational potential energy equivalent to $W \cdot h$, which can be transformed into kinetic energy if it is allowed to fall. Gravitational potential energy is usually expressed as $m \cdot g \cdot h$ (where $W = m \cdot g$; m is the mass of the object and g is the acceleration due to gravity).

Figure 7.3a shows a rubber ball held at rest at a height h_1 above the floor where the floor is the reference level ($h = 0$) for the measurement of gravitational potential energy. While it is held at rest, the ball has no kinetic energy, but its gravitational potential energy will be equal to $m \cdot g \cdot h_1$. If the ball is allowed to fall, its gravitational potential energy will be transformed into kinetic energy, i.e. its gravitational potential energy will decrease and its kinetic energy will increase. When the ball hits the floor, its gravitational potential energy will be zero and its kinetic energy will be equal to $m \cdot v^2 / 2$ where v is the velocity of the ball at impact, i.e.

$$m \cdot g \cdot h_1 = m \cdot v^2 / 2$$
$$v = \sqrt{(2g \cdot h_1)}$$

If $h_1 = 1$ m, then $v = \sqrt{(2 \times 9.81 \text{ m/s}^2 \times 1 \text{ m})} = 4.43$ m/s

Hysteresis, resilience and damping

In the preceding example, the ball strikes the floor with kinetic energy equivalent to the gravitational potential energy it possessed at release. During contact with the floor the ball will undergo a loading phase in which it is compressed and the kinetic energy of the ball is transformed into strain energy in the compressed ball. Following the loading phase, the ball undergoes an unloading phase, in which it recoils and the strain energy is released as kinetic energy in the form of the upward bounce of the ball. However, the ball will not bounce as high as the point from which it was dropped. This situation is shown in Figure 7.3a where h_1 is the drop height and h_2 is the bounce height. As the ball is at rest at A and B, some of the energy of the ball was dissipated during contact with the floor in the form of, for example, heat and sound. The amount of energy dissipated is reflected in the load deformation curves of the ball during loading and unloading (Figure 7.3b).

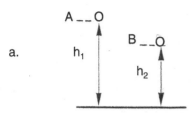

a.

h_1 : Drop Height

h_2 : Bounce Height

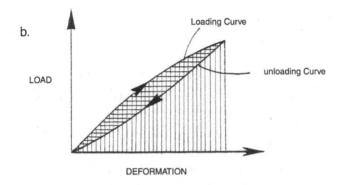

b.

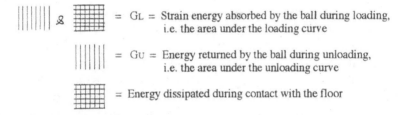

The resilience R of the ball is given by:

$$R = \frac{G_U}{G_L} \times 100\%$$

If $G_L = 180\,J$ and $G_U = 153\,J$, then:

$$R = \frac{153\,J}{180\,J} \times 100\%$$

$$R = 85\%$$

FIGURE 7.3 Load–deformation characteristics of a bouncing rubber ball.

The amount of strain energy absorbed by the ball during loading, the area under the loading curve, is greater than the amount of energy returned during unloading, the area under the unloading curve. The loop described by the loading and unloading curves is a hysteresis loop (from the Greek word *husteros* meaning later or delayed). The area of the hysteresis loop represents the energy dissipated. The

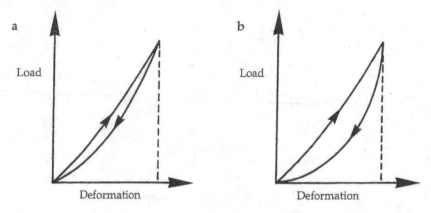

FIGURE 7.4 Load–deformation characteristics of materials. (a) High resilience and low damping. (b) Low resilience and high damping.

extent of hysteresis in a material is reflected in the resilience of the material which is defined as the amount of energy returned during unloading as a percentage of the amount of energy absorbed during loading. All materials exhibit hysteresis to a certain extent; there are no 100% resilient materials.

Figure 7.4a shows the load–deformation characteristics of highly resilient material such as some types of rubber, and Figure 7.4b shows the load–deformation characteristics of low-resilience material, such as some forms of vinyl acetate foam. Damping refers to a low level of resilience; a damping material returns very little energy during unloading compared to the amount of energy that it absorbs during loading. For protection during transportation, fragile goods are usually packed in materials with good damping properties. Similarly, in walking and running, shock-absorbing soles and insoles in shoes are used to protect the body from high-impact loads at heel-strike. In human movement, shock absorption refers to the dissipation of the work done on the body as a result of a collision with the environment in a way that prevents high impact loads. Shock absorption systems are low resilience energy absorption systems.

BOX 7.2

The human body converts chemical energy into three forms of mechanical energy: kinetic energy, gravitational potential energy and strain energy.

Power

Power is the rate of transformation of energy from one form to another. Mechanical power is the rate at which energy is transformed in the form of work, i.e. work rate. In the rest of this chapter, power refers to work rate. In the SI system, the unit of power is the watt (W). One watt (after James Watt 1736–1819) is a work rate of 1 J/s. Power can be measured over a period of time, referred to as average power, or instantaneously, referred to as instantaneous power.

Average power

In the example of kicking a soccer ball, the contact time t between the kicker's foot and the ball can be determined by applying Newton's second law of motion, i.e.

$$F \cdot t = m \cdot v \text{ (equation 7.2)}$$

$$t = \frac{m.v}{F} = \frac{0.45 \text{kg} \times 27.0 \text{m/s}}{607.5 \text{N}} = 0.02 \text{s}$$

As the kicker does 164 J of work on the ball in 0.02 s, then the average power P_a of the kick, i.e. the average rate at which the kicker transfers energy to the ball in the form of work, is given by

$$P_a = \frac{W}{t} = \frac{164 \text{J}}{0.02 \text{s}} = 8200 \text{W} = 8.2 \text{kW} \ (1 \text{kW} = 1 \text{kilowatt} = 1000 \text{W})$$

A soccer player kicking a stationary ball is similar, in terms of energy transfer, to a hammer hitting a nail (Figure 7.5). As the hammer contacts the nail, the hammer has a certain amount of translational kinetic energy due to the work done on it by the person swinging it. As the hammer is rapidly brought to rest, its translational kinetic energy is equally rapidly transferred to the nail in the form of work, which

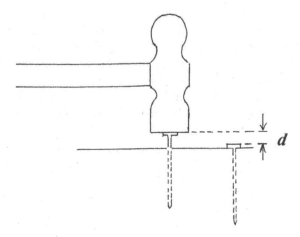

FIGURE 7.5 Impact of hammer on nail. d, distance that the nail is driven into the wood by the impact.

drives the nail a distance d into the wood. Some of the energy of the hammer may be dissipated as heat and sound. If it is assumed that all of the translational kinetic energy of the hammer is transferred to the nail in the form of work, and if

$m = 0.45$ kg $=$ the mass of the hammer
$v = 1.8$ m/s $=$ the velocity of the hammer on impact with the nail
$d = 0.01$ m

then from equation 7.6, the average force F exerted by the hammer on the nail is given by

$$F = \frac{m \cdot v^2}{2d} = \frac{0.45\,\text{kg} \times (1.8\,\text{m/ s})^2}{0.02\,\text{m}} = 72.9\,\text{N} = 7.43\,\text{kgf}$$

The duration of the impact t can be determined from Newton's second law of motion, i.e. $F \cdot t = m \cdot v - m \cdot u$, where $F = -72.9$ N, $u = 1.8$ m/s and $v = 0$.

$$t = \frac{-(0.45\,\text{kg} \cdot 1.8\,\text{m/ s})}{-72.9\,\text{N}} = 0.011\,\text{s}$$

The average power of the hammer strike on the nail is given by

$$P_a = \frac{W}{t} = \frac{F \cdot d}{t} = \frac{72.9\,\text{N} \times 0.01\,\text{m}}{0.011\,\text{s}} = 66.3\,\text{W}$$

Instantaneous power

In the example of kicking a soccer ball, the average power of the kick was 8.2 kW. Figure 7.6 shows the force-time graph and corresponding velocity-time graph and instantaneous power-time graph of the force exerted by the kicker on the ball. The corresponding data is shown in Table 7.1. The area between the force-time graph and the time axis represents the impulse of the force; the velocity of the ball increases as the impulse increases. The instantaneous power P_i of the kick, i.e. the instantaneous rate at which the kicker transfers energy to the ball in the form of work, is given by

$$P_i = F_i \cdot v_i$$

where F_i and v_i are the force and velocity of the ball at the instant of time t_i. For example, when $t_i = 0.01$ s, $F_i = 1130$ N and $v_i = 14.79$ m/s. Consequently, P_i is given by

$$P_i = 1130\ \text{N} \times 14.79\ \text{m/s} = 16712.7\ \text{W} = 16.713\ \text{kW}$$

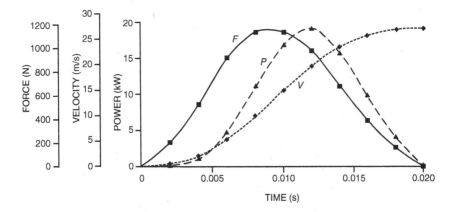

FIGURE 7.6 Force-time, velocity-time and instantaneous power-time graphs pertaining to a soccer ball that is kicked from a resting position. See data in Table 7.1. F, force; v, velocity; P, power.

TABLE 7.1 Force-time, velocity-time and instantaneous power-time data pertaining to a soccer ball that is kicked from a resting position (see Figure 7.6)

Time (s)	Force (N)	Velocity (m/s)	Instantaneous power (kW)
0	0	0	0
0.002	200	0.41	0.081
0.004	520	1.99	1.035
0.006	910	5.15	4.683
0.008	1130	9.77	11.039
0.010	1130	14.79	16.713
0.012	970	19.59	19.004
0.014	670	23.24	15.568
0.016	380	25.55	9.708
0.018	150	26.68	4.003
0.020	0	26.99	0

Peak instantaneous power, in the region of 19 kW, occurs at approximately $t_i = 0.012$ s (see Table 7.1 and Figure 7.6).

The transformation of relatively small amounts of energy can have a considerable effect when sufficient power is involved. For example, exposure of a piece of steel to a beam of light for 10 s has no visible effect on the steel. However, if the same amount of light is discharged in one picosecond (one millionth of one millionth of a second, 10^{-12} s), it will burn a hole in the steel (Frost 1967). This is the basis of laser technology.

BOX 7.3

Power is the rate of transformation of energy from one form to another. Mechanical power is the rate at which energy is transformed in the form of work. In the SI system, the unit of power is the watt.

Work of the moment of a force

Newton's second law of motion in relation to angular motion expresses the relationship between angular impulse and angular momentum, i.e.

$$M \cdot t = I \cdot \omega_2 - I \cdot \omega_1 \text{ (equation 6.1)}$$

where
M = resultant moment of force (greater than zero) acting on an object which has a moment of inertia I about a particular axis,
t = duration of the resultant moment,
ω_1 = angular velocity of the object at the start of the application of the resultant moment,
ω_2 = angular velocity of the object at the end of the application of the resultant moment.

If M is a constant moment, resulting in constant angular acceleration, the average angular velocity ω_a of the object during the period t is given by

$$\omega_a = \frac{\omega_1 + \omega_2}{2}$$

Eq. 7.7

If $\omega_1 = 0$, then

$$M \cdot t = I \cdot \omega \text{ (where } \omega = \omega_2)$$

Eq. 7.8

and

$$\omega_a = \frac{\omega}{2} \text{ (where } \omega = \omega_2)$$

Eq. 7.9

If θ is the angular distance in radians moved by the object during the period t, then

$$\omega_a = \frac{\theta}{t}$$

Eq. 7.10

It follows from equations 7.9 and 7.10 that

$$t = \frac{2\theta}{\omega}$$

Eq. 7.11

By substitution of t from equation 7.11 into equation 7.8,

$$\frac{2M \cdot \theta}{\omega} = I \cdot \omega$$

$$M \cdot \theta = \frac{I \cdot \omega^2}{2} \qquad \text{Eq. 7.12}$$

The quantity $M \cdot \theta$ is the work done by the moment of force on the object. As the unit of M is newton metres and the unit of θ is radians, the unit of $M \cdot \theta$ is joules, the same as the unit of work done by a force. The work done by the moment of a force is the product of the moment and the angular distance in radians moved by the object during the impulse of the moment. The quantity $I \cdot \omega^2/2$ is the change in rotational (angular) kinetic energy of the object resulting from the work done on it by the moment of force. The rotational kinetic energy of an object is the energy possessed by the object due to its angular velocity. An object with moment of inertia I and angular velocity ω about a particular axis has rotational kinetic energy equal to $I \cdot \omega^2/2$. A stationary object has no rotational kinetic energy as $\omega = 0$. Equation 7.12 is referred to as the work-energy equation in relation to the work of the moment of a force; it expresses the relationship between the work done on an object by the moment of a force and the resulting change in the rotational kinetic energy of the object (Watkins 2014).

At any particular instant in time, the total mechanical energy E of an object is the sum of its gravitational potential energy (*GPE*), translational kinetic energy (*TKE*) and rotational kinetic energy (*RKE*), i.e.

$$E = GPE + TKE + RKE \qquad \text{Eq. 7.13}$$

Internal and external work

All voluntary human movement is the result of work done by the skeletal muscles, i.e. muscle contractions transform chemical energy stored in the muscles into mechanical energy in the form of internal work W_I and external work W_E (Winter 1979). W_I is the work done on the body itself, i.e. changes in the mechanical energy of the body segments. W_E is the work done by the body in moving objects in the environment. Over a period of time t, W_I is given by

$$W_I = W_{GI} + W_{TI} + W_{RI} \qquad \text{Eq. 7.14}$$

where W_{GI} is the work done in changing the gravitational potential energy of the body, W_{TI} is the work done in changing the translational kinetic energy of the body and W_{RI} is the work done in changing the rotational kinetic energy of the body. Over the same period of time t, W_E is given by

$$W_E = W_{GE} + W_{TE} + W_{RE} \qquad \text{Eq. 7.15}$$

where W_{GE} is the work done in changing the gravitational potential energy of objects in the environment, W_{TE} is the work done in changing the translational kinetic energy of the objects and W_{RE} is the work done in changing the rotational kinetic energy of the objects. W_E includes, for example,

- Changes in the gravitational potential energy of other objects: e.g. lifting and lowering a box;
- Changes in the kinetic energy of other objects: e.g. throwing and catching a ball or accelerating the flywheel of a cycle ergometer;
- Work done against friction: e.g. pushing a box across a floor, pedalling a cycle ergometer against the friction brake mechanism or turning a screw.

Consequently, the total work done W_T by the human body and the corresponding average power output P_a during any particular period of time t are given by

$$W_T = W_I + W_E \qquad\qquad \text{Eq. 7.16}$$
$$P_a = W_T/t \qquad\qquad \text{Eq. 7.17}$$

Equation 7.17 should be used to determine the average power output of the human body over a particular period of time. To do so, it is necessary to measure $W_{GI}, W_{TI}, W_{RI}, W_{GE}, W_{TE}$ and W_{RE}. However, as it is difficult to measure all six work components, the total work done by the human body over any particular period of time is rarely if ever measured. Nevertheless, tests of human power output based on stair climbing (Margaria *et al.* 1966), running up a slope (Kyle and Caiozzo 1985) and vertical jumping (Davies and Rennie 1968) have been used for many years to assess human power output.

In Practical Worksheet 16, students determine average power output in stair climbing and running up a slope. In Practical Worksheet 17, students use a force platform to determine average and peak power output in a countermovement vertical jump. In Practical Worksheet 18, students determine the reliability of distance jumped in a standing long jump. In Practical Worksheet 19, students determine the concurrent validity of distance jumped in a standing long jump as a predictor of peak power in a countermovement vertical jump.

References

Davies, C.T.M. and Rennie, R. (1968) 'Human power output', *Nature* 217:770–771.

Frost, H.M. (1967) *An introduction to biomechanics*. Springfield, IL: Charles C Thomas.

Kyle, C.R. and Caiozzo, V. J. (1985) 'A comparison of the effect of external loading upon power output in stair climbing and running up a ramp', *European Journal of Applied Physiology* 54:99–103.

Margaria, R., Aghemo, P. and Rovelli, E. (1966) 'Measurement of muscular power (anaerobic) in man', *Journal of Applied Physiology* 21:1662–1664.

Watkins, J. (2014) *Fundamental biomechanics of sport and exercise*. London: Routledge.

Winter, D. A. (1979) 'A new definition of mechanical work in human movement', *Journal of Applied Physiology* 47:79–83.

Practical Worksheets

PRACTICAL WORKSHEET 1

Linear kinematic analysis of a 15 m sprint

Objective

To record the 5 m split times during a 15 m sprint and use the distance-time data to produce the distance-time, speed-time and acceleration-time graphs of the sprint.

Location

Indoor or outdoor area with minimum length of 30 m

Apparatus and equipment

Four sets of photocells linked to a timer

Method

Subject's clothing and footwear

Sports clothing and trainers

Layout of equipment

The four sets of photocells are arranged as in Figure PW1.1. Each set of photocells is arranged so that the photocells are placed approximately 3 m apart at each side of the running track. The photocells are mounted on tripods at a height of about 1 m. One set of photocells is located at the start, with the other sets located 5 m, 10 m and 15m from the start line.

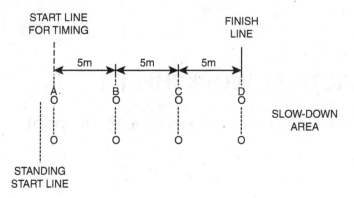

FIGURE PW1.1   Location of photocells (A, B, C, D).

Data collection and analysis

1 Using a standing start from 1 m behind the start line (so that the first set of photocells will start the timer as you run between them), perform three maximum-effort trials and record the 5 m, 10 m and 15 m times for each trial in Table PW1.1 of the data collection sheet.

2 Plot the distance–time data (distance on the vertical axis and time on the horizontal axis) of your fastest trial on centimetre squared graph paper and draw a smooth curve through the origin and the three data points to produce the distance–time graph. If necessary, extend the graph beyond the 3 s point on the time axis. A suitable scale to use would be 1 cm on the graph paper for 1 m for the distance axis and 5 cm on the graph paper for 1 s for the time axis.

3 From the distance–time graph, read the distance at 1, 2 and 3 s after the start and record these data in the second column of Table PW1.2 of the data collection sheet.

4 Calculate and record in the third column of Table PW1.2 the change in distance during each of the three 1 s intervals.

5 Record the average speed in each of the three 1 s intervals in the fourth column of Table PW1.2 (These will be the same numbers as in column 3).

6 Plot the average speed–time data (column 4 of Table PW1.2) on the same sheet of graph paper, choosing an appropriate scale for speed (vertical axis). A suitable scale would be 2 cm on the graph paper for 1 m/s for the speed axis. As the data represent average speeds, plot the data at the midpoints of the corresponding time intervals.

7 Draw a smooth curve through the origin and the three data points to produce the speed–time graph. Extend the graph beyond the 3 s point on the time axis.

8 From the speed-time graph, read the speed at 1, 2 and 3 s after the start and record these data in the second column of Table PW1.3 of the data collection sheet.

9 Calculate and record in the third column of Table PW1.3 the change in speed during each of the three 1 s intervals.

10 Record the average acceleration in each of the three 1 s intervals in the fourth column of Table PW1.3 (These will be the same numbers as in column 3).

11 Using the same axis and scale for acceleration as that used for speed, plot the average acceleration-time data (column 4 of Table PW1.3) on the same sheet of graph paper. As the data represent average accelerations, plot the data at the midpoints of the corresponding time intervals.

12 Draw a smooth curve through the origin and the three data points to produce the acceleration-time graph.

TABLE PW1.1 5 m, 10 m and 15 m times (s) in three maximum-effort trials

Distance(m)	Trial 1	Trial 2	Trial 3
5			
10			
15			

TABLE PW1.2 Average speed

Time interval(s)	Distance(m)	Change in distance(m)	Average speed(m/s)
1			
2			
3			

TABLE PW1.3 Average acceleration

Time interval(s)	Speed(m/s)	Change in speed(m/s)	Average acceleration (m/s^2)
1			
2			
3			

Presentation of results

1   Present the 5 m, 10 m and 15 m split times for your three maximum effort trials in Table PW1.1.
2   Present the average speed data for your fastest trial in Table PW1.2.
3   Present the average acceleration data for your fastest trial in Table PW1.3.
4   Present a figure showing the line-of-best-fit distance-time, speed time and acceleration-time graphs for your fastest trial.

Example results

Example data are shown in Tables PW1.4 to PW1.6. The distance-time, speed-time and acceleration-time graphs based on the data in Tables PW1.4 to PW1.6 are shown in Figure PW1.2. The speed-time graph indicates that speed continued to increase throughout the trial. This is clearly reflected in the progressive increase in the slope of the distance-time graph over the corresponding period. Whereas speed continued to increase throughout the trial, the slope of the speed-time graph progressively decreased, i.e. acceleration was always positive, but decreasing. This is clearly reflected in the acceleration-time graph.

TABLE PW1.4 5 m, 10 m and 15 m times (s) in three maximum-effort trials

Distance(m)	Trial 1	Trial 2	Trial 3
5	1.33	1.35	1.32
10	2.22	2.11	2.12
15	3.25	3.01	2.83

TABLE PW1.5 Average speed

Time(s)	Distance(m)	Change in distance(m)	Average speed(m/s)
1	3.45	3.45	3.45
2	9.25	5.80	5.80
3	16.25	7.00	7.00

TABLE PW1.6 Average acceleration

Time interval(s)	Speed(m/s)	Change in speed(m/s)	Average acceleration (m/s^2)
1	4.875	4.875	4.875
2	6.45	1.575	1.575
3	7.50	1.05	1.05

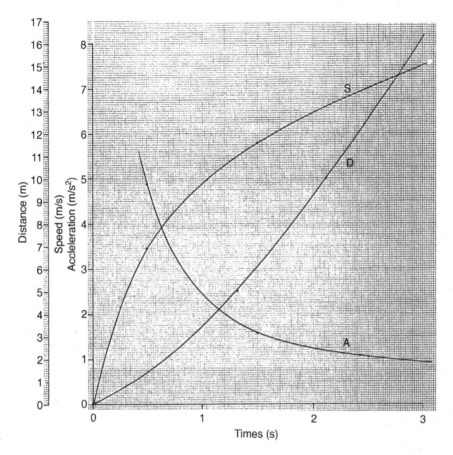

FIGURE PW1.2 Distance-time (D), speed-time (S) and acceleration-time (A) graphs based on the data in Tables PW1.4 to PW1.6.

PRACTICAL WORKSHEET 2

The effect of increase in speed on stride length, stride rate and relative stride length in running

Objective

To obtain stride length, stride rate and relative stride length data for subjects running on a treadmill over a speed range of 1.5 m/s–3.5 m/s and to produce the corresponding stride length-speed, stride rate-speed and relative stride length-speed graphs.

Location

Motion analysis laboratory

Apparatus and equipment

Variable speed treadmill with handrails, stop watches, steel tape

Method

Subject's clothing and footwear

Sports clothing and trainers

Data collection and analysis

Height of subject

The subject's height is measured (m) with the subject standing upright without shoes and looking straight ahead. The height is recorded in Table PW2.1.

Leg length

1   The subject lies supine with legs straight and together.
2   The subject relaxes legs so that legs rest naturally with feet turned out.
3   The length of each leg is measured with a steel tape; this is the distance between the anterior superior iliac spine and medial malleolus.
4   The subject's average leg length is recorded in the Table PW2.1.

Time measurements

1   For each subject, in a single trial, the time for 10 complete stride cycles at speeds of 1.5 m/s, 2.5 m/s and 3.5 m/s is measured and recorded in the results sheet.
2   At the start of each trial, the subject stands on the treadmill with hands on the handrails. The speed of the treadmill is gradually increased to 1.5 m/s (moderate walking pace) as the subject accommodates to the increase in speed.
3   After the subject has settled into a natural rhythm at a speed of 1.5 m/s, the time(s) for 10 complete stride cycles are measured using a stop watch (heel-strike to heel-strike of the same foot). The time for 10 complete stride cycles can be measured by any number of timers with the average time being recorded in Table PW2.1. For example, the class can be divided into groups of six people with each member of a group taking turns as subject, treadmill operator and timer.
4   After the time for 10 complete stride cycles at a speed of 1.5 m/s has been measured, the speed of the treadmill is gradually increased to 2.5 m/s (slow jog). After the subject has settled into a natural rhythm at a speed of 2.5 m/s, the time(s) for 10 complete stride cycles are measured and recorded in Table PW2.1.
5   The speed of the treadmill is then gradually increased to 3.5 m/s (moderate running pace) and the time for 10 complete stride cycles is measured as before and recorded in Table PW2.1. The speed of the treadmill is then gradually reduced to zero.
6   After the times for 10 complete stride cycles at all three speeds have been recorded, the stride rate, stride length, relative stride length with respect to height (RSL:H) and relative stride length with respect to leg length (RSL:L) are calculated for each speed as follows:

Stride rate (SR) $= 10$ cycles$/t$

where t = time for 10 complete stride cycles.
  Example:

  If $t = 9.56$ s at a speed of 1.5 m/s, then SR $= 10$ cycles$/9.56$ s $= 1.046$ Hz
  Stride length (SL) $=$ Speed$/$SR

Example:

If SR = 1.046 Hz at a speed of 1.5 m/s, then SL = 1.5 m/s / 1.046 Hz = 1.434 m/str

Relative stride length with respect to height$(RSL_H) = \dfrac{SL}{H}$

Example: If SL = 1.434 m/str and H = 1.694 m, then RSL_H = 0.846

Relative stride length with respect to leg length$(RSL_L) = \dfrac{SL}{L}$

Example: If SL = 1.434 m/str and L = 0.90 m, then RSL_L = 1.593

7 Record stride rate, stride length and relative stride length with respect to height and leg length in Table PW2.1.

Presentation of results

1 Present a results table showing individual and group (mean and standard deviation) results for the subjects in your group. Show the results for women and men separately, i.e. list the subjects as two groups.
2 Present two sets of graphs of the results:
   i Group mean results for stride rate and stride length (women and men separately). Plot speed (m/s) on the horizontal axis and stride rate (Hz) and stride length (m/str) on the vertical axis.
   ii Group mean results for relative stride length (women and men separately). Plot speed (m/s) on the horizontal axis and relative stride length (m/str) on the vertical axis.

NB: The unit of relative stride length for RSL_H is 'heights per stride' (length of stride relative to the subject's height) and for RSL_L is 'leg lengths per stride' (length of stride relative to the subject's average leg length).

Example results

Example data is shown in Table PW2.2. The corresponding group mean graphs for stride length-speed, stride rate-speed and relative stride length-speed are shown in Figure PW2.1. Figure PW2.1 shows that (i) the women had a shorter average stride length and a higher average stride rate than the men at each of the three speeds and (ii) the average relative stride length (with respect to height and leg length) at each speed was very similar for both groups.

TABLE PW2.1 Individual and group mean results for height, leg length, stride rate, stride length and relative stride length

Subject	H (m)	L (m)	1.5 m/s					2.5 m/s					3.5 m/s				
			Time (s)	SR (Hz)	SL (m/str)	RSL$_H$ (H/str)	RSL$_L$ (L/str)	Time (s)	SR (Hz)	SL (m/str)	RSL$_H$ (H/str)	RSL$_L$ (L/str)	Time (s)	SR (Hz)	SL (m/str)	RSL$_H$ (H/str)	RSL$_L$ (L/str)
Females																	
1.																	
2.																	
3.																	
4.																	
5.																	
6.																	
Mean																	
SD																	
Females																	
1.																	
2.																	
3.																	
4.																	
5.																	
6.																	
Mean																	
SD																	

H = height; L = average leg length; SR = stride rate; SL = stride length

RSL$_H$ = relative stride length in relation to height; RSL$_L$ = relative stride length in relation to average leg length

TABLE PW2.2 Individual and group mean results for height, leg length, stride rate, stride length and relative stride length

Subject	H (m)	L (m)	1.5 m/s					2.5 m/s					3.5 m/s				
			Time (s)	SR (Hz)	SL (m/str)	RSLH (H/str)	RSLL (L/str)	Time (s)	SR (Hz)	SL (m/str)	RSLH (H/str)	RSLL (L/str)	Time (s)	SR (Hz)	SL (m/str)	RSLH (H/str)	RSLL (L/str)
Females																	
1.	1.65	0.89	10.35	0.97	1.55	0.94	1.74	7.8	1.28	1.95	1.18	2.19	7.1	1.41	2.49	1.51	2.80
2.	1.69	0.90	9.56	1.05	1.43	0.84	1.59	7.66	1.31	1.91	1.13	2.12	7.09	1.41	2.48	1.46	2.76
3.	1.61	0.81	10.4	0.96	1.56	0.97	1.93	7.6	1.32	1.89	1.17	2.33	7.19	1.39	2.52	1.56	3.11
4.	1.65	0.87	9.46	1.06	1.42	0.86	1.62	6.97	1.43	1.75	1.06	2.0	6.47	1.55	2.26	1.37	2.58
5.	1.68	0.91	10.3	0.97	1.55	0.92	1.70	7.53	1.33	1.88	1.12	2.07	6.69	1.49	2.34	1.39	2.57
6.	1.65	0.87	9.50	1.05	1.43	0.87	1.64	7.0	1.43	1.75	1.06	2.01	6.0	1.67	2.1	1.27	2.41
Mean	1.66	0.88	9.93	1.01	1.49	0.9	1.70	7.43	1.35	1.86	1.12	2.12	6.76	1.49	2.37	1.43	2.71
SD	0.03	0.04	0.47	0.05	0.07	0.05	0.12	0.35	0.06	0.08	0.05	0.12	0.46	0.11	0.16	0.10	0.24
Males																	
1.	1.85	0.96	11.04	0.91	1.65	0.89	1.72	8.13	1.23	2.03	1.10	2.11	7.60	1.32	2.66	1.44	2.77
2.	1.83	0.95	11.0	0.91	1.65	0.90	1.73	8.0	1.18	2.12	1.16	2.22	8.09	1.24	2.83	1.55	2.96
3.	1.81	0.85	10.63	0.94	1.60	0.89	1.88	7.84	1.28	1.95	1.08	2.29	7.63	1.31	2.67	1.48	3.14
4.	1.69	0.89	10.94	0.91	1.65	0.98	1.86	8.16	1.23	2.03	1.20	2.29	7.47	1.34	2.61	1.55	2.94
5.	1.88	0.98	10.50	0.95	1.58	0.84	1.61	7.87	1.27	1.97	1.05	2.0	7.53	1.33	2.64	1.40	2.69
6.	1.81	0.96	10.15	0.99	1.52	0.84	1.58	7.62	1.31	1.91	1.06	1.98	7.15	1.40	2.50	1.38	2.59
Mean	1.81	0.93	10.71	0.94	1.61	0.89	1.73	8.02	1.25	2.0	1.11	2.15	7.58	1.32	2.65	1.47	2.85
SD	0.07	0.05	0.35	0.03	0.05	0.05	0.12	0.31	0.05	0.07	0.06	0.14	0.30	0.05	0.11	0.07	0.20

H = height; L = average leg length; SR = stride rate; SL = stride length

RSL_H = relative stride length in relation to height; RSL_L = relative stride length in relation to average leg length

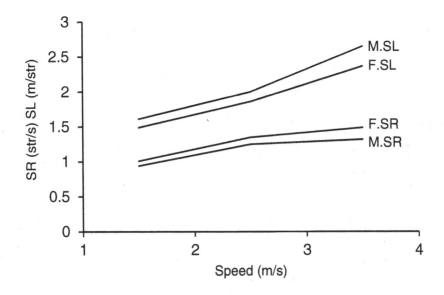

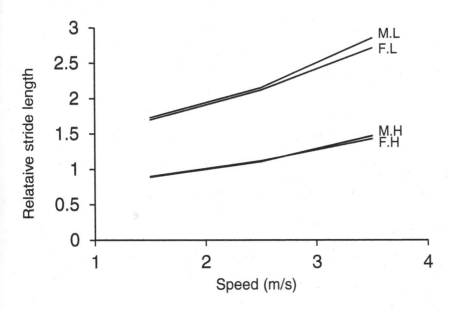

FIGURE PW2.1 (a) Group mean results for men (M) and women (F) for stride rate (SR) and stride length (SL) at speeds of 1.5 m/s, 2.5 m/s and 3.5 m/s. (b) Group mean results for men (M) and women (F) for relative stride length with respect to height (H) and average leg length (L) at speeds of 1.5 m/s, 2.5 m/s and 3.5 m/s.

PRACTICAL WORKSHEET 3

Determination of the coefficients of limiting friction and sliding friction between shoe soles and playing surfaces

Objective

To determine the coefficients of limiting (static) friction and sliding (dynamic) friction between shoe soles and playing surfaces.

Location

Sports hall with a wood surface
Sports hall with a polymeric rubber surface

Apparatus and equipment

1   Spring balance with a maximum force of 30 N graduated in 0.1 N; one balance for each group of 3–4 students.
2   Access to different types of shoes and surfaces.

Selection of shoes

Any type of shoe could be tested provided that the soles of the shoes are clean. Ideally, a variety of different types of sports shoes and non-sport shoes would be available. The sports shoes could include running shoes and shoes designed for particular sports. Example results for four types of shoe (running shoe, basketball shoe, badminton shoe, ordinary non-sport shoe) are presented in this worksheet.

Selection of surfaces

Ideally, access would be available to different sports surfaces, in particular, the two main types of sports hall surface, wood and polymeric rubber. When access to a sports hall or polymeric rubber running track is not available, the worksheet can be carried out with samples of surface material that can be clamped horizontally to an immoveable object such as a bench in a laboratory. The example results described in this worksheet were obtained for two surfaces (wood, polymeric rubber) using samples measuring approximately 0.2 m wide, 0.7 m long and 0.01 m thick.

Method

The effect of wear on shoe surfaces can be examined by testing new and worn shoes. Similarly, the effect of dry and wet conditions can be compared by testing the shoes when the soles and surfaces are dry and when they are wet.

1 The types of shoes and types of surfaces to be tested are listed in Table PW3.1.
2 The weight of each shoe is measured and recorded in Table PW3.1.
3 Each shoe must be dragged horizontally across each surface in line with the long axis of the shoe. The recommended method of applying a horizontal force to a shoe is to screw a small cup hook to the back of the heel of the shoe about 1 cm above the sole. A piece of string approximately 10 cm long with an eye at each end can then be used to link the shoe via the cup hook to the spring balance.
4 The first surface material to be tested is clamped in a horizontal position to a stable surface such as a tabletop. The spring balance is then used to apply a horizontal force to the first shoe as it rests on the surface. The force is increased very gradually while the person applying the force carefully observes the scale of the spring balance to note the maximum force, F_L, displayed just before the shoe begins to slide. This force is recorded. The procedure is repeated a number of times using different sections of the surface and different people applying the force. The mean of the F_L measurements is recorded in Table PW3.1. The procedure is repeated to observe the force, F_S, required to slide the shoe slowly but steadily. The mean of the F_S measurements is recorded in Table PW3.1.
5 The procedure described in paragraph 4 is repeated with each of the other shoes.
6 The procedure described in paragraphs 4 and 5 is then repeated using the other surface.
7 Using the data recorded in Table PW3.1, the coefficient of limiting friction, μ_L, and the coefficient of sliding friction, μ_S, for each shoe on each surface can then be calculated as follows.

$$\mu_L = \frac{F_L}{R}$$

$$\mu_S = \frac{F_S}{R}$$

TABLE PW3.1 Coefficients of limiting friction and sliding friction for four types of shoe on two surfaces

Shoe type†	Surface*								
	Wood					Rubber			
	R	F_L	μ_L	F_S	μ_S	F_L	μ_L	F_S	μ_S
	(N)	(N)		(N)		(N)		(N)	
Running	4.3	2.9	0.67	2.6	0.60	3.4	0.79	3.1	0.72
Basketball	5.5	2.8	0.51	2.3	0.42	4.8	0.76	3.7	0.67
Badminton	3.5	1.9	0.54	1.6	0.46	2.9	0.83	2.5	0.71
Non-sport	3.8	2.1	0.55	1.7	0.45	3.2	0.84	3.0	0.79

*Wood surface: indoor sprung wooden sports hall floor.
Rubber surface: indoor polymeric rubber running track.
† Running shoe: canvas upper with large, multi-patterned rubber tread.
Basketball shoe: canvas upper with narrow, uniform herringbone rubber tread.
Badminton shoe: canvas upper with uniform circular-dimpled rubber tread.
Non-sport shoe: leather upper with uniform close-grid PVC tread.
R = reaction force = weight of shoe.
F_L = maximum horizontal force displayed on spring balance just before the shoe begins to slide.
μ_L = coefficient of limiting friction.
F_S = horizontal force displayed on spring balance which maintains sliding.
μ_S = coefficient of sliding friction.

Presentation of results

1   Present a results table showing the reaction force (R) for each shoe, the mean limiting friction force (F_L) and mean sliding friction force (F_S) for each shoe on each surface, and the coefficients of limiting friction (μ_L) and sliding friction (μ_S) for each shoe on each surface.
2   Under the results table, briefly indicate the location and type of each surface tested and the types of shoes tested.

Example results

Example results are shown in Table PW3.1. The weights of the shoes were 3.5 N (badminton), 3.8 N (non-sport), 4.3 N (running) and 5.5 N (basketball). As shown in Figure PW3.1, μ_L and μ_S were higher for all four types of shoe on the polymeric surface than on the wood surface, μ_L was higher than μ_S for all four types of shoe on both surfaces and μ_L and μ_S for the running shoe were noticeably higher than the corresponding scores for the other three types of shoes on the wood surface, but not on the rubber surface.

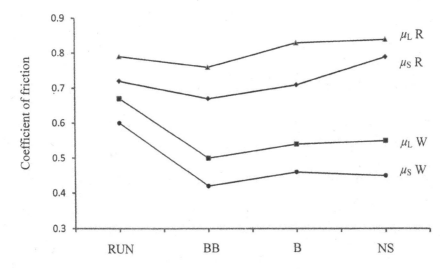

FIGURE PW3.1 Coefficients of limiting friction (μ_L) and sliding friction (μ_S) for the four shoes on the two surfaces. R, rubber surface; W, wood surface; RUN, running shoe; BB, basketball shoe; B, badminton shoe; NS, non-sport shoe.

PRACTICAL WORKSHEET 4

Force-time analysis of the ground reaction force in walking

Objective

To record the anteroposterior (F_X) and vertical (F_Y) components of the ground reaction force acting on a person during the ground contact phase of a single step when walking at a normal pace, and to perform a force-time analysis of the two recordings.

Location

Motion analysis laboratory

Apparatus and equipment

Force platform system

Method

Subject's clothing and footwear

Everyday clothing and shoes

Data collection and analysis

Mass and weight of the subject

1 Measure the subject's mass (kg), with subject standing upright without shoes.
2 Record the mass of the subject in Table PW4.1.
3 Calculate and record the weight (N) of the subject in Table PW4.1.

TABLE PW4.1 Analysis of the anteroposterior (F_X) and vertical (F_Y) ground reaction force components acting on the right foot of a person when walking at a normal, steady pace

Name of subject:

	Mass (kg)	Weight (N)
Mass of subject		

	Time (s)	Force (N)	Force (BW)
1. Heel contact (t_1, F_{Y1})		0	0
2. F_Y impact force peak (t_2, F_{Y2})			
3. Peak F_Y in the absorption phase (t_3, F_{Y3})			
4. End of the absorption phase (when $F_X = 0$) (t_4, F_{Y4})			
5. Peak F_Y in the propulsion phase (t_5, F_{Y5})			
6. Toe-off (t_6, F_{Y6})		0	0
7. Peak F_X in absorption phase (t_7, F_{Y7})			
8. Peak F_X in propulsion phase (t_8, F_{Y8})			

	Time (s)	Proportion of contact time (%)
9. Contact time (t_6-t_1)		100
10. Duration of absorption phase (t_4-t_1)		
11. Duration of propulsion phase (t_6-t_4)		
12. Time to F_Y impact force peak (t_2-t_1)		
13. Time to peak F_Y in the absorption phase (t_3-t_1)		
14. Time to peak F_Y in the propulsion phase (t_5-t_1)		
15. Time to peak F_X in the absorption phase (t_7-t_1)		
16. Time to peak F_X in the propulsion phase (t_8-t_1)		

	L_{RY} (N/s)	L_{RY} (BW/s)
17. Rate of F_Y loading (L_{RY}) during impact $(F_{Y2}/(t_2-t_1))$		

Ground reaction force-time components

Record the anteroposterior (F_X) and vertical (F_Y) ground reaction force-time components during contact time of the right foot.

1   On a signal from the system operator, the subject walks at a normal steady pace (approximately 1.2 m/s) across the force plate, making sure that only the right foot contacts the force plate.

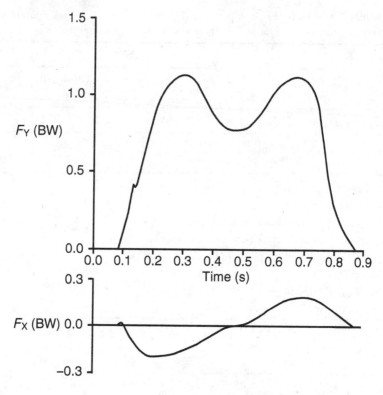

FIGURE PW4.1 Anteroposterior (F_X) and vertical (F_Y) ground reaction force-time components acting on the right foot of a person when walking at a normal, steady pace.

2 The operator prints the anteroposterior (F_X) and vertical (F_Y) force-time components of the ground reaction force acting on the right foot during contact with the force plate. Figure PW4.1 shows typical F_X-time and F_Y-time records.

Analysis of the F_X-time and F_Y-time records

1 From the F_X-time and F_Y-time records, estimate the forces (N) and times (s) corresponding to the variables listed 1 to 8 in Table PW4.1. Record these forces and times in Table PW4.1.

2 Calculate the forces in units of body weight and record the forces in Table PW4.1.

3 Using the time data in Table PW4.1 for points 1 to 8, calculate and record the time variables 9–16 in Table PW4.1.

4 Calculate and record in Table PW4.1 the rate of F_Y loading (L_{RY}) during impact (the period t_1 to t_2) in N/s and BW/s.

Presentation of results

Your submission should consist of:

1   A figure of the F_X and F_Y force-time records showing the time points 1 to 8.
2   A table of results showing the force and time analysis of the F_X and F_Y force-time records.

Example results

Figure PW4.2 shows the time points 1 to 8 on the F_X and F_Y force-time records of Figure PW4.1.

Table PW4.2 shows the force and time analysis of the F_X and F_Y force-time records of Figure PW4.2.

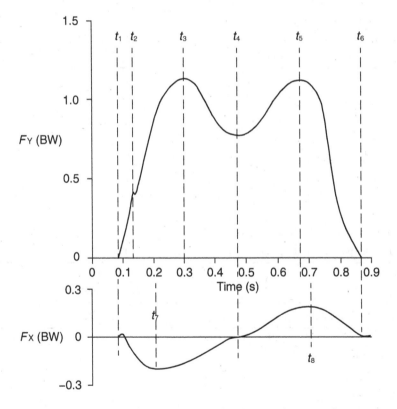

FIGURE PW4.2   Anteroposterior (F_X) and vertical (F_Y) ground reaction force-time components acting on the right foot of a person when walking at a normal, steady pace. t_1, heel contact; t_2, F_Y impact force peak; t_3, peak F_Y in the absorption phase; t_4, end of the absorption phase; t_5, peak F_Y in the propulsion phase; t_6, toe-off; t_7, peak F_X in the absorption phase; t_8, peak F_X in the propulsion phase.

TABLE PW4.2 Analysis of the anteroposterior (F_X) and vertical (F_Y) ground reaction force components acting on the right foot of a person when walking at a normal, steady pace

Name of subject:

	Mass (kg)	Weight (N)	
Mass of subject	71.0	695.5	

	Time (s)	Force (N)	Force (BW)
1. Heel contact (t_1, F_{Y1})	0.084	0	0
2. F_Y impact force peak (t_2, F_{Y2})	0.134	288.1	0.41
3. Peak F_Y in the absorption phase (t_3, F_{Y3})	0.297	779.9	1.12
4. End of the absorption phase (when $F_X = 0$) (t_4, F_{Y4})	0.469	531.6	0.76
5. Peak F_Y in the propulsion phase (t_5, F_{Y5})	0.672	775.0	1.11
6. Toe-off (t_6, F_{Y6})	0.870	0	0
7. Peak F_X in absorption phase (t_7, F_{Y7})	0.208	−132.1	0.18
8. Peak F_X in propulsion phase (t_8, F_{Y8})	0.701	136.1	0.19

	Time (s)	Proportion of contact time (%)
9. Contact time ($t_6 - t_1$)	0.786	100
10. Duration of absorption phase ($t_4 - t_1$)	0.385	49.0
11. Duration of propulsion phase ($t_6 - t_4$)	0.401	51.0
12. Time to F_Y impact force peak ($t_2 - t_1$)	0.050	6.4
13. Time to peak F_Y in the absorption phase ($t_3 - t_1$)	0.213	27.1
14. Time to peak F_Y in the propulsion phase ($t_5 - t_1$)	0.588	74.8
15. Time to peak F_X in the absorption phase ($t_7 - t_1$)	0.124	15.8
16. Time to peak F_X in the propulsion phase ($t_8 - t_1$)	0.617	78.4

	L_{RY} (N/s)	L_{RY} (BW/s)
17. Rate of F_Y loading (L_{RY}) during impact ($F_{Y2}/(t_2 - t_1)$)	5762.0	8.28

PRACTICAL WORKSHEET 5

Force-time analysis of the ground reaction force in running

Objective

To record the anteroposterior (F_X) and vertical (F_Y) components of the ground reaction force acting on a runner during the ground contact phase of a single step when running at a moderate pace and to perform a force-time analysis of the two recordings.

Location

Motion analysis laboratory

Apparatus and equipment

Force platform system

Method

Subject's clothing and footwear

Sports clothing and trainers

Data collection and analysis

Mass and weight of the subject

1 Measure the subject's mass (kg) with subject standing upright without shoes.
2 Record the mass of the subject in Table PW5.1.
3 Calculate and record the weight (N) of the subject in Table PW5.1.

TABLE PW5.1 Analysis of the anteroposterior (F_X) and vertical (F_Y) ground reaction force components acting on the right foot of a runner when running at a moderate pace

Name of subject:		
	Mass (kg)	Weight (N)
Mass of subject		

	Time (s)	Force (N)	Force (BW)
1. Heel contact (t_1, F_{Y1})		0	0
2. F_Y impact force peak (IFP) (t_2, F_{Y2})			
3. End of the passive phase (t_3, F_{Y3})			
4. End of the absorption phase (when $F_X = 0$) (t_4, F_{Y4})			
5. Toe-off (t_5, F_{Y5})		0	0
6. Peak F_X in absorption phase (t_6, F_{Y6})			
7. Peak F_X in propulsion phase (t_7, F_{Y7})			

	Time (s)	Proportion of contact time (%)
8. Contact time ($t_5 - t_1$)		100
9. Time to IFP ($t_2 - t_1$)		
10. Duration of passive phase ($t_3 - t_1$)		
11. Duration of active phase ($t_5 - t_3$)		
12. Duration of absorption phase ($t_4 - t_1$)		
13. Duration of propulsion phase ($t_5 - t_4$)		

	L_{RY} (N/s)	L_{RY} (BW/s)
14. Rate of F_Y loading (L_{RY}) during impact ($F_{Y2}/(t_2 - t_1)$)		

Ground reaction force-time components

Record the anteroposterior (F_X) and vertical (F_Y) ground reaction force-time components during contact time of the right foot.

1   On a signal from the system operator, the subject runs across the force plate at a moderate speed (approximately 3.5 m/s), making sure that only the right foot contacts the force plate.
2   The operator prints the anteroposterior (F_X) and vertical (F_Y) force-time components of the ground reaction force acting on the right foot during contact with the force plate. Figure PW5.1 shows typical F_X-time and F_Y-time records.

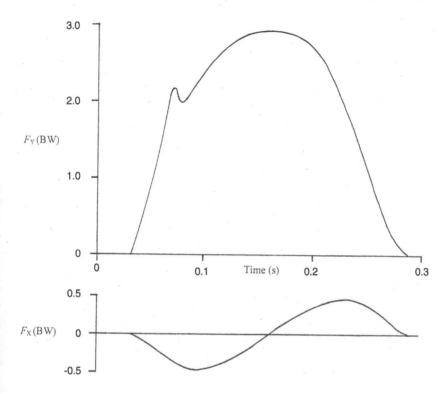

FIGURE PW5.1   Anteroposterior (F_X) and vertical (F_Y) ground reaction force-time components acting on the right foot of a runner when running at a moderate pace.

Analysis of the F_X-time and F_Y-time records

1   From the F_X-time and F_Y-time records, estimate the forces (N) and times (s) corresponding to the time points listed 1 to 7 in Table PW5.1. Record these forces and times in Table PW5.1.

2   Calculate the forces in units of body weight and record the forces in Table PW5.1.

3   Using the time data in Table PW5.1 for points 1 to 7, calculate and record the time variables 8 to 13 in Table PW5.1.

4   Calculate and record in Table PW5.1 the rate of F_Y loading (L_{RY}) during impact (the period t_1 to t_2) in N/s and BW/s.

Presentation of results

Your submission should consist of:

1   A figure of the F_X and F_Y force-time records showing the time points 1 to 7.

2   A table of results showing the force and time analysis of the F_X and F_Y force-time records.

Example results

Figure PW5.2 shows the time points 1 to 7 on the F_X and F_Y force-time records of Figure PW5.1.

Table PW5.2 shows the force and time analysis of the F_X and F_Y force-time records of Figure PW5.2.

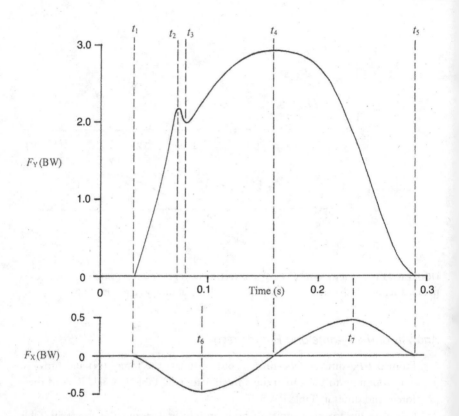

FIGURE PW5.2 Anteroposterior (F_X) and vertical (F_Y) ground reaction force-time components acting on the right foot of a runner when running at a moderate pace. t_1, heel contact; t_2, F_Y impact force peak; t_3, end of passive phase; t_4, end of the absorption phase; t_5, toe-off; t_6, peak F_X in absorption phase; t_7, peak F_X in the propulsion phase.

TABLE PW5.2 Analysis of the anteroposterior (F_X) and vertical (F_Y) ground reaction force components acting on the right foot of a runner when running at a moderate pace

Name of subject:			
	Mass (kg)	Weight (N)	
Mass of subject	75.2	737.7	

	Time (s)	Force (N)	Force (BW)
1. Heel contact (t_1, F_{Y1})	0.030	0	0
2. F_Y impact force peak (IFP) (t_2, F_{Y2})	0.071	1615.6	2.19
3. End of the passive phase (t_3, F_{Y3})	0.078	1475.4	2.00
4. End of the absorption phase (when $F_X = 0$) (t_4, F_{Y4})	0.159	2161.4	2.93
5. Toe-off (t_5, F_{Y5})	0.288	0	0
6. Peak F_X in absorption phase (t_6, F_{Y6})	0.095	339.3	0.46
7. Peak F_X in propulsion phase (t_7, F_{Y7})	0.232	346.7	0.47

	Time (s)	Proportion of contact time (%)
8. Contact time ($t_5 - t_1$)	0.258	100
9. Time to IFP ($t_2 - t_1$)	0.041	15.9
10. Duration of passive phase ($t_3 - t_1$)	0.048	18.6
11. Duration of active phase ($t_5 - t_3$)	0.210	81.4
12. Duration of absorption phase ($t_4 - t_1$)	0.129	50.0
13. Duration of propulsion phase ($t_5 - t_4$)	0.129	50.0

	L_{RY} (N/s)	L_{RY} (BW/s)
14. Rate of F_Y loading (L_{RY}) during impact ($F_{Y2}/(t_2 - t_1)$)	39 404.9	53.4

PRACTICAL WORKSHEET 6

Linear impulse analysis of the ground reaction force in running

Objectives

To record the anteroposterior (F_X) and vertical (F_Y) components of the ground reaction force acting on the right foot of a subject when running at a moderate speed and to perform an impulse analysis of the two recordings.

Location

Motion analysis laboratory

Apparatus and equipment

Force platform system
   Photocells
   Timer

Method

Subject's clothing

Shorts, shirt and trainers

Data collection

Record the anteroposterior (F_X) and vertical (F_Y) components of the ground reaction force acting on the right foot of the subject when running at a moderate speed.

1   In each trial a subject is required to run in a straight line through two sets of photocells at hip height to land the right foot on the platform which is located between the two sets of photocells.

2   The first set of photocells is situated 3 m from the centre of the platform and the second set of photocells is situated 3 m beyond the centre of the platform. The time, t, required to run between the two sets of photo cells is measured by the timer. The timer is started by the runner running through the first set of photocells and stopped by the runner running through the second set of photocells. The average speed v of the runner between the two sets of photocells is calculated by dividing the distance between the two sets of photocells, $d = 6$ m, by the time t.

3   Each subject should have sufficient practice to consistently land on the force platform with the right foot and to achieve a steady running speed between the two sets of photocells.

4   Prior to the running trials, each subject's weight is measured by the force platform. On a signal from the force platform system operator, the subject steps onto the platform and stands perfectly still. The operator records the vertical component of the ground reaction force for a few seconds at 1000 Hz and then signals the subject to step off the platform. The ground reaction force recording is then displayed and the weight of the subject is measured by averaging a 0.5 s portion of the record.

5   In each running trial the anteroposterior (F_X) and vertical (F_Y) components of the ground reaction force acting on the right foot of the runner during the single step on the platform are recorded at 1000 Hz. Each subject performs a number of running trials until a trial is obtained in which the whole of the right foot lands on the platform and the speed of the subject is, subjectively, fairly steady. An impulse analysis is then carried out on the anteroposterior and vertical force-time records.

Data analysis

1   Data analysis will be described in relation to the example results shown in Tables PW6.1 and PW6.2.

2   The weight W (N) of the subject is measured and recorded in an Excel spreadsheet as shown in Table PW6.1.

3   The mass m (kg) of the subject is calculated ($m = W/9.81$) and recorded in Table PW6.1.

4   Running consists of a series of step cycles (alternate right leg and left leg cycles) with each step cycle, t_L, consisting of contact time, t_C, when the foot is in contact with the ground, followed by flight time, t_F, when both feet are off the ground prior to the start of the next step cycle. Figure PW6.1 shows the F_X and F_Y force-time graphs of the subject's right foot cycle that are analyzed in Tables PW6.1 and PW6.2. Figure PW6.1 also shows the corresponding step cycle time ($t_L = 0.321$ s), contact time ($t_C = 0.190$ s) and flight time ($t_F = 0.131$ s).

5 The F_X and F_Y force-time records should be time-sliced to retain the force-time data from about 0.1 s before the start of t_C to about 0.1 s after the end of t_P. The time-sliced force-time data should be copied into the first two columns of the Excel spreadsheet. As the volume of data produced in the analysis is likely to be considerable, it is recommended that sheet 1 of the spreadsheet should be used to analyze the anteroposterior force (F_X) record and sheet 2 be used to analyze the vertical force (F_Y) record.

6 With a sampling frequency of 1000 Hz, a step cycle time of 0.321 s would require 321 rows in the Excel spreadsheet. In the example results in Tables PW6.1 and 6.2, the sampling frequency has been reduced from 1000 Hz to 200 Hz so that the example analysis can be presented more concisely. Consequently, there are 39 rows of data in Table PW6.1 (analysis of t_C) and 65 rows in Table PW6.2 (analysis of t_C and t_P). The reduction of the sampling frequency decreases the accuracy of the analysis, but the method of analysis is unchanged.

7 Analysis of the F_X record is shown in Table PW6.1. In column 3 of Table PW6.1 the impulse of F_X in each time interval is calculated by multiplying the average force in the time interval by the length of the time interval. In the first time interval in Table PW6.1 (between 0.855 s and 0.86 s) the force at the start of the time interval is zero (start of heel-strike). The force at the end of the time interval is −43.257 N. Consequently, the average force over the time interval is −21.628 N and the impulse of the average force in the time interval is −21.628 N × 0.005 s = −0.1081 N·s.

8 In column 4 of Table PW6.1 the cumulative impulse of F_X is calculated by summing the impulses in column 3 from heel-strike to toe-off, i.e. the duration of t_C. At the end of the first time interval the impulse is −0.1081 N·s, i.e. 0 + (−0.1081) N·s = −0.1081 N·s. At the end of the second time interval (0.86 s to 0.865 s) the cumulative impulse is −0.1081 N·s + (−0.2812) N·s = −0.3893 N·s.

9 In column 5 of Table PW6.1, the cumulative change in the anteroposterior velocity of the CG is calculated by dividing the cumulative impulse data in column 4 by the mass of the subject. As shown in Table PW6.1, Figure PW6.1 and Figure PW6.2, F_X is negative during roughly the first half of t_C (from heel-strike at 0.855 s to 0.945 s) and positive in the second half (from 0.945 s to toe-off at 1.045 s). The period when F_X is negative is referred to as the absorption phase and the period when F_X is positive is referred to as the propulsion phase. In the absorption phase the anteroposterior velocity decreases and in the propulsion phase the anteroposterior velocity increases. As shown in Table PW6.1 and Figure PW6.2, the anteroposterior velocity of the CG decreased by 0.1894 m/s in the absorption phase and increased by 0.1965 m/s during the propulsion phase. The decrease of 0.1894 m/s in the absorption phase is 4.83% of the average speed of 3.92 m/s. The increase of 0.1965 m/s in the propulsion phase is 5.01% of the average speed of 3.92 m/s.

10 Change in anteroposterior velocity during t_C is determined by the impulse of F_X. In contrast, change in vertical velocity is determined by the impulse of the resultant vertical force acting on the CG, i.e. the resultant of F_Y and body weight. Analysis of the F_Y record is shown in Table PW6.2 and Figure PW6.3.

11   The subject's weight is copied into all of the cells in column 3 of Table PW6.2.

12   In column 4 of Table PW6.2, the resultant vertical force acting on the subject at each instant in time is calculated by subtracting body weight (column 3) from the vertical component of the ground reaction force (column 2). A negative resultant force indicates downward acceleration of the CG or upward deceleration of the CG. A positive resultant force indicates downward deceleration of the CG or upward acceleration of the CG.

13   In column 5 of Table PW6.2 the impulse of the resultant vertical force in each time interval is calculated by multiplying the average resultant force in the time interval by the length of the time interval. In the first time interval in Table PW6.2 (between 0.855 s and 0.86 s), the resultant force at the start of the time interval is −596.94 N. The resultant force at the end of the time interval is −342.36 N. Consequently, the average resultant force over the time interval is −469.65 N and the impulse of the average resultant force in the time interval is −469.65 N × 0.005 s = −2.3482 N·s.

14   In column 6 of Table PW6.2, the cumulative impulse of the resultant vertical force is calculated by summing the impulses in column 5 throughout t_L. At the end of the first time interval the impulse is −2.3482 N·s, i.e. 0 + (−2.3482) N·s = −2.3482 N·s. At the end of the second time interval (0.86 s to 0.865 s) the cumulative impulse = −2.3482 N·s + (−0.9920) N·s = −3.3402 N·s.

15   In column 7 of Table PW6.2 the cumulative change in the vertical velocity of the CG is calculated by dividing the cumulative impulse data in column 6 by the mass of the subject. As the vertical velocity of the CG at heel-strike is not zero (the CG will be moving downward at heel-strike like a bouncing ball), the velocity data must be adjusted so that the velocity data and time data are properly synchronized. Table PW6.2 shows that the cumulative impulse during t_C is 78.0845 N·s (at 1.045 s). If the first half of this impulse arrests the downward velocity of the CG (absorption phase) and the second half of the impulse generates upward velocity of the CG (propulsion phase) equivalent to that lost during the absorption phase, then the end of the absorption phase will occur when the cumulative impulse is 39.04 N·s. Interpolation of the cumulative impulse − time data in Table PW6.2 indicates that the end of the absorption phase occurs at 0.9419 s. Interpolation of the cumulative velocity − time data in Table PW6.2 indicates that the velocity of the CG at 0.9419 s is 0.635 m/s. However the actual velocity of the CG at 0.9419 s (the end of the absorption phase) is zero. Consequently to synchronize the cumulative velocity data with the time data, it is necessary to subtract 0.635 m/s from each of the cumulative velocity data in column 7. This adjustment is shown in column 8 of Table PW6.2. Figure PW6.3 shows the adjusted cumulative velocity − time graph in relation to the F_Y-time graph. Maximum downward velocity was 0.689 m/s (at 0.865 s), maximum upward velocity was 0.889 m/s (at 1.01 s) and upward velocity at take-off was 0.648 m/s (at 1.045 s). The adjusted velocity-time graph also shows the uniform acceleration of the CG due to gravity during t_F; vertical velocity changes from 0.648 m/s at take-off at 1.045 s through zero at

approximately 1.11 s, the highest point of the CG during t_F, to –0.627 m/s at the end of t_F. The velocity at the start of t_C is –0.635, which is consistent with the velocity of –0.627 m/s at the end of t_F.

16   In column 9 of Table PW6.2 the change in vertical displacement of the CG during each time interval is calculated by multiplying the average speed in the time interval by the length of the time interval. In the first time interval in Table PW6.2 (between 0.855 s and 0.86 s) the speed at the start of the time interval is –0.635 m/s. The speed at the end of the time interval is –0.673 m/s. Consequently, the average speed over the time interval is –0.654 m/s and the change in vertical displacement of the CG in the time interval is –0.654 m/s × 0.005 s = –0.00327 m.

17   In column 10 of Table PW6.2 the cumulative change in vertical displacement of the CG is calculated by summing the displacements in column 9 throughout t_L. At the end of the first time interval the vertical displacement is –0.00327 m, i.e. 0 + (–0.00327) m = –0.00327 m. At the end of the second time interval (0.86 s to 0.865 s) the cumulative vertical displacement is –0.00327 + (–0.00341) m = –0.00668 m. Figure PW6.3 shows the cumulative vertical displacement-time graph throughout t_L. Relative to the vertical displacement of the CG at heel-strike, maximum displacement downward was 0.0373 m (at 0.94 s), displacement at take-off was 0.0271 m (at 1.045 s) and maximum upward displacement, the highest point of the CG during t_F, was 0.0485 m (at 1.11 s).

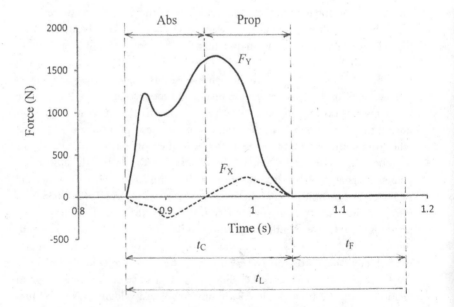

FIGURE PW6.1   Anteroposterior (F_X) and vertical (F_Y) components of the ground reaction force during the step cycle of the right foot of a female student running at 3.92 m/s. t_L, step cycle time; t_C, ground contact time; t_F, flight time. $t_L = t_C + t_F$. Abs, absorption phase; Prop, propulsion phase.

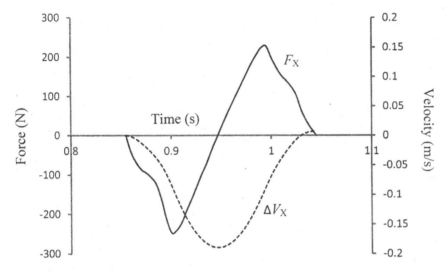

FIGURE PW6.2   Force-time graph of the anteroposterior component of the ground reaction force (F_X) and the corresponding change in anteroposterior velocity-time graph (ΔV_X) during ground contact of the right foot of a female student running at 3.92 m/s.

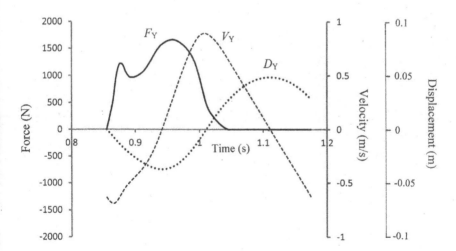

FIGURE PW6.3   Force-time graph of the vertical component of the ground reaction force (F_Y) and the corresponding velocity-time (V_Y) and displacement-time (D_Y) graphs during the step cycle of the right foot of a female student running at 3.92 m/s.

TABLE PW6.1 Analysis of the anteroposterior component (F_X) of the ground reaction force acting on the right foot of a female student running at 3.92 m/s

Name of subject: Alice		Type of foot contact: Heel-striker		
Weight (N): 596.94		Mass (kg): 60.85		
Trial time (s): 1.53		Average speed (m/s): 3.92		

Time (s)	FX (N)	Impulse (N·s)	Cumulative Impulse (N·s)	Cumulative velocity (m/s)
0.855	0	0	0	0
0.86	−43.257	−0.1081	−0.1081	−0.0018
0.865	−69.212	−0.2812	−0.3893	−0.0064
0.87	−86.515	−0.3893	−0.7786	−0.0128
0.875	−95.166	−0.4542	−1.2328	−0.0203
0.88	−107.279	−0.5061	−1.7389	−0.0286
0.885	−124.582	−0.5796	−2.3186	−0.0381
0.89	−162.648	−0.7181	−3.0367	−0.0499
0.895	−214.557	−0.9430	−3.9797	−0.0654
0.9	−247.433	−1.1550	−5.1347	−0.0844
0.905	−240.512	−1.2199	−6.3545	−0.1044
0.91	−221.478	−1.1550	−7.5095	−0.1234
0.915	−190.333	−1.0295	−8.5390	−0.1403
0.92	−160.918	−0.8781	−9.4172	−0.1548
0.925	−129.773	−0.7267	−10.1439	−0.1667
0.93	−98.627	−0.5710	−10.7149	−0.1761
0.935	−70.942	−0.4239	−11.1388	−0.1830
0.94	−38.067	−0.2725	−11.4113	−0.1875
0.945	−8.651	−0.1168	−11.5281	−0.1894
0.95	21.629	0.0324	−11.4957	−0.1889
0.955	50.179	0.1795	−11.3162	−0.1860
0.96	77.863	0.3201	−10.9961	−0.1807
0.965	103.818	0.4542	−10.5419	−0.1732
0.97	129.772	0.5840	−9.9579	−0.1636
0.975	155.727	0.7137	−9.2441	−0.1519
0.98	181.681	0.8435	−8.4006	−0.1380
0.985	204.175	0.9646	−7.4360	−0.1222
0.99	223.209	1.0685	−6.3675	−0.1046
0.995	228.399	1.1290	−5.2385	−0.0861
1.0	200.715	1.0728	−4.1657	−0.0685
1.005	174.760	0.9387	−3.2270	−0.0530
1.01	153.997	0.8219	−2.4051	−0.0395
1.015	140.154	0.7354	−1.6697	−0.0274
1.02	124.582	0.6618	−1.0079	−0.0166
1.025	103.818	0.5710	−0.4369	−0.0072
1.03	65.751	0.4239	−0.0129	−0.0002
1.035	38.067	0.2595	0.2466	0.0041
1.04	17.303	0.1384	0.3850	0.0063
1.045	0	0.0433	0.4282	0.0070

TABLE PW6.2 Analysis of the vertical component (F_Y) of the ground reaction force acting on the right foot of a female student running at 3.92 m/s

Name of subject: Alice
Weight (N): 596.94
Trial time (s): 1.53

Type of foot contact: Heel-striker
Mass (kg): 60.85
Average speed (m/s): 3.92

Time (s)	F_Y (N)	BW (N)	F_Y − BW (N)	Impulse (N·s)	C Imp* (N·s)	C Vel* (m/s)	C VelA* (m/s)	C Disp* (m)	C Disp* (m)
0.855	0	596.94	−596.94	0	0	0	−0.635	0	0
0.86	254.58	596.94	−342.36	−2.3482	−2.3482	−0.0386	−0.6736	−0.00327	−0.00327
0.865	542.51	596.94	−54.43	−0.9920	−3.3402	−0.0549	−0.6899	−0.00341	−0.00668
0.87	993.73	596.94	396.79	0.8559	−2.4843	−0.0408	−0.6758	−0.00341	−0.01009
0.875	1211.43	596.94	614.49	2.5282	0.0439	0.0007	−0.6343	−0.00327	−0.01337
0.88	1206.17	596.94	609.23	3.0593	3.1032	0.0510	−0.5840	−0.00304	−0.01642
0.885	1070.98	596.94	474.04	2.7082	5.8113	0.0955	−0.5395	−0.00281	−0.01922
0.89	983.19	596.94	386.25	2.1507	7.9621	0.1308	−0.5041	−0.00261	−0.02183
0.895	967.39	596.94	370.45	1.8917	9.8538	0.1619	−0.4731	−0.00244	−0.02428
0.9	979.68	596.94	382.74	1.8830	11.7368	0.1929	−0.4421	−0.00229	−0.02656
0.905	1009.53	596.94	412.59	1.9883	13.7251	0.2256	−0.4094	−0.00213	−0.02869
0.91	1053.42	596.94	456.48	2.1727	15.8978	0.2613	−0.3737	−0.00196	−0.03065
0.915	1114.87	596.94	517.93	2.4360	18.3338	0.3013	−0.3337	0.00177	−0.03242
0.92	1202.65	596.94	605.71	2.8091	21.1429	0.3474	−0.2875	−0.00155	−0.03397
0.925	1299.22	596.94	702.28	3.2699	24.4129	0.4012	−0.2338	−0.00130	−0.03528
0.93	1404.56	596.94	807.62	3.7747	28.1876	0.4632	−0.1717	−0.00101	−0.03629
0.935	1492.35	596.94	895.41	4.2575	32.4452	0.5332	−0.1017	−0.00068	−0.03697

(Continued)

TABLE PW6.2 (Continued)

Time (s)	F_Y (N)	BW (N)	$F_Y - BW$ (N)	Impulse (N·s)	C Imp* (N·s)	C Vel* (m/s)	C VelA* (m/s)	C Disp* (m)	C Disp* (m)
0.94	1562.57	596.94	965.63	4.6526	37.0978	0.6096	-0.0253	-0.00032	-0.03729
0.945	1606.47	596.94	1009.53	4.9379	42.0357	0.6908	0.0558	0	-0.03721
0.95	1641.58	596.94	1044.64	5.1354	47.1711	0.7752	0.1402	0.00049	-0.03672
0.955	1659.14	596.94	1062.20	5.2671	52.4382	0.8617	0.2267	0.00092	-0.03581
0.96	1662.65	596.94	1065.71	5.3197	57.7580	0.9492	0.3142	0.00135	-0.03446
0.965	1641.58	596.94	1044.64	5.2758	63.0339	1.0359	0.4009	0.00179	-0.03267
0.97	1606.47	596.94	1009.53	5.1354	68.1693	1.1203	0.4853	0.00222	-0.03045
0.975	1559.06	596.94	962.12	4.9291	73.0984	1.2013	0.5663	0.00263	-0.02782
0.98	1497.61	596.94	900.67	4.6569	77.7554	1.2778	0.6428	0.00302	-0.02480
0.985	1422.12	596.94	825.18	4.3146	82.0700	1.3487	0.7137	0.00339	-0.02141
0.99	1316.78	596.94	719.84	3.8625	85.9326	1.4122	0.7772	0.00372	-0.01768
0.995	1167.54	596.94	570.60	3.2261	89.1587	1.4652	0.8302	0.00402	-0.01366
1.0	956.86	596.94	359.92	2.3263	91.4850	1.5034	0.8684	0.00425	-0.00942
1.005	719.84	596.94	122.90	1.2070	92.6920	1.5233	0.8883	0.00439	-0.00503
1.01	491.60	596.94	-105.34	0.0439	92.7359	1.5240	0.8890	0.00444	-0.00058
1.015	344.12	596.94	-252.82	-0.8954	91.8405	1.5093	0.8742	0.00441	0.00383
1.02	256.33	596.94	-340.61	-1.4835	90.3569	1.4849	0.8499	0.00431	0.00814
1.025	184.35	596.94	-412.59	-1.8830	88.4740	1.4540	0.8190	0.00417	0.01231

1.03	121.14	596.94	-475.8	-2.2209	86.2530	1.4175	0.7825	0.00400	0.01631
1.035	68.47	596.94	-528.47	-2.5106	83.7423	1.3762	0.7412	0.00381	0.02012
1.04	28.09	596.94	-568.85	-2.7433	80.9990	1.3311	0.6961	0.00359	0.02371
1.045	0	596.94	-596.94	-2.9144	78.0845	1.2832	0.6482	0.00336	0.02708
1.05	0	596.94	-596.94	-2.9847	75.0998	1.2342	0.5992	0.00312	0.03019
1.055	0	596.94	-596.94	-2.9847	72.1151	1.1851	0.5501	0.00287	0.03307
1.06	0	596.94	-596.94	-2.9847	69.1304	1.1361	0.5011	0.00263	0.03569
1.065	0	596.94	-596.94	-2.9847	66.1457	1.0870	0.4520	0.00238	0.03808
1.07	0	596.94	-596.94	-2.9847	63.1610	1.0379	0.4030	0.00214	0.04022
1.075	0	596.94	-596.94	-2.9847	60.1763	0.9889	0.3539	0.00189	0.04211
1.08	0	596.94	-596.94	-2.9847	57.1916	0.9398	0.3048	0.00165	0.04376
1.085	0	596.94	-596.94	-2.9847	54.2069	0.8908	0.2558	0.00140	0.04516
1.09	0	596.94	-596.94	-2.9847	51.2222	0.8417	0.2067	0.00115	0.04631
1.095	0	596.94	-596.94	-2.9847	48.2375	0.7927	0.1577	0.00091	0.04722
1.1	0	596.94	-596.94	-2.9847	45.2528	0.7436	0.1086	0.00066	0.04789
1.105	0	596.94	-596.94	-2.9847	42.2681	0.6946	0.0596	0.00042	0.04831
1.11	0	596.94	-596.94	-2.9847	39.28345	0.6455	0.0105	0.00017	0.04848
1.115	0	596.94	-596.94	-2.9847	36.29875	0.5965	-0.0384	0	0.04841
1.12	0	596.94	-596.94	-2.9847	33.31405	0.5474	-0.0875	-0.00031	0.04810
1.125	0	596.94	-596.94	-2.9847	30.32935	0.4984	-0.1365	-0.00056	0.04754

(Continued)

TABLE PW6.2 (Continued)

Time (s)	F_Y (N)	BW (N)	F_Y – BW (N)	Impulse (N·s)	C Imp* (N·s)	C Vel* (m/s)	C VelA* (m/s)	C Disp* (m)	C Disp* (m)
1.13	0	596.94	−596.94	−2.9847	27.34465	0.4494	−0.1856	−0.00080	0.04674
1.135	0	596.94	−596.94	−2.9847	24.35995	0.4003	−0.2346	−0.00105	0.04568
1.14	0	596.94	−596.94	−2.9847	21.37525	0.3512	−0.2837	−0.00129	0.04439
1.145	0	596.94	−596.94	−2.9847	18.39055	0.3022	−0.3327	−0.00154	0.04285
1.15	0	596.94	−596.94	−2.9847	15.40585	0.2531	−0.3818	−0.00178	0.04106
1.155	0	596.94	−596.94	−2.9847	12.42115	0.2041	−0.4308	−0.00203	0.03903
1.16	0	596.94	−596.94	−2.9847	9.43645	0.1550	−0.4799	−0.00227	0.03675
1.165	0	596.94	−596.94	−2.9847	6.45175	0.1060	−0.5289	−0.00252	0.03423
1.17	0	596.94	−596.94	−2.9847	3.46705	0.0569	−0.5780	−0.00277	0.03146
1.175	0	596.94	−596.94	−2.9847	0.48235	0.0079	−0.6270	−0.00301	0.02845

* C Imp: cumulative impulse
C Vel: cumulative velocity
C VelA: cumulative velocity adjusted
Disp: displacement
C Disp: cumulative displacement

Presentation of results

1 Present your F_X-time and F_Y-time graphs on a single figure as shown in Figure PW6.1.

2 Present your impulse analyses of your F_X-time and F_Y-time records as shown in Tables PW6.1 and PW6.2.

3 Present your F_X-time graph and corresponding velocity-time graph on a single figure as shown in Figure PW6.2.

4 Present your F_Y-time graph and corresponding velocity-time and displacement-time graphs on a single figure as shown in Figure PW6.3.

Example results

Example results are shown in Tables PW6.1 and 6.2 and in Figures PW6.1, PW6.2 and PW6.3.

PRACTICAL WORKSHEET 7

Linear impulse analysis of the ground reaction force in a countermovement vertical jump

Objectives

To record the vertical (F_Y) component of the ground reaction force acting on a subject during the performance of a countermovement vertical jump and to carry out a linear impulse analysis of the F_Y-time record.

Location

Motion analysis laboratory

Apparatus and equipment

Force platform system

Method

Subject's clothing

Shorts, shirt and trainers

Data collection

Record the vertical component of the ground reaction force acting on a subject while performing a countermovement jump on a force platform.

1   Each subject should practice the jump a number of times before any trials are recorded. The jump is a countermovement jump without the use of the arms.

The subject adopts a relaxed standing position on the force platform with hands on hips (to eliminate the use of the arms) and feet shoulder width apart. The subject stands as still as possible for at least two seconds before the jump and then, in a single continuous movement, flexes his/her hips, knees and ankles (the countermovement) to move into a half squat position (knee angle approximately 90°) and immediately follows the half squat with a vertical jump for maximal height to land back on the force platform. The hands remain on the hips throughout the entire movement.

2   After two or three practice trials, two trials are recorded.

3   On a signal from the force platform system operator, the subject steps onto the platform. After the subject has adopted the start position, the system operator starts recording the vertical component of the ground reaction force at 1000 Hz. On another signal from the system operator, the subject performs a jump. When the subject regains a stationary standing position after landing, the system operator stops the recording and signals to the subject to step off the platform. After a 30 s recovery period, a second trial is recorded.

4   The trial with the longer flight time (which is likely to be associated with a higher jump) is selected for analysis.

Data analysis

1   Data analysis will be described in relation to the example vertical ground reaction force-time graph shown in Figure PW7.1.

2   The force-time graph of the jump should be displayed and the weight W (N) of the subject should be determined by averaging a 0.5 s section of the force-time

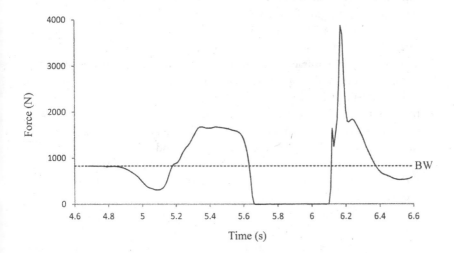

FIGURE PW7.1 Vertical ground reaction force-time recording of the performance of a countermovement vertical jump (hands on hips) from the start of movement to approximately 0.5 s after landing by a male student. BW, body weight.

recording during the period when the subject was standing still before the jump. Record the weight of the subject in an Excel spreadsheet, as shown in Table PW7.1.

3   Calculate the mass m of the subject where $m = W/9.81$ N. Record the subject's mass as shown in Table PW7.1.

4   The force-time graph should be time-sliced to retain the force-time data from about 0.2 s before the start of the countermovement to just after landing. The time-sliced force-time data should be copied into the first two columns of the Excel spreadsheet as shown in Table PW7.1. In the example results in Table PW7.1, the period of the time slice is 1.87 s (from 4.73 s to 6.59 s). With a sampling frequency of 1000 Hz, a time period of 1.87 s would require 1870 rows in the Excel spreadsheet. In the example results in Table PW7.1, the sampling frequency has been reduced from 1000 Hz to 100 Hz so that the example analysis can be presented more concisely. Consequently, there are 187 rows of data in Table PW7.1. The reduction of the sampling frequency decreases the accuracy of the analysis, but the method of analysis is unchanged.

5   The subject's weight should be copied into all of the cells in column 3 of Table PW7.1.

6   In column 4 of Table PW7.1, the resultant vertical force acting on the centre of gravity (CG) of the subject at each instant in time is calculated by subtracting body weight (column 3) from the vertical component of the ground reaction force (column 2). A negative resultant force indicates downward acceleration of the CG or upward deceleration of the CG. A positive resultant force indicates downward deceleration of the CG or upward acceleration of the CG.

7   In column 5 of Table PW7.1, the impulse of the resultant vertical force in each time interval is calculated by multiplying the average resultant force in the time interval by the length of the time interval. In the second time interval in Table PW7.1 (between 4.74 s and 4.75 s) the resultant force at the start of the time interval is zero. The resultant force at the end of the time interval is −0.48 N. Consequently, the average resultant force over the time interval is −0.024 N and the impulse of the average resultant force in the time interval = −0.024 N × 0.01 s = −0.00024 N·s.

8   In column 6 of Table PW7.1, the cumulative impulse of the resultant vertical force is calculated by summing the impulses in column 5 from the start to the end of the time slice. At the end of the second time interval the impulse is −0.00024 N·s, i.e. 0 + (−0.00024) N·s = −0.00024 N·s. At the end of the third time interval (4.75 s to 4.76 s) the cumulative impulse is −0.00024 N·s + (−0.01036) N·s = −0.0106 N·s.

9   In column 7 of Table PW7.1, the cumulative vertical velocity of the CG is calculated by dividing the cumulative impulse data in column 6 by the mass of the subject. As expected, the data in column 7 shows that the velocity of the CG was close to zero (to three decimal places) as the subject was standing still before the jump (4.73 s to 4.84 s). After the start of the counter-movement (at 4.85 s) the CG accelerated downward (downward velocity

increasing) and reached a maximum velocity downward of −1.0970 m/s at 5.18 s. This was followed by a period of deceleration downward in which the downward velocity of the CG was reduced to zero (the lowest point in the countermovement) at approximately 5.375 s. This was followed by a period of upward acceleration of the CG culminating in a maximum upward velocity of 2.2686 m/s at 5.63 s and a take-off velocity of 2.0157 m/s at 5.67 s; see Figure PW7.2.

10 In column 8 of Table PW7.1, the change in vertical displacement of the CG during each time interval is calculated by multiplying the average velocity in the time interval by the length of the time interval. The velocity at the start of the time interval 4.87 s to 4.88 s is −0.01017 m/s. The velocity at the end of the time interval is −0.01333 m/s. Consequently, the average velocity over the time interval is −0.01175 m/s and the change in vertical displacement of the CG in the time interval is −0.01175 m/s × 0.01 s = −0.001175 m.

11 In column 9 of Table PW7.1, the cumulative change in vertical displacement of the CG is calculated by summing the displacements in column 8 from the start to the end of the time slice. At 4.88 s, the cumulative displacement is −0.00059 m. The displacement in the time interval 4.88 s to 4.89 s is −0.00016 m. Consequently, the cumulative displacement at 4.89 s is −0.00059 m + (−0.00016 m) = −0.00075 m.

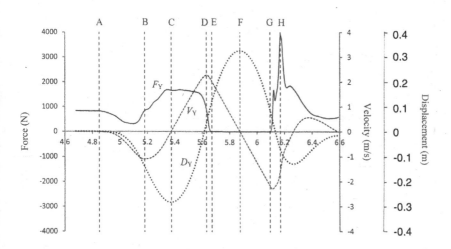

FIGURE PW7.2 Vertical ground reaction force-time graph (F_Y) and corresponding velocity-time graph (V_Y) and displacement-time graph (D_Y) of the countermovement vertical jump and landing shown in Figure PW7.1. A, start of countermovement; B, maximum velocity downward; C, maximum displacement downward; D, maximum velocity upward; E, take-off; F, maximum displacement upward; G, landing; H, peak force during landing.

TABLE PW7.1 Integration of the vertical ground reaction force–time recording of the countermovement jump shown in Figure PW7.1

Name of subject: John
Weight (N): 828.63
Mass of subject (kg): 84.468

Time (s)	F_Y (N)	BW (N)	$F_Y - BW$ (N)	Impulse (N·s)	C Impulse* (N·s)	C Velocity (m/s)	Disp† (m)	C Disp (m)
4.73	828.63	828.63	0	0	0	0	0	0
4.74	828.582	828.63	0	0	0	0	0	0
4.75	828.63	828.63	-0.048	-0.00024	-0.00024	0	0	0
4.76	826.606	828.63	-2.024	-0.01036	-0.0106	-0.00013	0	0
4.77	826.137	828.63	-2.493	-0.02259	-0.03319	-0.00039	0	0
4.78	823.454	828.63	-5.176	-0.03835	-0.07153	-0.00085	0	0
4.79	817.534	828.63	-11.096	-0.08136	-0.15289	-0.00181	0	0
4.80	820.629	828.63	-8.001	-0.09548	-0.24838	-0.00294	0	0
4.81	820.666	828.63	-7.964	-0.07982	-0.3282	-0.00389	0	0
4.82	820.87	828.63	-7.760	-0.07862	-0.40682	-0.00482	0	-0.00012
4.83	822.936	828.63	-5.694	-0.06727	-0.47409	-0.00561	0	-0.00018
4.84	823.649	828.63	-4.981	-0.05337	-0.52747	-0.00624	0	-0.00024
4.85	820.269	828.63	-8.361	-0.06671	-0.59418	-0.00703	0	-0.0003
4.86	816.887	828.63	-11.743	-0.10052	-0.6947	-0.00822	0	-0.00038
4.87	807.541	828.63	-21.089	-0.16416	-0.85886	-0.01017	0	-0.00047
4.88	796.315	828.63	-32.315	-0.26702	-1.12588	-0.01333	-0.00012	-0.00059
4.89	784.915	828.63	-43.715	-0.38015	-1.50603	-0.01783	-0.00016	-0.00075
4.90	769.427	828.63	-59.203	-0.51459	-2.02062	-0.02392	-0.00021	-0.00095

4.91	749.169	828.63	−79.461	−0.69332	−2.71394	−0.03213	−0.00028	−0.00123
4.92	732.137	828.63	−96.493	−0.87977	−3.59371	−0.04255	−0.00037	−0.00161
4.93	705.918	828.63	−122.712	−1.09603	−4.68973	−0.05552	−0.00049	−0.00210
4.94	685.638	828.63	−142.992	−1.32852	−6.01825	−0.07125	−0.00063	−0.00273
4.95	662.123	828.63	−166.507	−1.5475	−7.56575	−0.08957	−0.00080	−0.00353
4.96	637.232	828.63	−191.398	−1.7895	−9.35527	−0.11076	−0.001	−0.00454
4.97	605.012	828.63	−223.618	−2.07508	−11.4304	−0.13532	−0.00123	−0.00577
4.98	567.158	828.63	−261.472	−2.42545	−13.8558	−0.16404	−0.0015	−0.00726
4.99	523.508	828.63	−305.122	−2.83297	−16.6888	−0.19758	−0.00181	−0.00907
5.00	482.057	828.63	−346.573	−3.25848	−19.9472	−0.23615	−0.00217	−0.01124
5.01	439.931	828.63	−388.699	−3.67636	−23.6236	−0.27968	−0.00258	−0.01382
5.02	402.077	828.63	−426.553	−4.07626	−27.6999	−0.32793	−0.00304	−0.01686
5.03	375.783	828.63	−452.847	−4.397	−32.0969	−0.37999	−0.00354	−0.0204
5.04	358.866	828.63	−469.764	−4.61306	−36.7099	−0.4346	−0.00407	−0.02447
5.05	347.741	828.63	−480.889	−4.75327	−41.4632	−0.49087	−0.00463	−0.0291
5.06	336.964	828.63	−491.666	−4.86278	−46.326	−0.54844	−0.0052	−0.03429
5.07	321.436	828.63	−507.194	−4.9943	−51.3203	−0.60757	−0.00578	−0.04007
5.08	310.674	828.63	−517.956	−5.12575	−56.446	−0.66825	−0.00638	−0.04645
5.09	310.121	828.63	−518.509	−5.18233	−61.6283	−0.72961	−0.00699	−0.05344
5.10	309.584	828.63	−519.046	−5.18778	−66.8161	−0.79102	−0.0076	−0.06104
5.11	322.666	828.63	−505.964	−5.12505	−71.9412	−0.8517	−0.00821	−0.06926
5.12	343.416	828.63	−485.214	−4.95589	−76.8971	−0.91037	−0.00881	−0.07807
5.13	383.243	828.63	−445.387	−4.65301	−81.5501	−0.96546	−0.00938	−0.08745

(Continued)

TABLE PW7.1 (Continued)

Time (s)	F_Y (N)	BW (N)	F_Y – BW (N)	Impulse (N·s)	C Impulse* (N·s)	C Velocity (m/s)	Disp† (m)	C Disp (m)
5.14	445.732	828.63	-382.898	-4.14143	-85.6915	-1.01448	-0.0099	-0.09735
5.15	547.871	828.63	-280.759	-3.31829	-89.0098	-1.05377	-0.01034	-0.10769
5.16	664.803	828.63	-163.827	-2.22293	-91.2327	-1.08009	-0.01067	-0.11836
5.17	762.159	828.63	-66.471	-1.15149	-92.3842	-1.09372	-0.01087	-0.12923
5.18	839.401	828.63	10.771	-0.2785	-92.6627	-1.09702	-0.01095	-0.14018
5.19	874.75	828.63	46.12	0.28455	-92.3782	-1.09365	-0.01095	-0.15113
5.20	888.803	828.63	60.173	0.531465	-91.8468	-1.08736	-0.01091	-0.16204
5.21	908.132	828.63	79.502	0.698375	-91.1484	-1.07909	-0.01083	-0.17287
5.22	961.513	828.63	132.883	1.061925	-90.0865	-1.06652	-0.01073	-0.1836
5.23	1036.73	828.63	208.1	1.704915	-88.3816	-1.04633	-0.01056	-0.19416
5.24	1116.87	828.63	288.24	2.4817	-85.8999	-1.01695	-0.01032	-0.20448
5.25	1180.82	828.63	352.19	3.20215	-82.6977	-0.97904	-0.00998	-0.21446
5.26	1231.97	828.63	403.34	3.77765	-78.9201	-0.93432	-0.00957	-0.22403
5.27	1267.63	828.63	439	4.2117	-74.7084	-0.88446	-0.00909	-0.23312
5.28	1315.72	828.63	487.09	4.63045	-70.0779	-0.82964	-0.00857	-0.24169
5.29	1380.33	828.63	551.7	5.19395	-64.884	-0.76815	-0.00799	-0.24968
5.30	1449.52	828.63	620.89	5.86295	-59.021	-0.69874	-0.00733	-0.25701
5.31	1519.22	828.63	690.59	6.5574	-52.4636	-0.62111	-0.0066	-0.26361
5.32	1587.35	828.63	758.72	7.24655	-45.2171	-0.53532	-0.00578	-0.2694
5.33	1649.69	828.63	821.06	7.8989	-37.3182	-0.4418	-0.00489	-0.27428

5.34	1678.66	828.63	850.03	8.35545	-28.9627	-0.34288	-0.00392	-0.2782
5.35	1682.91	828.63	854.28	8.52155	-20.4412	-0.242	-0.00292	-0.28113
5.36	1680.52	828.63	851.89	8.53085	-11.9103	-0.141	-0.00192	-0.28304
5.37	1668.26	828.63	839.63	8.4576	-3.4527	-0.04088	-0.00091	-0.28395
5.38	1658.41	828.63	829.78	8.34705	4.8943	0.057943	0	-0.28387
5.39	1655.56	828.63	826.93	8.28355	13.1779	0.156011	0.00107	-0.2828
5.40	1656.98	828.63	828.35	8.2764	21.4543	0.253993	0.00205	-0.28075
5.41	1661.13	828.63	832.5	8.30425	29.7585	0.352306	0.003031	-0.27772
5.42	1670.18	828.63	841.55	8.37025	38.1288	0.451399	0.004019	-0.2737
5.43	1681.25	828.63	852.62	8.47085	46.5996	0.551684	0.005015	-0.26868
5.44	1681.61	828.63	852.98	8.528	55.1276	0.652645	0.006022	-0.26266
5.45	1676	828.63	847.37	8.50175	63.6294	0.753296	0.00703	-0.25563
5.46	1673.8	828.63	845.17	8.4627	72.0921	0.853484	0.008034	-0.2476
5.47	1668.9	828.63	840.27	8.4272	80.5193	0.953252	0.009034	-0.23856
5.48	1662.99	828.63	834.36	8.37315	88.8924	1.05238	0.010028	-0.22854
5.49	1654.87	828.63	826.24	8.303	97.1954	1.150678	0.011015	-0.21752
5.50	1649.31	828.63	820.68	8.2346	105.4301	1.248166	0.011994	-0.20553
5.51	1642.4	828.63	813.77	8.17225	113.6023	1.344915	0.012965	-0.19256
5.52	1630.24	828.63	801.61	8.0769	121.6792	1.440536	0.013927	-0.17863
5.53	1618.1	828.63	789.47	7.9554	129.6346	1.534718	0.014876	-0.16376
5.54	1609.7	828.63	781.07	7.8527	137.4873	1.627685	0.015812	-0.14795
5.55	1602.17	828.63	773.54	7.77305	145.2604	1.719709	0.016737	-0.13121
5.56	1589.9	828.63	761.27	7.67405	152.9344	1.81056	0.017651	-0.11356

(Continued)

TABLE PW7.1 (Continued)

Time (s)	F_Y (N)	BW (N)	$F_Y - BW$ (N)	Impulse (N·s)	C Impulse* (N·s)	C Velocity (m/s)	Disp† (m)	C Disp (m)
5.57	1571.87	828.63	743.24	7.52255	160.457	1.899618	0.018551	−0.09501
5.58	1541.61	828.63	712.98	7.2811	167.7381	1.985818	0.019427	−0.07558
5.59	1490.14	828.63	661.51	6.87245	174.6105	2.067179	0.020265	−0.05531
5.60	1410.47	828.63	581.84	6.21675	180.8273	2.140778	0.02104	−0.03427
5.61	1292.78	828.63	464.15	5.22995	186.0572	2.202695	0.021717	−0.01256
5.62	1125.36	828.63	296.73	3.8044	189.8616	2.247734	0.022252	0.00969
5.63	885.13	828.63	56.50	1.76615	191.6278	2.268643	0.022582	0.03227
5.64	566.33	828.63	−262.29	−1.02897	190.5988	2.256461	0.022626	0.05490
5.65	161.98	828.63	−666.64	−4.64472	185.9541	2.201474	0.02229	0.07719
5.66	7.42	828.63	−821.21	−7.43931	178.5148	2.113401	0.02157	0.09876
5.67	0	828.63	−828.63	−8.24922	170.2655	2.01574	0.020646	0.11941
5.68	0	828.63	−828.63	−8.2863	161.9792	1.91764	0.019667	0.13907
5.69	0	828.63	−828.63	−8.2863	153.6929	1.81954	0.018686	0.15776
5.70	0	828.63	−828.63	−8.2863	145.4066	1.72144	0.017705	0.17547
5.71	0	828.63	−828.63	−8.2863	137.1203	1.623341	0.01672	0.19219
5.72	0	828.63	−828.63	−8.2863	128.834	1.525241	0.01574	0.20793
5.73	0	828.63	−828.63	−8.2863	120.5477	1.42714	0.014762	0.222699
5.74	0	828.63	−828.63	−8.2863	112.2614	1.329041	0.013781	0.236479
5.75	0	828.63	−828.63	−8.2863	103.9751	1.230941	0.0128	0.249279
5.76	0	828.63	−828.63	−8.2863	95.6888	1.132841	0.011819	0.261098

5.77	0	828.63	-828.63	87.4025	-8.2863	1.034741	0.010838	0.271936
5.78	0	828.63	-828.63	79.1162	-8.2863	0.936642	0.009857	0.281793
5.79	0	828.63	-828.63	70.8299	-8.2863	0.838542	0.00887	0.290669
5.80	0	828.63	-828.63	62.5436	-8.2863	0.740442	0.007895	0.298564
5.81	0	828.63	-828.63	54.2573	-8.2863	0.642342	0.006914	0.305478
5.82	0	828.63	-828.63	45.9710	-8.2863	0.544242	0.005933	0.311411
5.83	0	828.63	-828.63	37.6847	-8.2863	0.446142	0.004952	0.316363
5.84	0	828.63	-828.63	29.3984	-8.2863	0.348042	0.003971	0.320334
5.85	0	828.63	-828.63	21.1121	-8.2863	0.249943	0.00299	0.323324
5.86	0	828.63	-828.63	12.8258	-8.2863	0.151843	0.002009	0.325332
5.87	0	828.63	-828.63	4.5395	-8.2863	0.053743	0.001028	0.32636
5.88	0	828.63	-828.63	-3.7467	-8.2863	-0.04436	0	0.326407
5.89	0	828.63	-828.63	-12.0331	-8.2863	-0.14246	-0.00093	0.325473
5.90	0	828.63	-828.63	-20.3194	-8.2863	-0.24056	-0.00192	0.323558
5.91	0	828.63	-828.63	-28.6057	-8.2863	-0.33866	-0.0029	0.320662
5.92	0	828.63	-828.63	-36.892	-8.2863	-0.43676	-0.00388	0.316785
5.93	0	828.63	-828.63	-45.1783	-8.2863	-0.53486	-0.00486	0.311927
5.94	0	828.63	-828.63	-53.4646	-8.2863	-0.63296	-0.00584	0.306088
5.95	0	828.63	-828.63	-61.7509	-8.2863	-0.73106	-0.00682	0.299268
5.96	0	828.63	-828.63	-70.0372	-8.2863	-0.82916	-0.0078	0.291467
5.97	0	8	28.63	-8.2863	-828.63	-78.3235	-0.92726	-0.00878
5.98	0	828.63	-828.63	-86.6098	-8.2863	-1.02536	-0.00976	0.272922
5.99	0	828.63	-828.63	-94.8961	-8.2863	-1.12346	-0.01074	0.262178

(Continued)

TABLE PW7.1 (Continued)

Time (s)	F_v (N)	BW (N)	F_v – BW (N)	Impulse (N·s)	C Impulse* (N·s)	C Velocity (m/s)	Disp† (m)	C Disp (m)
6.0	0	828.63	–828.63	–8.2863	–103.182	–1.22156	–0.01173	0.250453
6.01	0	828.63	–828.63	–8.2863	–111.469	–1.31966	–0.01271	0.237747
6.02	0	828.63	–828.63	–8.2863	–119.755	–1.41776	–0.01369	0.224059
6.03	0	828.63	–828.63	–8.2863	–128.041	–1.51586	–0.01467	0.209391
6.04	0	828.63	–828.63	–8.2863	–136.328	–1.61396	–0.01565	0.193742
6.05	0	828.63	–828.63	–8.2863	–144.614	–1.71205	–0.01663	0.177112
6.06	0	828.63	–828.63	–8.2863	–152.9	–1.81015	–0.01761	0.159501
6.07	0	828.63	–828.63	–8.2863	–161.186	–1.90825	–0.01859	0.140909
6.08	0	828.63	–828.63	–8.2863	–169.473	–2.00635	–0.01957	0.121336
6.09	0	828.63	–828.63	–8.2863	–177.759	–2.10445	–0.02055	0.100782
6.10	1.79	828.63	–826.837	–8.27733	–186.036	–2.20245	–0.02153	0.079248
6.11	351.35	828.63	–477.282	–6.52059	–192.557	–2.27964	–0.02241	0.056837
6.12	1647.61	828.63	818.98	1.70849	–190.848	–2.25942	–0.0227	0.034142
6.13	1255.33	828.63	426.7	6.2284	–184.62	–2.18568	–0.02223	0.011916
6.14	1514.15	828.63	685.52	5.5611	–179.059	–2.11984	–0.02153	–0.00961
6.15	1847.57	828.63	1018.94	8.5223	–170.537	–2.01895	–0.02069	–0.03031
6.16	2691.9	828.63	1863.27	14.41105	–156.126	–1.84834	–0.01934	–0.04964
6.17	3874.25	828.63	3045.62	24.54445	–131.581	–1.55776	–0.01703	–0.06667
6.18	3677.97	828.63	2849.34	29.4748	–102.106	–1.20882	–0.01383	–0.08051
6.19	2724.28	828.63	1895.65	23.72495	–78.3814	–0.92794	–0.01068	–0.09119
6.2	2057.51	828.63	1228.88	15.62265	–62.7588	–0.74299	–0.00835	–0.09954
6.21	1801.43	828.63	972.8	11.0084	–51.7504	–0.61266	–0.00678	–0.10632

6.22	1788.26	828.63	959.63	−42.0882	9.66215	−0.49827	−0.00555	−0.11188
6.23	1826.88	828.63	998.25	−32.2988	9.7894	−0.38238	−0.0044	−0.11628
6.24	1848.44	828.63	1019.81	−22.2085	10.0903	−0.26292	−0.00323	−0.11951
6.25	1819.99	828.63	991.36	−12.1527	10.05585	−0.14387	−0.00203	−0.12154
6.26	1754.29	828.63	925.66	−2.56759	9.5851	−0.0304	−0.00087	−0.12241
6.27	1687.38	828.63	858.75	6.354457	8.92205	0.07522	0.000224	−0.12219
6.28	1613.39	828.63	784.76	14.57201	8.21755	0.172515	0.001239	−0.12095
6.29	1528.74	828.63	700.11	21.99636	7.42435	0.260411	0.002165	−0.11878
6.3	1445.46	828.63	616.83	28.58106	6.5847	0.338365	0.002994	−0.11579
6.31	1344.32	828.63	515.69	34.24366	5.6626	0.405404	0.003719	−0.11207
6.32	1244.16	828.63	415.53	38.89976	4.6561	0.460527	0.00433	−0.10774
6.33	1154.7	828.63	326.07	42.60776	3.708	0.504425	0.004825	−0.10292
6.34	1075.12	828.63	246.49	45.47056	2.8628	0.538317	0.005214	−0.0977
6.35	993.827	828.63	165.197	47.52899	2.058435	0.562686	0.005505	−0.0922
6.36	922.577	828.63	93.947	48.82471	1.29572	0.578026	0.005704	−0.08649
6.37	854.212	828.63	25.582	49.42236	0.597645	0.585102	0.005816	−0.08068
6.38	793.825	828.63	−34.805	49.37624	−0.04611	0.584556	0.005848	−0.07483
6.39	743.958	828.63	−84.672	48.77886	−0.59739	0.577483	0.00581	−0.06902
6.4	705.119	828.63	−123.511	47.73794	−1.04092	0.56516	0.005713	−0.06331
6.41	672.045	828.63	−156.585	46.33746	−1.40048	0.54858	0.005569	−0.05774
6.42	654.07	828.63	−174.56	44.68174	−1.65573	0.528978	0.005388	−0.05235
6.43	639.487	828.63	−189.143	42.86322	−1.81852	0.507449	0.005182	−0.04717
6.44	627.623	828.63	−201.007	40.91247	−1.95075	0.484355	0.004959	−0.04221
6.45	613.218	828.63	−215.412	38.83038	−2.0821	0.459705	0.00472	−0.03749
6.46	599.145	828.63	−229.485	36.60589	−2.22449	0.43337	0.004465	−0.03302

(Continued)

TABLE PW7.1 (Continued)

Time (s)	F_Y (N)	BW (N)	$F_Y - BW$ (N)	Impulse (N·s)	C Impulse* (N·s)	C Velocity (m/s)	Disp† (m)	C Disp (m)
6.47	577.434	828.63	−251.196	−2.40341	34.20249	0.404916	0.004191	−0.02883
6.48	562.862	828.63	−265.768	−2.58482	31.61767	0.374315	0.003896	−0.02494
6.49	551.335	828.63	−277.295	−2.71532	28.90235	0.342169	0.003582	−0.02135
6.5	541.664	828.63	−286.966	−2.82131	26.08105	0.308768	0.003255	−0.0181
6.51	537.095	828.63	−291.535	−2.89251	23.18854	0.274525	0.002916	−0.01518
6.52	533.873	828.63	−294.757	−2.93146	20.25708	0.23982	0.002572	−0.01261
6.53	536.604	828.63	−292.026	−2.93392	17.32317	0.205086	0.002225	−0.01039
6.54	536.107	828.63	−292.523	−2.92275	14.40042	0.170484	0.001878	−0.00851
6.55	539.689	828.63	−288.941	−2.90732	11.4931	0.136065	0.001533	−0.00698
6.56	545.653	828.63	−282.977	−2.85959	8.633512	0.10221	0.001191	−0.00578
6.57	556.199	828.63	−272.431	−2.77704	5.856472	0.069334	0.000858	−0.00493
6.58	565.884	828.63	−262.746	−2.67589	3.180587	0.037654	0.000535	−0.00439
6.59	585.579	828.63	−243.051	−2.52899	0.651602	0.007714	0.000227	−0.00417

* C Impulse: cumulative impulse.
C Velocity: cumulative velocity.
Disp: displacement.
C Disp: cumulative displacement.
† Displacement data listed in the table as zero are zero to at least four places of decimals.

TABLE PW7.2 Linear kinematic events in the vertical movement of the centre of gravity (CG) of the subject during performance of the countermovement jump and landing shown in Figure PW7.1. The events are labelled in Figure PW7.2.

		Time (s)	V_Y (m/s)	D_Y (m)
A:	Start of countermovement.	4.85	0	0
A to B:	Acceleration downward.			
B:	Maximum velocity downward.	5.18	−1.0970	−0.1402
B to C:	Deceleration downward.			
C:	Maximum displacement downward.	5.3750	0	−0.2839
C to D:	Acceleration upward.			
D:	Maximum velocity upward.	5.63	2.2686	−0.0323
D to E:	Deceleration upward.			
E:	Take-off.	5.67	2.0157	0.1194
E to G:	Flight.			
F:	Maximum displacement upward: highest point of CG during flight.	5.8750	0	0.3264
G:	Landing.	6.09	−2.1044	0.1008
H:	Peak force during landing = 3874.25 N.	6.17	−1.5578	−0.0667

12   The key linear kinematic events in the countermovement jump are presented in Table PW7.2.

13   Jump height (h_J), i.e. the maximum vertical displacement of the CG relative to the stationary starting position, is the sum of take-off height (h_{TO}) and flight height (h_F) where h_{TO} is the height of the CG at take-off and h_F is the maximum vertical displacement after take-off. As shown in Table PW7.2, $h_{TO} = 0.1194$ m and $h_J = 0.3264$ m. Consequently, $h_F = 0.207$ m.

Presentation of results

1   Present your individual vertical ground reaction force-time graph, as shown in Figure PW7.1.

2   Present the results of your integration of the vertical ground reaction force-time recording at 100 Hz, as shown in Table PW7.1.

3   Present the vertical ground reaction force-time graph and corresponding velocity-time and displacement-time graphs, shown in Figure PW7.2.

4   Present the key kinematic events resulting from your analysis, as shown in Table PW7.2.

Example results

Example results are shown in Figure PW7.1, Table PW7.1, Figure PW7.2 and Table PW7.2.

PRACTICAL WORKSHEET 8

Comparative linear impulse analysis of the ground reaction forces in countermovement vertical jumps with and without an arm swing

Objectives

To record the vertical (F_Y) component of the ground reaction force acting on a subject during the performance of a countermovement vertical jump with an arm swing and a countermovement vertical jump without an arm swing and to carry out a comparative linear impulse analysis of the F_Y-time records.

Location

Motion analysis laboratory

Apparatus and equipment

Force platform system

Method

Subject's clothing

Shorts, shirt and trainers

Data collection

Record the vertical component of the ground reaction force acting on a subject while performing a countermovement vertical jump with an arm swing and a countermovement vertical jump without an arm swing.

1   In a countermovement jump with an arm swing, the subject adopts a relaxed standing position on the force platform with feet shoulder width apart. With straight arms, the subject then fully extends his/her shoulders (arms swing forward and upward) to raise his/her arms symmetrically above his/her head. This position is held as still as possible for at least two seconds. On a signal from the force platform operator, the subject then flexes his/her shoulders to swing the arms forward, downward and backward, and simultaneously flexes his/her hips, knees and ankles to move into a half squat position (knee angle approximately 90°). These movements constitute the countermovement. The countermovement is immediately followed by a maximal effort vertical jump involving a vigorous downward, forward and upward swing of the arms and vigorous extension of the hips, knees and ankles. The subject should land back on the force platform.

2   In a countermovement jump without an arm swing, the subject keeps hands on hips throughout the entire movement.

3   Each subject should have sufficient practice of both types the jump to consistently land on the platform.

4   On a signal from the force platform system operator, the subject steps onto the platform. After the subject has adopted the start position, the system operator starts recording the vertical component (F_Y) of the ground reaction force at 1000 Hz. On another signal from the system operator, the subject performs a jump. When the subject regains a stationary standing position after landing, the system operator stops the recording and signals to the subject to step off the platform.

5   Each subject performs two trials without an arm swing and two trials with an arm swing with 30 s recovery period between trials. For each type of jump, the trial with the longer flight time (which is likely to be associated with a higher jump) is selected for analysis.

Data analysis

1   Figure PW8.1 shows the vertical ground reaction force-time graphs of one male subject in a countermovement with an arm swing and in a countermovement without an arm swing. For graphical comparison, the two records were synchronized at take-off.
    The method of integrating each of the force-time recordings is the same as in Practical Worksheet 7 and will be described in relation to the jump with an arm swing (Figure PW8.2).

2   The force-time graph of the jump should be displayed and the weight W (N) of the subject should be determined by averaging a 0.5 s section of the force-time recording during the period when the subject was standing still before the jump. Record the weight of the subject in an Excel spreadsheet, as shown in Table PW8.1.

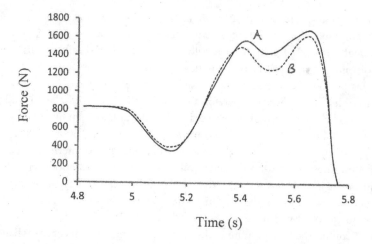

FIGURE PW8.1 Vertical ground reaction force-time graphs of a countermovement vertical jump with an arm swing and a countermovement vertical jump without an arm swing by a male student. A, with an arm swing; B without an arm swing.

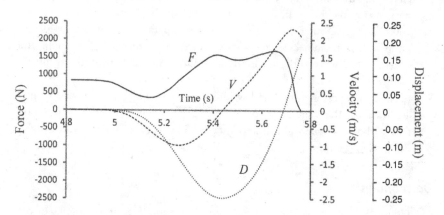

FIGURE PW8.2 Vertical ground reaction force-time graph (*F*) and corresponding velocity-time graph (*V*) and displacement-time graph (*D*) of the countermovement vertical jump with an arm swing.

3 Calculate the mass m of the subject where $m = W/9.81$ N. Record the subject's mass as shown in Table PW8.1.

4 The force-time graph should be time-sliced to retain the force-time data from about 0.2 s before the start of the countermovement to just after landing. The time-sliced force-time data should be copied into the first two columns of the Excel spreadsheet as shown in Table PW8.1. The period of the time slice is 0.94 s (from 4.82 s to 5.76 s).

TABLE PW8.1 Integration of the vertical ground reaction force–time recording of the countermovement jump with an arm swing shown in Figure PW8.1

Name of subject: John
Weight (N): 828.81
Mass of subject (kg): 84.49

Time (s)	F_Y (N)	BW (N)	$F_Y - BW$ (N)	Impulse (N·s)	C Impulse* (N·s)	C Velocity (m/s)	Disp† (m)	C Disp (m)
4.82	828.53	828.81	−0.28	0	0	0	0	0
4.84	829.661	828.81	0.851	0.00571	0.00571	0	0	0
4.86	828.616	828.81	−0.194	0.00657	0.01228	0.00014	0	0
4.88	829.432	828.81	0.622	0.00428	0.01656	0.00019	0	0
4.9	828.27	828.81	−0.54	0.00082	0.01738	0.00020	0	0
4.92	826.699	828.81	−2.111	−0.02651	−0.00913	−0.00011	0	0
4.94	818.9	828.81	−9.91	−0.12021	−0.12934	−0.00153	0	0
4.96	801.482	828.81	−27.33	−0.37238	−0.50172	−0.00594	0	0
4.98	780.086	828.81	−48.72	−0.76052	−1.26224	−0.01494	−0.00021	−0.00029
5.0	730.456	828.81	−98.35	−1.47078	−2.73302	−0.03235	−0.00047	−0.00076
5.02	662.099	828.81	−166.7	−2.65065	−5.38367	−0.06372	−0.00096	−0.00172
5.04	590.453	828.81	−238.4	−4.05068	−9.43435	−0.11166	−0.00175	−0.00347
5.06	518.255	828.81	−310.6	−5.48912	−14.9235	−0.17663	−0.00288	0.00635
5.08	449.787	828.81	−379	−6.89578	−21.8193	−0.25825	−0.00435	−0.01070
5.1	401.029	828.81	−427.8	−8.06804	−29.8873	−0.35374	−0.00612	−0.01682
5.12	368.449	828.81	−460.4	−8.88142	−38.7687	−0.45886	−0.00813	−0.02495

(Continued)

TABLE PW8.1 (Continued)

Time (s)	F_Y (N)	BW (N)	$F_Y - BW$ (N)	Impulse (N·s)	C Impulse* (N·s)	C Velocity (m/s)	Disp† (m)	C Disp (m)
5.14	353.176	828.81	−475.6	−9.35995	−48.1287	−0.56964	−0.01028	−0.03523
5.16	365.972	828.81	−462.8	−9.38472	−57.5134	−0.68071	−0.0125	−0.04774
5.18	422.992	828.81	−405.8	−8.68656	−66.1999	−0.78352	−0.01464	−0.06238
5.2	499.362	828.81	−329.4	−7.35266	−73.5526	−0.87055	−0.01654	−0.07892
5.22	589.858	828.81	−239	−5.684	−79.2366	−0.93782	−0.01808	−0.09700
5.24	707.658	828.81	−121.2	−3.60104	−82.8376	−0.98044	−0.01918	−0.11619
5.26	842.486	828.81	13.676	−1.07476	−83.9124	−0.99316	−0.01974	−0.13592
5.28	961.519	828.81	132.71	1.46385	−82.4486	−0.97584	−0.01969	−0.15561
5.3	1074.88	828.81	246.07	3.78779	−78.6608	−0.93101	−0.01907	−0.17468
5.32	1190.93	828.81	362.12	6.0819	−72.5789	−0.85902	−0.0179	−0.19258
5.34	1293.01	828.81	464.2	8.2632	−64.3157	−0.76122	−0.0162	−0.20878
5.36	1393.15	828.81	564.34	10.2854	−54.0303	−0.63949	−0.01401	−0.2227
5.38	1489.23	828.81	660.42	12.2476	−41.7827	−0.49453	−0.01134	−0.23413
5.4	1552.3	828.81	723.49	13.8391	−27.9436	−0.33073	−0.00825	−0.24238
5.42	1568.04	828.81	739.23	14.6272	−13.3164	−0.15761	−0.00488	−0.24727
5.44	1538.61	828.81	709.8	14.4903	1.17394	0.01389	−0.00144	−0.24870
5.46	1486.65	828.81	657.84	13.6764	14.85034	0.17576	0.00189	−0.24681
5.48	1441.9	828.81	613.09	12.7093	27.55964	0.32618	0.00502	−0.24179
5.5	1431.1	828.81	602.29	12.1538	39.71344	0.47003	0.00796	−0.23383

5.52	1442.45	828.81	613.64	12.1593	51.87274	0.61395	0.01084	-0.22299
5.54	1470.61	828.81	641.8	12.5544	64.42714	0.76254	0.01376	-0.20922
5.56	1518.29	828.81	689.48	13.3128	77.73994	0.92010	0.01682	-0.19239
5.58	1569.36	828.81	740.55	14.3003	92.04024	1.08936	0.02009	-0.17230
5.6	1609.59	828.81	780.78	15.2133	107.2535	1.26942	0.02358	-0.14871
5.62	1647.49	828.81	818.68	15.9946	123.2481	1.45873	0.02728	-0.12143
5.64	1680.33	828.81	851.52	16.702	139.9501	1.65641	0.03115	-0.09028
5.66	1682.01	828.81	853.2	17.0472	156.9973	1.85817	0.03514	-0.05513
5.68	1608.77	828.81	779.96	16.3316	173.3289	2.05147	0.03909	-0.01604
5.7	1412.17	828.81	583.36	13.6332	186.9621	2.21283	0.04264	0.02660
5.72	998.26	828.81	169.45	7.5281	194.4902	2.30193	0.045148	0.07174
5.74	299.28	828.81	-529.5	-3.60073	190.8895	2.25931	0.045612	0.11736
5.76	0	828.81	-828.8	-13.5833	177.3062	2.09854	0.043579	0.16094

★ C Impulse: cumulative impulse.
C Velocity: cumulative velocity.
Disp: displacement.
C Disp: cumulative displacement.
† Displacement data listed in the table as zero are zero to at least four places of decimals.

5 With a sampling frequency of 1000 Hz, a time period of 0.94 s would require 940 rows in the Excel spreadsheet. In Table PW8.1, the sampling frequency has been reduced from 1000 Hz to 50 Hz so that the analysis can be presented more concisely. Consequently, there are 48 rows of data in Table PW8.1 with 47 time intervals: 47×0.02 s $= 0.94$ s.

6 The lower the sampling frequency, the greater the likelihood that a specific event, such as maximum velocity downward, maximum velocity upward, take-off velocity, maximum displacement downward, maximum displacement upward and displacement at take-off, will occur between data points, i.e. between rows in Table PW8.1. The actual values and times of these events could be estimated by interpolation of the data, but the magnitudes and times of these events referred to below are taken directly from Table PW8.1 and, as such, are approximate values.

7 The subject's weight should be copied into all of the cells in column 3 of Table PW8.1.

8 In column 4 of Table PW8.1, the resultant vertical force acting on the centre of gravity (CG) of the subject at each instant in time is calculated by subtracting body weight (column 3) from the vertical component of the ground reaction force (column 2).

9 In column 5 of Table PW8.1, the impulse of the resultant vertical force in each time interval is calculated by multiplying the average resultant force in the time interval by the length of the time interval. In the first time interval in Table PW8.1 (between 4.82 s and 4.84 s) the resultant force at the start of the time interval is −0.28 N. The resultant force at the end of the time interval is 0.851 N. Consequently, the average resultant force over the time interval is 0.285 N and the impulse of the average resultant force in the time interval = 0.285 N $\times$ 0.02 s $= 0.00571$ N·s.

10 In column 6 of Table PW8.1, the cumulative impulse of the resultant vertical force is calculated by summing the impulses in column 5 from the start to the end of the time slice. At the end of the first time interval the impulse is 0.00571 N·s, i.e. $0 + 0.00571$ N·s $= 0.00571$ N·s. At the end of the second time interval (4.84 s to 4.86 s) the cumulative impulse is 0.00571 N·s $+ 0.00657$ N·s $= 0.01228$ N·s.

11 In column 7 of Table PW8.1, the cumulative vertical velocity of the CG is calculated by dividing the cumulative impulse data in column 6 by the mass of the subject. The velocity data shows that after the start of the countermovement (at 4.90 s) the CG accelerated downward (downward velocity increasing) and reached a maximum velocity downward of −0.9932 m/s at 5.26 s. This was followed by a period of deceleration downward in which the downward velocity of the CG was reduced to zero (the lowest point in the countermovement) at approximately 5.43 s. This was followed by a period of upward acceleration of the CG culminating in a maximum upward velocity of 2.3019 m/s at 5.72 s and a take-off velocity of 2.0985 m/s at 5.76 s; see Figure PW8.2.

12 In column 8 of Table PW8.1, the change in vertical displacement of the CG during each time interval is calculated by multiplying the average velocity in the time interval by the length of the time interval. The velocity at the start of the time interval (4.98 s to 5.0 s is –0.01494 m/s. The velocity at the end of the time interval is –0.03235 m/s. Consequently, the average velocity over the time interval is –0.02364 m/s and the change in vertical displacement of the CG in the time interval is –0.02364 m/s × 0.02 s = –0.00047 m.

13 In column 9 of Table PW8.1, the cumulative change in vertical displacement of the CG is calculated by summing the displacements in column 8 from the start to the end of the time slice. At 4.98 s, the cumulative displacement is –0.00029 m. The displacement in the time interval 4.98 s to 5.0 s is –0.00047 m. Consequently, the cumulative displacement at 5.0 s is –0.00029 m + (–0.00047 m) = –0.00076 m.

14 The displacement data shows that the maximum downward displacement of the CG was –0.2487 m at 5.44 s (the end of the countermovement) and displacement at take-off was 0.1609 m at 5.76 s; see Table PW8.1 and Figure PW8.2.

15 Flight height can be estimated from take-off velocity by applying the equation for uniformly accelerated motion $v^2 - u^2 = 2 \cdot a \cdot s$, where u is take-off velocity = 2.0985 m/s, v is velocity at the peak of the flight = 0, a is acceleration = –9.81 m/s^2 and s is flight height. Consequently,

$$s = \frac{v^2 - u^2}{2 \cdot a} = -\left(\frac{2.0985^2}{19.62} \right) = \frac{-4.4037}{-19.62} = 0.2244\,\text{m}$$

16 The integration of the force-time recording of the countermovement without an arm swing is shown in Table PW8.2 and Figure PW8.3.

17 The key linear kinematic events in the two countermovement jumps are presented in Table PW8.3.

Presentation of results

1 Present your individual vertical ground reaction force-time graphs for a countermovement with arm swing and a countermovement without arm swing, as shown in Figure PW8.1.

2 Present the results of your integration of the vertical ground reaction force-time recordings at 50 Hz, as shown in Tables PW8.1 and 8.2.

3 Present the vertical ground reaction force-time graph and corresponding velocity-time and displacement-time graphs for each jump, as shown in Figures PW8.2 and PW8.3.

4 Present the key kinematic events resulting from your analysis of the two jumps, as in Table PW8.3.

TABLE PW8.2 Integration of the vertical ground reaction force–time recording of the countermovement jump without an arm swing shown in Figure PW8.1

Name of subject: John
Weight (N): 828.81
Mass of subject (kg): 84.49

Time (s)	F_Y (N)	BW (N)	$F_Y - BW$ (N)	Impulse (N·s)	C Impulse* (N·s)	C Vel (m/s)	Disp† (m)	C Disp (m)
4.82	828.22	828.81	-0.59	0	0	0	0	0
4.84	828.26	828.81	-0.55	-0.0114	-0.0114	-0.0001	0	0
4.86	828.32	828.81	-0.49	-0.0104	-0.0218	-0.0003	0	0
4.88	828.24	828.81	-0.57	-0.0106	-0.0324	-0.0004	0	0
4.9	828.87	828.81	0.06	-0.0051	-0.0375	-0.0004	0	0
4.92	826.649	828.81	-2.161	-0.021	-0.0585	-0.0007	0	0
4.94	823.887	828.81	-4.923	-0.0708	-0.1293	-0.0015	0	0
4.96	820.315	828.81	-8.495	-0.1342	-0.2635	-0.0031	0	-0.0001
4.98	804.427	828.81	-24.383	-0.3288	-0.5923	-0.007	-0.0001	-0.0002
5	765.137	828.81	-63.673	-0.8806	-1.4729	-0.0174	-0.00024	-0.0004
5.02	699.638	828.81	-129.17	-1.9285	-3.4013	-0.0403	-0.00058	-0.001
5.04	627.232	828.81	-201.58	-3.3075	-6.7088	-0.0794	-0.0012	-0.0022
5.06	547.158	828.81	-281.65	-4.8323	-11.541	-0.1366	-0.00216	-0.0044
5.08	478.057	828.81	-350.75	-6.3241	-17.865	-0.2114	-0.00348	-0.0079
5.1	432.077	828.81	-396.73	-7.4749	-25.34	-0.2999	-0.00511	-0.013
5.12	398.866	828.81	-429.94	-8.2668	-33.607	-0.3978	-0.00698	-0.02
5.14	396.964	828.81	-431.85	-8.6179	-42.225	-0.4998	-0.00898	-0.0289
5.16	405.674	828.81	-423.14	-8.5498	-50.775	-0.601	-0.01101	-0.0399

5.18	435.584	828.81	−393.23	−8.1636	−58.938	−0.6976	−0.01299	−0.0529
5.2	502.416	828.81	−326.39	−7.1962	−66.134	−0.7827	−0.0148	−0.0677
5.22	595.732	828.81	−233.08	−5.5947	−71.729	−0.849	−0.01632	−0.084
5.24	704.803	828.81	−124.01	−3.5709	−75.3	−0.8912	−0.0174	−0.1014
5.26	842.486	828.81	13.676	−1.1033	−76.403	−0.9043	−0.01796	−0.1194
5.28	995.803	828.81	166.993	1.80669	−74.597	−0.8829	−0.01787	−0.1373
5.3	1133.513	828.81	304.703	4.71696	−69.88	−0.8271	−0.0171	−0.1544
5.32	1243.87	828.81	415.06	7.19763	−62.682	−0.7419	−0.01569	−0.1701
5.34	1346.511	828.81	517.701	9.32761	−53.354	−0.6315	−0.01373	−0.1838
5.36	1423.72	828.81	594.91	11.1261	−42.228	−0.4998	−0.01131	−0.1951
5.38	1469.52	828.81	640.71	12.3562	−29.872	−0.3536	−0.00853	−0.2036
5.4	1497.35	828.81	668.54	13.0925	−16.78	−0.1986	−0.00552	−0.2092
5.42	1468.66	828.81	639.85	13.0839	−3.6956	−0.0437	−0.00242	−0.2116
5.44	1395.52	828.81	566.71	12.0656	8.36998	0.09906	0.000553	−0.211
5.46	1328.41	828.81	499.6	10.6631	19.0331	0.22527	0.003243	−0.2078
5.48	1276.98	828.81	448.17	9.4777	28.5108	0.33745	0.005627	−0.2022
5.5	1251.18	828.81	422.37	8.7054	37.2162	0.44048	0.007779	−0.1944
5.52	1251.61	828.81	422.8	8.4517	45.6679	0.54051	0.00981	−0.1846
5.54	1271.8	828.81	442.99	8.6579	54.3258	0.64298	0.011835	−0.1727
5.56	1335.99	828.81	507.18	9.5017	63.8275	0.75544	0.013984	−0.1587
5.58	1421.31	828.81	592.5	10.9968	74.8243	0.8856	0.01641	−0.1423
5.6	1513.24	828.81	684.43	12.7693	87.5936	1.03673	0.019223	−0.1231
5.62	1581.7	828.81	752.89	14.3732	101.967	1.20685	0.022436	−0.1007

(Continued)

TABLE PW8.2 (Continued)

Time (s)	F_Y (N)	BW (N)	$F_Y - BW$ (N)	Impulse (N·s)	C Impulse* (N·s)	C Vel (m/s)	Disp† (m)	C Disp (m)
5.64	1620.9	828.81	792.09	15.4498	117.417	1.38971	0.025966	-0.0747
5.66	1611.61	828.81	782.8	15.7489	133.165	1.57611	0.029658	-0.0451
5.68	1510.47	828.81	681.66	14.6446	147.81	1.74944	0.033255	-0.0118
5.7	1295.36	828.81	466.55	11.4821	159.292	1.88534	0.036348	0.02455
5.72	926.335	828.81	97.525	5.64075	164.933	1.9521	0.038374	0.06292
5.74	307.4165	828.81	-521.39	-4.2387	160.694	1.90193	0.03854	0.10146
5.76	0	828.81	-828.81	-13.502	147.192	1.74213	0.036441	0.1379

* C Impulse: cumulative impulse.
C Velocity: cumulative velocity.
Disp: displacement.
† Displacement data listed in the table as zero are zero to at least four places of decimals.
C Disp: cumulative displacement.

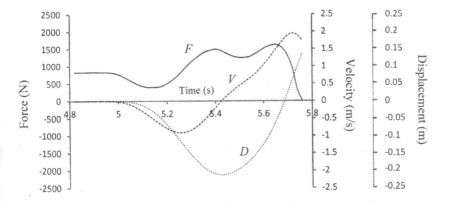

FIGURE PW8.3 Vertical ground reaction force-time graph (*F*) and corresponding velocity-time graph (*V*) and displacement-time graph (*D*) of the countermovement vertical jump without an arm swing.

TABLE PW8.3 Linear kinematic events in the vertical movement of the centre of gravity (*CG*) of the subject during performance of the countermovement vertical jump without an arm swing and the countermovement vertical jump with an arm swing

	Without arm swing	With arm swing	Δ(%)★
Maximum velocity downward (m/s)	0.9043	0.9932	9.83
Maximum velocity upward (m/s)	1.9521	2.3019	17.92
Take-off velocity (m/s)	1.7421	2.0985	20.46
Maximum displacement downward (m)	0.2116	0.2487	17.53
Take-off height (m)	0.1379	0.1609	16.68
Flight height (m)	0.1547	0.2244	45.05
Jump height (m)	0.2926	0.3853	31.68

★ (With − Without) × 100
    Without

Example results

Example results are shown in Figures PW8.1 to PW8.3 and Tables PW8.1 to PW8.3. The results show that jump height in the jump with arm swing was 31.68% higher than in the jump without arm swing (0.3853 m and 0.2926 m, respectively). The increase in jump height with arm swing was the result of a 16.68% increase in take-off height (0.1609 m and 0.1379 m respectively) and a 45.05% increase in flight height (0.2244 m and 0.1547 m respectively). The 45.05% increase in flight height was the result of a 20.46% increase in take-off velocity.

PRACTICAL WORKSHEET 9

Linear impulse analysis of the ground reaction force in a standing long jump

Objectives

To record the anteroposterior (F_X) and vertical (F_Y) components of the ground reaction force acting on a subject during the performance of a standing long jump and to perform an impulse analysis of the two recordings.

Location

Motion analysis laboratory

Apparatus and equipment

Force platform system

Method

Subject's clothing

Shorts, shirt and trainers

Data collection

Record the anteroposterior (F_X) and vertical (F_Y) components of the ground reaction force acting on a subject during the performance of a standing long jump with an arm swing.

1   In a standing long jump with an arm swing, the subject adopts a relaxed standing position on the force platform with feet shoulder width apart and toes touching

a line on the force platform perpendicular to the direction of the jump. With straight arms, the subject then fully extends the shoulders (arms swing forward and upward) to raise the arms symmetrically above the head. This position is held as still as possible for at least two seconds. On a signal from the force platform operator, the subject then flexes the shoulders to swing the arms forward, downward and backward, and simultaneously flexes the hips, knees and ankles to move into a half squat position (knee angle approximately 90°) with the trunk leaning forward. These movements are immediately followed by a maximal effort forward jump involving a vigorous downward and forward swing of the arms and vigorous extension of the hips, knees and ankles. The subject should land on both feet as far forward of the start position as possible in a stable position.

2   Each subject should have sufficient practice of the standing long jump to consistently land in a stable position.

3   On a signal from the force platform system operator, the subject steps onto the platform. After the subject has adopted the start position, the system operator starts recording the anteroposterior (F_X) and vertical (F_Y) components of the ground reaction force at 1000 Hz. On another signal from the system operator, the subject performs a jump. The system operator stops the recording after the subject lands. An assistant marks a line on the floor at the back of the rearmost heel after landing. The length of the jump from the start line to the rearmost heel line is measured and recorded.

4   Each subject performs two trials with 30 s recovery period between trials. The force-time recordings of the longest jump are selected for analysis.

Data analysis

1   Figure PW9.1 shows the vertical (F_Y) and anteroposterior (F_X) ground reaction force-time graphs of a standing long jump with arm swing by a male student. Analysis of the recordings will be described in relation to the results presented in Table PW9.1 and Table PW9.2.

2   The F_Y-time recording should be displayed and the weight W (N) of the subject should be determined by averaging a 0.5 s section of the recording during the period when the subject was standing still before the jump. Record the weight of the subject in an Excel spreadsheet, as shown in Table PW9.1.

3   Calculate the mass m of the subject where $m = W/9.81$ N. Record the subject's mass as shown in Table PW9.1.

4   The force-time graph should be time-sliced to retain the force-time data from about 0.1 s before the start of the movement to about 0.1 s after take-off. The time-sliced force-time data should be copied into the first two columns of the Excel spreadsheet as shown in Table PW9.1. The period of the time slice is 0.92 s (from 3.22 s to 4.14 s).

5   With a sampling frequency of 1000 Hz, a time period of 0.92 s would require 920 rows in the Excel spreadsheet. In Table PW9.1, the sampling frequency has been reduced from 1000 Hz to 50 Hz so that the analysis can be presented

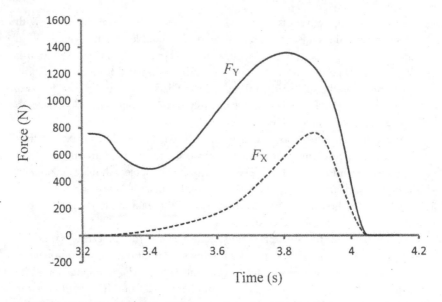

FIGURE PW9.1 Vertical (F_Y) and anteroposterior (F_X) ground reaction force-time graphs of a standing long jump with arm swing by a male student.

more concisely. Consequently, there are 47 rows of data in Table PW9.1 with 46 time intervals: 46×0.02 s $= 0.92$ s.

6 The lower the sampling frequency, the greater the likelihood that a specific event, such as maximum velocity downward, maximum velocity upward, take-off velocity, maximum displacement downward, maximum displacement upward and displacement at take-off, will occur between data points, i.e. between rows in Table PW9.1. The actual values and times of these events could be estimated by interpolation of the data, but the magnitudes and times of these events referred to below are taken directly from Table PW9.1 and, as such, are approximate values.

7 The subject's weight should be copied into all of the cells in column 3 of Table PW.1.

8 In column 4 of Table PW9.1, the resultant vertical force acting on the centre of gravity (CG) of the subject at each instant in time is calculated by subtracting body weight (column 3) from the vertical component of the ground reaction force (column 2).

9 In column 5 of Table PW9.1, the impulse of the resultant vertical force in each time interval is calculated by multiplying the average resultant force in the time interval by the length of the time interval. In the first time interval in Table PW9.1 (between 3.22 s and 3.24 s) the resultant force at the start of the time interval is zero. The resultant force at the end of the time interval is -2.39 N. Consequently, the average resultant force over the time interval is -1.195. N and the impulse of the average resultant force in the time interval $= -1.195$ N $\times 0.02$ s $= -0.0239$ N·s.

10 In column 6 of Table PW9.1, the cumulative impulse of the resultant vertical force is calculated by summing the impulses in column 5 from the start to

TABLE PW9.1 Integration of the vertical ground reaction force-time recording of the standing long jump shown in Figure PW9.1

Name of subject: Michael
Weight (N): 757.27
Mass of subject (kg): 77.19

Time (s)	F_Y (N)	BW (N)	F_Y – BW (N)	Impulse (N·s)	C Impulse* (N·s)	C Velocity (m/s)	Disp† (m)	C Disp (m)
3.22	757.27	757.27	0	0	0	0	0	0
3.24	754.88	757.27	−2.39	−0.0239	−0.0239	−0.00031	0	0
3.26	744.7	757.27	−12.57	−0.1496	−0.1735	−0.00225	0	0
3.28	711.47	757.27	−45.8	−0.5837	−0.7572	−0.00981	−0.00012	−0.00015
3.3	639.63	757.27	−117.64	−1.6344	−2.3916	−0.03098	−0.00041	−0.00056
3.32	585.55	757.27	−171.72	−2.8936	−5.2852	−0.06847	−0.00099	−0.00155
3.34	545.63	757.27	−211.64	−3.8336	−9.1188	−0.11813	−0.00187	−0.00342
3.36	518.41	757.27	−238.86	−4.505	−13.6238	−0.1765	−0.00295	−0.00636
3.38	500.45	757.27	−256.82	−4.9568	−18.5806	−0.24071	−0.00417	−0.01054
3.4	495.26	757.27	−262.01	−5.1883	−23.7689	−0.30793	−0.00549	−0.01602
3.42	499.85	757.27	−257.42	−5.1943	−28.9632	−0.37522	−0.00683	−0.02285
3.44	518.2	757.27	−239.07	−4.9649	−33.9281	−0.43954	−0.00815	−0.031
3.46	546.43	757.27	−210.84	−4.4991	−38.4272	−0.49783	−0.00937	−0.04038
3.48	582.86	757.27	−174.41	−3.8525	−42.2797	−0.54774	−0.01046	−0.05083
3.5	623.47	757.27	−133.8	−3.0821	−45.3618	−0.58766	−0.01135	−0.06218
3.52	670.47	757.27	−86.8	−2.206	−47.5678	−0.61624	−0.01204	−0.07422
3.54	723.15	757.27	−34.12	−1.2092	−48.777	−0.63191	−0.01248	−0.08671
3.56	786.01	757.27	28.74	−0.0538	−48.8308	−0.63261	−0.01265	−0.09935
3.58	848.17	757.27	90.9	1.1964	−47.6344	−0.61711	−0.0125	−0.11185
3.6	914.42	757.27	157.15	2.4805	−45.1539	−0.58497	−0.01202	−0.12387
3.62	975.79	757.27	218.52	3.7567	−41.3972	−0.5363	−0.01121	−0.13508
3.64	1037.44	757.27	280.17	4.9869	−36.4103	−0.4717	−0.01008	−0.14516
3.66	1101.2	757.27	343.93	6.241	−30.1693	−0.39084	−0.00863	−0.15379
3.68	1157.77	757.27	400.5	7.4443	−22.725	−0.2944	−0.00685	−0.16064
3.7	1210.75	757.27	453.48	8.5398	−14.1852	−0.18377	−0.00478	−0.16542
3.72	1257.96	757.27	500.69	9.5417	−4.6435	−0.06016	−0.00244	−0.16786
3.74	1294.26	757.27	536.99	10.3768	5.7333	0.07427	0.00014	−0.16772
3.76	1323.31	757.27	566.04	11.0303	16.7636	0.21717	0.00291	−0.1648
3.78	1343.65	757.27	586.38	11.5242	28.2878	0.36647	0.00583	−0.15897
3.8	1355.33	757.27	598.06	11.8444	40.1322	0.51991	0.00886	−0.1501
3.82	1355.33	757.27	598.06	11.9612	52.0934	0.67487	0.01194	−0.13816
3.84	1342.16	757.27	584.89	11.8295	63.9229	0.82812	0.01503	−0.12313
3.86	1317.24	757.27	559.97	11.4486	75.3715	0.97644	0.01804	−0.10508

(Continued)

TABLE PW9.1 (Continued)

Time (s)	F_Y (N)	BW (N)	F_Y − BW (N)	Impulse (N·s)	C Impulse* (N·s)	C Velocity (m/s)	Disp† (m)	C Disp (m)
3.88	1280.79	757.27	523.52	10.8349	86.2064	1.11680	0.02093	−0.08415
3.9	1225.1	757.27	467.83	9.9135	96.1199	1.24523	0.02362	−0.06053
3.92	1145.36	757.27	388.09	8.5592	104.6791	1.35612	0.02601	−0.03451
3.94	1038.05	757.27	280.78	6.6887	111.3678	1.44277	0.02798	−0.00653
3.96	885.58	757.27	128.31	4.0909	115.4587	1.49577	0.02938	0.02286
3.98	660.62	757.27	−96.65	0.3166	115.7753	1.49987	0.02995	0.05281
4.0	390.45	757.27	−366.82	−4.6347	111.1406	1.43983	0.02939	0.08221
4.02	160.32	757.27	−596.95	−9.6377	101.5029	1.31497	0.02754	0.10976
4.04	20.04	757.27	−737.27	−13.3422	88.1607	1.14212	0.02457	0.13433
4.06	0	757.27	−757.27	−14.9454	73.2153	0.94850	0.02090	0.15523
4.08	0	757.27	−757.27	−15.1454	58.0699	0.752298	0.017008	0.17224
4.1	0	757.27	−757.27	−15.1454	42.9245	0.556089	0.013084	0.18533
4.12	0	757.27	−757.27	−15.1454	27.7791	0.35988	0.00916	0.194491
4.14	0	757.27	−757.27	−15.1454	12.6337	0.16367	0.005235	0.199726

* C Impulse: cumulative impulse.
C Velocity: cumulative velocity.
Disp: displacement.
C Disp: cumulative displacement.
† Displacement data listed in the table as zero are zero to at least four places of decimals.

TABLE PW9.2 Integration of the anteroposterior ground reaction force-time recording of the countermovement jump shown in Figure PW9.1

Name of subject: Michael
Weight (N): 757.27
Mass of subject (kg): 77.19

Time (s)	F_X (N)	Impulse (N·s)	C Impulse* (N·s)	C Velocity (m/s)	Displacement† (m)	C Displacement (m)
3.22	0	0	0	0	0	0
3.24	0.87	0.0087	0.0087	0.000113	0	0
3.26	1.75	0.0262	0.0349	0.000452	0	0
3.28	2.63	0.0438	0.0787	0.00102	0	0
3.3	6.13	0.0876	0.1663	0.002154	0	0
3.32	10.5	0.1663	0.3326	0.004309	0	0.000118
3.34	15.76	0.2626	0.5952	0.007711	0.00012	0.000238
3.36	21	0.3676	0.9628	0.012473	0.000202	0.00044
3.38	28.44	0.4944	1.4572	0.018878	0.000314	0.000753
3.4	35.89	0.6433	2.1005	0.027212	0.000461	0.001214
3.42	43.77	0.7966	2.8971	0.037532	0.000647	0.001862
3.44	52.52	0.9629	3.86	0.050006	0.000875	0.002737

Time (s)	F_x (N)	Impulse (N·s)	C Impulse* (N·s)	C Velocity (m/s)	Displacement† (m)	C Displacement (m)
3.46	62.59	1.1511	5.0111	0.064919	0.001149	0.003886
3.48	73.53	1.3612	6.3723	0.082553	0.001475	0.005361
3.5	85.79	1.5932	7.9655	0.103193	0.001857	0.007219
3.52	98.04	1.8383	9.8038	0.127009	0.002302	0.009521
3.54	112.05	2.1009	11.9047	0.154226	0.002812	0.012333
3.56	127.8	2.3985	14.3032	0.185299	0.003395	0.015728
3.58	144.44	2.7224	17.0256	0.220567	0.004059	0.019787
3.6	163.69	3.0813	20.1069	0.260486	0.004811	0.024597
3.62	185.58	3.4927	23.5996	0.305734	0.005662	0.03026
3.64	211.84	3.9742	27.5738	0.35722	0.00663	0.036889
3.66	245.1	4.5694	32.1432	0.416417	0.007736	0.044625
3.68	283.62	5.2872	37.4304	0.484913	0.009013	0.053639
3.7	326.51	6.1013	43.5317	0.563955	0.010489	0.064127
3.72	375.53	7.0204	50.5521	0.654905	0.012189	0.076316
3.74	422.8	7.9833	58.5354	0.758329	0.014132	0.090448
3.76	471.82	8.9462	67.4816	0.874227	0.016326	0.106774
3.78	526.1	9.9792	77.4608	1.003508	0.018777	0.125551
3.8	576.87	11.0297	88.4905	1.146398	0.021499	0.14705
3.82	630.77	12.0764	100.5669	1.302849	0.024492	0.171543
3.84	684.04	13.1481	113.715	1.473183	0.02776	0.199303
3.86	729.55	14.1359	127.8509	1.656314	0.031295	0.230598
3.88	757.32	14.8687	142.7196	1.848939	0.035053	0.265651
3.9	757.19	15.1451	157.8647	2.045144	0.038941	0.304592
3.92	716.93	14.7412	172.6059	2.236117	0.042813	0.347404
3.94	610.13	13.2706	185.8765	2.408039	0.046442	0.393846
3.96	465.41	10.7554	196.6319	2.547375	0.049554	0.4434
3.98	320.26	7.8567	204.4886	2.649159	0.051965	0.495365
4.0	190.72	5.1098	209.5984	2.715357	0.053645	0.54901
4.02	80.53	2.7125	212.3109	2.750497	0.054659	0.603669
4.04	10	0.9053	213.2162	2.762226	0.055127	0.658796
4.06	0	0.1	213.3162	2.763521	0.055257	0.714054
4.08	0	0	213.3162	2.763521	0.05527	0.769324
4.1	0	0	213.3162	2.763521	0.05527	0.824594
4.12	0	0	213.3162	2.763521	0.05527	0.879865
4.14	0	0	213.3162	2.763521	0.05527	0.935135

* C Impulse: cumulative impulse.
C Velocity: cumulative velocity.
C Displacement: cumulative displacement.
† Displacement data listed in the table as zero are zero to at least four places of decimals.

the end of the time slice. At the end of the first time interval the cumulative impulse is −0.0239 N·s, i.e. 0 + (−0.0239) N·s = −0.0239 N·s. At the end of the second time interval (3.24 s to 3.26 s) the cumulative impulse is −0.0239 N·s + (−0.1496) N·s = −0.1735 N·s.

11 In column 7 of Table PW9.1, the cumulative vertical velocity of the CG is calculated by dividing the cumulative impulse data in column 6 by the mass of the subject. The velocity data shows that after the start of the movement (at 3.22 s) the CG accelerated downward (downward velocity increasing) and reached a maximum velocity downward of −0.6326 m/s at 3.56 s. This was followed by a period of deceleration downward in which the downward velocity of the CG was reduced to zero at approximately 3.723 s. This was followed by a period of upward acceleration of the CG culminating in a maximum upward velocity of 1.4998 m/s at 3.98 s and a take-off velocity of 0.9485 m/s at 4.06 s; see Figure PW9.2.

12 In column 8 of Table PW9.1, the change in vertical displacement of the CG during each time interval is calculated by multiplying the average velocity in the time interval by the length of the time interval. The velocity at the start of the time interval 3.28 s to 3.0 s is −0.00981 m/s. The velocity at the end of the time interval is −0.03098 m/s. Consequently, the average velocity over the time interval is −0.02039 m/s and the change in vertical displacement of the CG in the time interval is −0.02039 m/s × 0.02 s = −0.00041 m.

13 In column 9 of Table PW9.1, the cumulative change in vertical displacement of the CG is calculated by summing the displacements in column 8 from the start to the end of the time slice. At 3.3 s, the cumulative displacement is −0.00056 m. The displacement in the time interval 3.3 s to 3.32 s is −0.00099 m. Consequently, the cumulative displacement at 3.32 s is −0.00056 m + (−0.00099 m) = −0.0001545 m.

14 The displacement data shows that the maximum downward displacement of the CG was −0.16786m at 3.72 s and displacement at take-off was 0.1552 m at 4.06 s; see Table PW9.1 and Figure PW9.2.

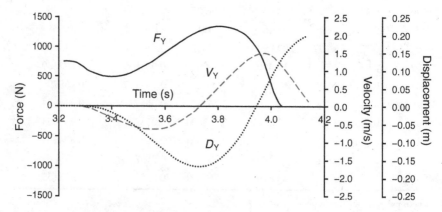

FIGURE PW9.2 Vertical ground reaction force-time graph (F_Y) and corresponding velocity-time (V_Y) and displacement-time (D_Y) graphs of the standing long jump.

15 Analysis of the F_X-time recording is presented in Table PW9.2. In column 3 of Table PW9.2, the impulse of F_X in each time interval is calculated by multiplying the average force in the time interval by the length of the time interval. In the first time interval in Table PW9.2 (between 3.22 s and 3.34 s) the force at the start of the time interval is zero. The force at the end of the time interval is 0.87 N. Consequently, the average force over the time interval is 0.435 N and the impulse of the average force in the time interval is 0.435 N × 0.02 s = 0.0087 N·s.

16 In column 4 of Table PW9.2 the cumulative impulse of F_X is calculated by summing the impulses in column 3 from the start to the end of the time slice. At the end of the first time interval the cumulative impulse is 0.0087 N·s, i.e. 0 + 0.0087 N·s = 0.0087 N·s. At the end of the second time interval (3.24 s to 3.26 s) the cumulative impulse is 0.0087 N·s + 0.0262 N·s = 0.0349 N·s.

17 In column 5 of Table PW9.2, the cumulative change in the anteroposterior velocity of the CG is calculated by dividing the cumulative impulse data in column 4 by the mass of the subject. As shown in Table PW9.2 and Figure PW9.3, F_X is positive throughout the time slice. Consequently anteroposterior velocity progressively increases in the direction of the jump (forward) during the same period, culminating in a maximum velocity of 2.7635 m/s at take-off (at 4.06 s). The anteroposterior velocity during the flight phase is the same as at take-off as the effect of air resistance during the flight phase would be negligible; see Figure PW9.3.

18 In column 6 of Table PW9.2, the change in anteroposterior displacement of the CG in each time interval is calculated by multiplying the average velocity in the time interval by the length of the time interval. The velocity at the start of the time interval 3.34 s to 3.36 s is 0.00771 m/s. The velocity at the end of the time interval is 0.01247 m/s. Consequently, the average velocity over the time interval is 0.01009 m/s and the change in anteroposterior displacement of the CG in the time interval is 0.01009 m/s × 0.02 s = 0.000202 m.

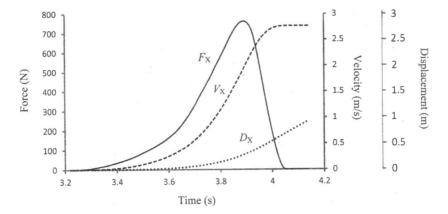

FIGURE PW9.3 Anteroposterior ground reaction force-time graph (F_X) and corresponding velocity-time (V_X) and displacement-time (D_X) graphs of the standing long jump.

19 In column 7 of Table PW9.2, the cumulative change in anteroposterior displacement of the CG is calculated by summing the displacements in column 6 from the start to the end of the time slice. At 3.34 s, the cumulative displacement is 0.000238 m. The displacement in the time interval 3.34 s to 3.36 s is 0.000202 m. Consequently, the cumulative displacement at 3.36 s is 0.000238 m + 0.000202 m = 0.00044 m. Table PW9.2 shows that forward displacement of the CG progressively increased from the start of movement to take-off. Anterior displacement of the CG at take-off was 0.7140 m and continued to increase throughout the flight phase; see Figure PW9.3.

20 The trajectory of the CG in the median plane from the start of movement to just after take-off is shown in Figure PW9.4.

Presentation of results

1 Present your individual vertical and anteroposterior ground reaction force-time graphs for a standing long jump as shown in Figure PW9.1.

2 Present the results of your integration of the vertical ground reaction force-time record and the results of your integration of the anteroposterior ground reaction force-time record at 50 Hz, as shown in Tables PW9.1 and 9.2.

3 Present the vertical ground reaction force-time graph and corresponding velocity-time and displacement-time graphs, as in Figure PW9.2.

4 Present the anteroposterior ground reaction force-time graph and corresponding velocity-time and displacement-time graphs, as in Figure PW9.3.

5 Present a graph of the trajectory of the CG in the median plane, as in Figure PW9.4.

Example results

Example results are shown in Table PW9.1, Table PW9.2 and Figures PW9.1 to PW9.4.

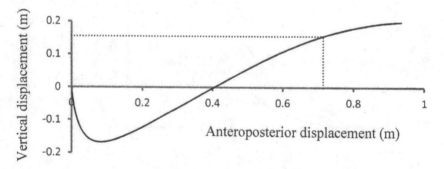

FIGURE PW9.4 Median plane trajectory of the whole body centre of gravity (CG) in the standing long jump. The position of the CG at take-off (D_X = 0.714 m; D_Y = 0.155 m) is indicated by the intersection of the dotted lines.

PRACTICAL WORKSHEET 10

Determination of reactive strength index in rebound vertical jumping

Introduction

1   In most movements, especially whole body movements, the muscles function in eccentric-concentric cycles, i.e. the muscles contract eccentrically (develop tension and lengthen) immediately before contracting concentrically (develop tension and shorten). The eccentric-concentric cycle is often referred to as the stretch-shorten cycle. In comparison with purely concentric contractions, the stretch-shorten cycle is more effective in terms of force production and more efficient in terms of energy expenditure.

    The stretch-shorten cycle is evident in everyday activities, such as walking and running, with cycles of absorption and propulsion corresponding to cycles of eccentric and concentric muscle contractions. However, the stretch-shorten cycle is usually more noticeable in very forceful movements such as throwing and jumping that involve distinct countermovements.

2   In a stretch-shorten cycle, the higher the rate of stretching in the eccentric phase, the higher the force generated in both the eccentric and concentric phases. However, the amount of force generated in the eccentric phase and, consequently, in the concentric phase, is limited by the eccentric strength of the muscles. In plyometric strength training, which is based on exercises involving repeated rapid eccentric-concentric cycles of muscle contractions, the objective is to gradually increase the eccentric strength of the muscles which, in turn, will increase the concentric strength of the muscles.

3   For any particular plyometric exercise, the reactive strength index (*RSI*) provides an indication of the optimal training load. For example, for a plyometric exercise based on rebound vertical jumping, the drop height that results in the highest *RSI* is the optimal drop height. As jump height improves with training, the optimal drop height is reassessed by reassessing RSI.

4 In a rebound vertical jump, also referred to as a drop jump and depth jump, the subject steps off a raised platform of known height and, on landing on the ground, rebounds as quickly as possible to jump as high as possible, and then lands with as similar a body position as possible to that at take-off. Ground contact time during the rebound (t_C) and flight time during the subsequent jump (t_F) are measured. Jump height (h_J) is calculated from flight time by applying the equation of uniformly accelerated motion $h_J = g \cdot t_F^2/8$ where g is the acceleration due to gravity = 9.81 m/s². Reactive strength index (*RSI*) is calculated by dividing jump height by contact time, i.e. $RSI = h_J/t_C$. Consequently, for a given drop height, the shorter the contact time and the higher the jump height, the higher the *RSI*.

Objective

To determine optimal drop height for rebound vertical jump-based plyometric strength training by measuring reactive strength index (*RSI*) over a range of drop heights.

Location

Motion analysis laboratory

Apparatus and equipment

Force platform system or contact mat and timer

Method

Subject's clothing

Shorts, shirt and trainers

Data collection

Record contact time and flight time in rebound vertical jumps from a number of drop heights.

1 Each subject should have sufficient practice of performing maximum effort rebound jumps, for the drop heights to be used to assess *RSI*, to consistently land with as similar a body position as possible to that at take-off. The importance of a similar body position at take-off and landing is that *RSI* depends upon h_J which, in turn, depends upon t_F which, in turn, depends upon body position at take-off and landing. The more similar the body position

at take-off and landing, the more symmetrical will be the trajectory of the whole body centre of gravity (CG) each side of the point of maximum height during flight and, consequently, the more valid the estimate of t_F in relation to the theoretical flight time that the corresponding take-off velocity should produce.

2   The example results presented in Tables PW10.1 and PW10.2 were obtained for four drop heights: 0.1 m, 0.2 m, 0.3 m and 0.4 m. Four wooden boxes of height 0.1 m, 0.2 m, 0.3 m and 0.4 m were used for this purpose. In turn, each box was placed directly alongside the longer side of a force platform

TABLE PW10.1 Contact time (t_C), flight time (t_F), jump height (h_J) and reactive strength index (RSI) for one male subject in two trials at four drop heights

Name of subject: Craig
Weight (N): 739.67
Mass of subject (kg): 75.4

				Drop height (m)							
	0.1 Trial			0.2 Trial			0.3 Trial			0.4 Trial	
	1	2	Mean	1	2	Mean	1	2	Mean	1	2	Mean
t_C (s)	0.242	0.235	0.238	0.253	0.229	0.241	0.256	0.248	0.252	0.253	0.249	0.251
t_F (s)	0.476	0.497	0.486	0.533	0.520	0.527	0.552	0.554	0.553	0.510	0.498	0.504
h_J (m)	0.278	0.303	0.290	0.349	0.331	0.340	0.374	0.377	0.375	0.319	0.304	0.331
RSI (m/s)	1.15	1.29	1.22	1.38	1.45	1.41	1.46	1.52	1.49	1.26	1.22	1.24

TABLE PW10.2 Individual and group mean results for reactive strength index at four drop heights for a group of six male students

Subject	Drop height (m)			
	0.1	0.2	0.3	0.4
1	1.22	1.41	1.49	1.24
2	1.35	1.48	1.42	1.28
3	0.96	1.14	1.21	1.08
4	1.13	1.22	1.32	0.98
5	1.34	1.37	1.48	1.37
6	1.28	1.42	1.52	1.46
Mean	1.21	1.34	1.41	1.24
SD	0.15	0.13	0.12	0.18

(0.4 m × 0.6 m) so that the subject stepped forward off the box without stepping down or jumping up and fell directly onto the force platform. On contact with the force platform, the subject was encouraged to minimize contact time on the platform, jump as high as possible following the rebound and land with the same body position as at take-off. Arm swing was not prescribed to increase the likelihood of a subject being able to control the rebound jump and land with a similar body position to that at take-off.

3   After sufficient warm-up and submaximal practice of drop jumping, the first subject is requested to stand on the force platform. The force platform system operator records the vertical ground reaction force at 1000 Hz for about three seconds and then instructs the subject to step off the platform. The force platform system operator measures the weight of the subject by averaging a 0.5 s section of the vertical ground reaction force-time record. The subject's weight is recorded in a results sheet (Table PW10.1). The subject is then requested to adopt a relaxed standing position on the first box (height = 0.1 m) close to the edge of the box that is alongside the force platform. The force platform system operator starts recording the vertical component of the ground reaction force at 1000 Hz. On a signal from the force platform system operator, the subject performs a trial and establishes a relaxed standing position on the platform after landing from the rebound jump. The force platform system operator stops the recording and saves the recording for subsequent analysis. The subject then performs a second trial at the same height with a 1 min recovery between trials. The procedure of measuring body weight and recording two trials at the first drop height is then repeated with each of the other subjects. After all subjects (group of 4–6 subjects) have performed two trials at the first drop height, the procedure of recording two trials is repeated at each of the other drop heights for all subjects.

4   Instead of a force platform system, a contact mat and timer can be used to measure contact time and flight time. Whereas body weight is not required in the calculation of RSI, it is always useful to record body weight when assessing RSI to be able to examine the relationship between body weight and RSI over time.

Data analysis

1   Figure PW10.1 shows a typical vertical force-time graph for a male subject (mass = 75.4 kg) in a rebound jump and landing from a drop height of 0.3 m. Figure PW10.1 shows the two times, contact time (t_C) and flight time (t_F), that are required to calculate RSI.

2   For each subject in each trial, contact time and flight time are obtained by inspection of the corresponding force-time records. The contact times and flight times for each subject are recorded in the subject's results sheet; see

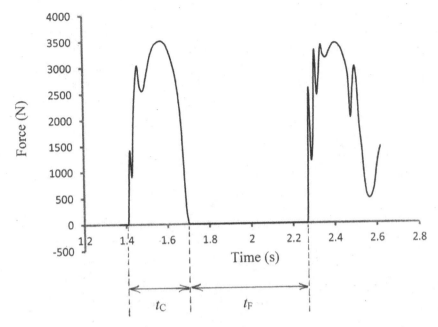

FIGURE PW10.1   Typical vertical ground reaction force–time graph in a rebound jump and landing from a drop height of 0.3 m by a male student. t_C, contact time; t_F, flight time.

Table PW10.1. The subject's results sheet is then completed by calculating and recording jump height and *RSI* in each trial together with the means for contact time, flight time, height jumped and RSI at each drop height.

3   The individual means and group mean results for *RSI* at each drop height are presented in a table and a figure; see Table PW10.2 and Figure PW10.2.

Presentation of results

1   Present an example of a vertical force–time record from one of your trials as shown in Figure PW10.1.
2   Present your individual results as shown in Table PW10.1.
3   Present the individual means for all subjects and group means for *RSI* at each drop height as shown in Table PW10.2.
4   Present a figure showing the individual means for all subjects and group means for *RSI* against drop height as shown in Figure PW10.2.

Example results

Example results are shown in Table PW10.1, Table 10.2, Figure PW10.1 and Figure PW10.2. Table PW10.1 shows the results for a single male subject at four drop heights: 0.1 m, 0.2 m, 0.3 m and 0.4 m. Table PW10.2 and Figure PW10.2 shows the individual means and group mean results for *RSI* at the four drop heights for a group of six male subjects. Table PW10.2 and Figure PW10.2 show that the optimal drop height for subjects 1, 3, 4, 5 and 6 was 0.3 m and that the optimal drop height for subject 2 was 0.2 m. The highest group mean *RSI* was for the drop height of 0.3 m and the lowest group mean RSI was for the drop height of 0.1 m.

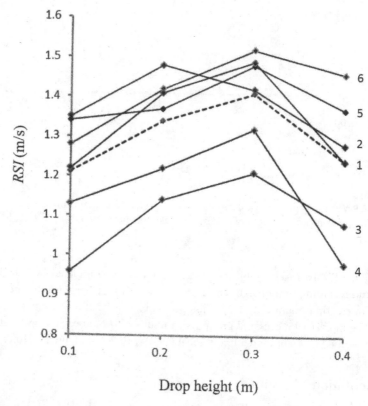

FIGURE PW10.2 Individual (solid lines) and group (dotted line) mean results for reactive strength index at four drop heights for a group of six male students.

PRACTICAL WORKSHEET 11

Hip and knee angular kinematics of a penalty kick in rugby

Objectives

To video a subject performing a penalty kick in rugby and analyze the video to produce angular displacement-time and angular velocity-time graphs of the hip and knee joints of the kicking leg.

Location

Grass rugby pitch with posts or sports hall with nets

Apparatus and equipment

Video camera and computer with appropriate motion analysis software.

Method

Subject's clothing and preparation of the subject

In the analysis of the video it is necessary to record, in each frame, the sagittal plane X (anteroposterior) and Y (vertical) coordinates of the approximate centres of the shoulder joint, hip joint, knee joint and ankle joint on the right side of the body. Consequently, the subject should wear tight-fitting shorts, a tight-fitting singlet and shoes (boots for an outdoor grass pitch, indoor football shoes for sports hall) without socks so that the joints are not covered by clothing. The approximate plane of each joint should be marked with a water-soluble coloured pen as shown in Figure PW11.1.

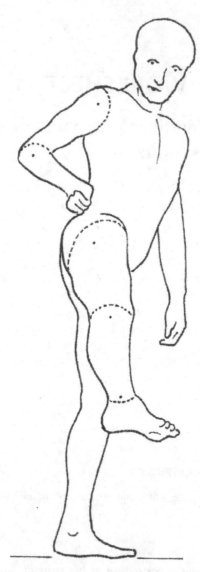

FIGURE PW11.1   Joint plane markings of the right shoulder, right hip, right knee and right ankle joints.

Video-recording of a penalty kick

1   Ideally, the location for video-recording the kicks should be a dry outdoor grass pitch. If this is not possible, a sports hall with a net hanging 3 m–4 m in front of the ball can be used.
2   If a grass pitch is available, each kick should be taken from the 22 m line, in the middle of the posts.

3 The camera is set up at a distance of approximately 10 m to the right of the ball (for a right-footed kicker), with the optical axis of the camera parallel to the goal line and passing through the ball.

4 The subject performs a number of practice penalty kicks, i.e. s/he tries to kick the ball over the bar and through the posts. As the subject performs the practice trials, the camera operator should adjust the zoom of the camera to ensure that all of the movement of the subject is visible from the start of the backswing of the kicking leg, at the start of the kicking action, to the end of the follow-through of the kicking leg.

5 After sufficient practice, on the command from the camera operator, the subject performs a number of trials which are recorded. A recovery period of at least 1 min should be given between recorded trials.

Video analysis

1 Ideally, a successful trial (in which the ball passes over the bar and through the posts) is selected for analysis. Figure PW11.2 shows a picture sequence of the trial that was analyzed to produce the results shown in Figures PW11.3 to PW11.5. The sampling frequency was 100 Hz.

FIGURE PW11.2 Stick figure sequence at 50 Hz of a 19-year-old male subject performing a penalty kick in rugby.

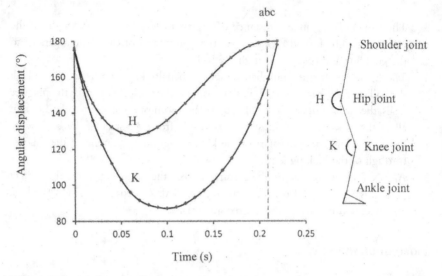

FIGURE PW11.3 Angular displacement-time graphs of the movement of the hip (H) and knee (K) joints of the kicking leg of a 19-year-old male subject performing a penalty kick in rugby from the start of the backswing to just after separation of foot and ball. abc, approximate ball contact.

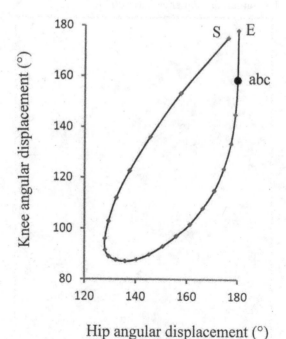

FIGURE PW11.4 Hip angular displacement-knee angular displacement diagram of the movement of the hip (H) and knee (K) joints of a 19-year-old male subject performing a penalty kick in rugby from the start of backswing of the kicking leg (S) to just after separation of foot and ball (E). abc, approximate ball contact.

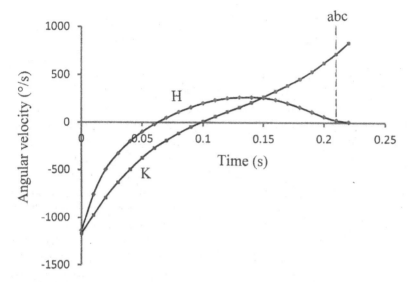

FIGURE PW11.5   Angular velocity–time graphs of the movement of the hip (H) and knee (K) joints of the kicking leg of a 19-year-old male subject performing a penalty kick in rugby from the start of the backswing to just after separation of foot and ball. abc, approximate ball contact.

2   Analyze the video from the start of the backswing of the kicking leg in the kicking action (frame 6 in Figure PW11.2) to the end of the follow-through of the kicking leg (not shown in Figure PW11.2).

3   In the first frame, use the origin function to set the origin for the measurement of X and Y coordinates of points in the display. The location of the origin may be set automatically or manually depending upon the motion analysis system in use.

4   In each frame, use the joint plane markers to estimate and digitize the estimated joint centres of the right shoulder joint, hip joint, knee joint and ankle joint (Figure PW11.1). The digitized points will automatically be stored by the motion analysis system.

5   Use the relevant menu in the motion analysis software to define the hip angle and the knee angle. In the results shown in Figures PW11.3–PW11.5, the hip angle and knee angle were defined as shown in Figure PW11.3. An increase in the hip angle indicted hip flexion and an increase in the knee angle indicated knee extension.

6   Use the relevant menu to calculate and plot the angular displacement–time and angular velocity–time histories of the movement of the hip and knee joints.

Presentation of results

Present your results as shown in Figures PW11.3–PW11.5.

Example results

Example results are shown in Figures PW11.3–PW11.5. Figure PW11.3 shows the angular displacement-time graphs of the movement of the hip joint and the knee joint from the start of the backswing of the kicking leg in the kicking action to just after separation of the ball from the foot following the kick. The duration of the kicking action was 0.22 s. The range of motion of the hip joint was approximately 52° (128° at 0.06 s, 180° at 0.22 s) and the range of motion of the knee joint was approximately 91° (87° at 0.1 s, 178° at 0.22 s). Figure PW11.4 shows hip angular displacement plotted against knee angular displacement. Figures PW11.3 and PW11.4 show three main phases of the kicking action: backswing, transition, forward-swing. The backswing phase is characterized by simultaneous hip extension and knee flexion, culminating in maximum hip extension (0 s to 0.07 s). This is followed by a transition phase in which hip displacement changes from extension to flexion and knee flexion reaches its maximum (0.07 s to 0.1 s). The transition phase is followed by the forward-swing phase (0.1 s to 0.2 s) involving simultaneous hip flexion and knee extension culminating in ball contact. The greater angular displacement of the knee joint in the forward-swing phase (approximately 75°) compared to that of the hip joint (approximately 45°) is reflected in Figure PW11.5 which shows the hip angular velocity-time and knee angular velocity-time graphs. During the second half of the forward swing phase, hip angular velocity progressively decreases to zero and knee angular velocity progressively increases through ball contact.

PRACTICAL WORKSHEET 12

Determination of the position of the whole-body centre of gravity of the human body by the direct method using a one-dimension reaction board

Objectives

1   To determine the position of the whole body centre of gravity in the anatomical position.
2   To examine the effect of changes in body shape on the position of the whole body centre of gravity relative to the anatomical position.

Location

Motion analysis laboratory

Apparatus and equipment

One-dimension reaction board (approximately 2.5 m × 0.5 m) with a centimetre scale running left to right on one side, one set of weighing scales.

Method

Subject's clothing

Shorts and shirt

Data collection and analysis

1   Record in Table PW12.1 the height h (cm) and weight W (kgf) of the subject without shoes.
2   Record in Table PW12.1 the distance l between the knife edge supports of the reaction board.

3 Support the reaction board in a horizontal position with knife edge support B resting on the weighing scales (Figure PW12.1a).

4 Record in Table PW12.1 the vertical force S_1 (kgf) exerted on the scales, i.e. the vertical support force acting on knife edge support B.

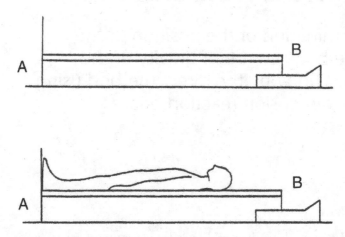

FIGURE PW12.1 (a) Reaction board resting horizontally with knife edge support B resting on the weighing scales. (b) Reaction board resting horizontally with knife edge support B resting on the weighing scales with the subject lying on the board in position 1.

TABLE PW12.1 Individual results

Name of subject:
Weight of subject W (kgf):
Height of subject h (cm)
l (cm):
S_1 (kgf):

Body position	S_2 (kgf)	d (cm)	d%	Δd (cm)	Δd%
1				0	0
2					
3					
4					
5					
6					

S_2, vertical force on knife edge support B with the subject lying on the board in the corresponding position; d, distance between knife-edge support A and the vertical plane containing the whole body centre of gravity of the subject; d%, d as a percentage of height h; Δd, change in d with respect to position 1; Δd%, Δd as a percentage of h.

5   Position 1: anatomical reference position.
   i   Subject lies on the board with arms by sides and soles of feet in the same plane as knife edge support A (Figure PW12.1b).
   ii   Record in Table PW12.1 the force S_2 on the scales.
   iii   Calculate the horizontal distance d (cm) between knife edge support A and the parallel vertical plane containing the whole body centre of gravity of the subject using equation PW12.1.

$$d = \frac{l(S_2 - S_1)}{W} \quad \text{Eq. PW12.1}$$

   iv   Record d in Table PW12.1.
   v   Calculate d as a percentage of h and record the result in Table PW12.1.
6   Position 2: From position 1, fold arms across chest (Figure PW12.2a).
   i   Record S_2 in Table PW12.1.
   ii   Calculate d (cm) using equation PW12.1 and record the result in Table PW12.1.
   iii   Calculate d as a percentage of h and record the result in Table PW12.1.
   iv   Calculate the change in d (Δd, cm) between Positions 1 and 2 and record the result in Table PW12.1.
   v   Calculate Δd as a percentage of h and record the result in Table PW12.1.
7   Position 3: From position 1, fully abduct both arms (Figure PW12.2b).
   i   Record S_2 in Table PW12.1.
   ii   Calculate d (cm) using equation PW12.1 and record the result in Table PW12.1.
   iii   Calculate d as a percentage of h and record the result in Table PW12.1.
   iv   Calculate Δd between Positions 1 and 3 and record the result in Table PW12.1.
   v   Calculate Δd as a percentage of h and record the result in Table PW12.1.
8   Position 4: From position 1, fully flex hips and knees (Figure PW12.2c).
   i   Record S_2 in Table PW12.1.
   ii   Calculate d (cm) using equation PW12.1 and record the result in Table PW12.1.
   iii   Calculate d as a percentage of h and record the result in Table PW12.1.
   iv   Calculate Δd between Positions 1 and 4 and record the result in Table PW12.1
   v   Calculate Δd as a percentage of h and record the result in Table PW12.1.
9   Position 5: From position 1, fully abduct both arms and fully flex hips and knees (Figure PW12.2d).
   i   Record S_2 in Table PW12.1.
   ii   Calculate d (cm) using equation PW12.1 and record the result in Table PW12.1.
   iii   Calculate d as a percentage of h and record the result in Table PW12.1.

     iv   Calculate Δd between Positions 1 and 5 and record the result in Table PW12.1.

     v   Calculate Δd as a percentage of h and record the result in Table PW12.1.

10   Position 6: From position 1, sit-up to touch toes (Figure PW12.2e).

     i   Record S_2 in Table PW12.1.

     ii   Calculate d (cm) using equation PW12.1 and record the result in Table PW12.1.

     iii Calculate d as a percentage of h and record the result in Table PW12.1.

     iv   Calculate Δd between Positions 1 and 6 and record the result in Table PW12.1.

     v   Calculate Δd as a percentage of h and record the result in Table PW12.1.

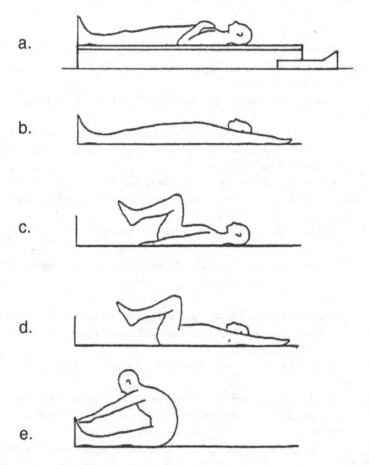

a.

b.

c.

d.

e.

FIGURE PW12.2 Reaction board resting horizontally with knife edge support B resting on the weighing scales with the subject lying on the board. (a) Position 2: arms folded across chest. (b) Position 3: arms extended above the head. (c) Position 4: hips and knees flexed. (d) Position 5: arms extended above the head and hips and knees flexed. (e) Position 6: sitting up with fingers touching the toes.

Presentation of results

1   Present your individual results in Table PW12.1.
2   Present the results for all of the subjects in your group and the group mean data in Table PW12.2.

TABLE PW12.2 Individual and group results

Subjects	h (cm)	W (kgf)	Position 1		Position 2		Position 3		Position 4		Position 5		Position 6	
			d %	Δd %	d %	Δd %	d %	Δd %	d %	Δd %	d %	Δd %	d %	Δd %
Women														
1			0											
2			0											
3			0											
4			0											
5			0											
Mean			0											
SD			0											
Men														
1			0											
2			0											
3			0											
4			0											
5			0											
Mean			0											
SD			0											

h, height of subject; W, weight of subject; d%, d as a percentage of h; Δd%, change in d with respect to position 1 as a percentage of h.

Example results

Example data are shown in Table PW12.3 and Table PW12.4. Table PW12.4 shows group mean results for 10 students (5 women and 5 men). The group mean data show that the change in the position of the whole body centre of gravity is on average very similar for the men and women subjects even though there is considerable variation in height and weight.

TABLE PW12.3 Individual results

Name of subject: Anne
Weight W (kgf): 67.0
Height h (cm) 167.0
l (cm): 244.0
S_1 (kgf): 10.0

Body position	S_2 (kgf)	d (cm)	$d\%$	Δd (cm)	$\Delta d\%$
1	36.0	94.7	56.7	0	0
2	36.5	96.5	57.8	1.8	1.08
3	37.5	100.1	59.9	5.4	3.23
4	41.5	114.7	68.7	20.0	12.0
5	42.0	116.5	69.7	21.8	13.05
6	29.0	69.2	41.4	−25.5	−15.3

S_2, vertical force on knife edge support B with the subject lying on the board in the corresponding position; d, distance between knife-edge support A and the vertical plane containing the whole body centre of gravity of the subject; $d\%$, d as a percentage of height h; Δd, change in d with respect to position 1; $\Delta d\%$, Δd as a percentage of h.

TABLE PW12.4 Individual and group results

Subjects	h (cm)	W (kgf)	Position 1		Position 2		Position 3		Position 4		Position 5		Position 6	
			$d\%$	$\Delta d\%$	$d\%$	$\Delta d\%$	$d\%$	$\Delta d\%$	$d\%$	$\Delta d\%$	$d\%$	$\Delta d\%$	$d\%$	$\Delta d\%$
Women														
Anne	167	67	56.7	0	57.8	1.08	59.9	3.23	68.7	12.0	69.7	13.05	41.4	−15.3
Sarah	153.4	52	54.8	0	56.1	1.24	58.5	3.71	64.8	9.9	67.3	12.45	39.9	−14.9
Dawn	157	52.5	57.8	0	58.9	1.21	61	3.25	68.6	10.8	71	13.23	42.1	−15.6
Susan	172	68	53.2	0	54.2	1.04	56.3	3.13	64.7	11.5	66.7	13.56	41.7	−11.5
Kylie	167	61	55.6	0	56.6	0.96	59.5	3.89	65.4	9.75	67.3	11.7	41	−14.7
Mean	163.3	60.1	55.6	0	56.7	1.11	59.0	3.44	66.4	10.8	68.4	12.8	41.2	−14.4
SD	7.76	7.65	1.76	0	1.78	0.12	1.77	0.34	2.04	0.95	1.85	0.73	0.84	1.67
Men														
Paul	176.5	77	58.3	0	59.2	0.9	62.8	4.49	68.2	9.88	71.8	13.5	45.8	−12.6
Richard	181.3	76	61.9	0	62.9	0.88	65.5	3.54	69.1	7.08	72.6	10.6	46	−15.9
Bruce	189.4	80.5	59.8	0	60.4	0.63	63.1	3.27	68.9	9.13	72.8	13.0	44.8	−14.9
David	171	78	58.7	0	60.2	0.54	62.4	3.72	68.4	9.66	73.6	14.9	43.1	−15.6
John	169	68	59.6	0	60.5	0.89	62.2	2.66	68.6	8.99	70.4	10.8	43.3	−16.3
Mean	177.4	75.9	59.7	0	60.6	0.77	63.2	3.54	68.6	8.95	72.2	12.6	44.6	−15.1
SD	1.65	0.94	0.28	0	0.27	0.03	0.27	0.13	0.07	0.22	0.24	0.36	0.27	0.3

h, height of subject; W, weight of subject; $d\%$, d as a percentage of h; $\Delta d\%$, change in d with respect to position 1 as a percentage of h.

PRACTICAL WORKSHEET 13

Comparison of the direct and segmental analysis methods of determining the position of the whole-body centre of gravity of the human body

Objective

To compare the direct and segmental analysis methods of determining the transverse plane containing the centre of gravity of the human body in the anatomical position using a one-dimension reaction board.

Location

Motion analysis laboratory

Apparatus and equipment

One-dimension reaction board (approximately 2.5 m × 0.5 m) with a centimetre scale running left to right on one side, one set of weighing scales.

Method

Subject's clothing

Shorts and a sleeveless top so that the following points on the skin on the left side of the body can be easily identified:

- A point on the skin of the left arm at a distance of 3 cm below the tip of the acromion process, i.e. 3 cm to the left of the acromion process when the subject is lying horizontally in the anatomical position. This point will indicate the plane of the left shoulder joint centre when lying on the reaction board.
- The tip of the styloid process of the left ulna. This point will indicate the plane of the left wrist when lying on the reaction board.

- The tip of the left greater tuberosity. This point will indicate the plane of the left hip joint centre when lying on the reaction board.
- The tip of the lateral malleolus of the left fibula. This point will indicate the plane of the left ankle joint centre when lying on the reaction board.

Data collection

1   Record in Table PW13.1 the weight W (kgf) of the subject (shorts, sleeveless top, no shoes).
2   Record in Table PW13.1 the height h (cm) of the subject (no shoes).
3   Record in Table PW13.1 the distance l (cm) between the two knife edge supports of the reaction board.
4   Support the board in a horizontal position with knife edge support B resting on the scales (Figure PW13.1a)
5   Record in Table PW13.1 the vertical force S_1 (kgf) exerted on the scales.

TABLE PW13.1 Individual results

Subject
W (kgf)
h (cm)
l (cm)
S_1 (kgf)
S_2 (kgf)
d_M (cm)
d_H (cm)
d_U (cm)
d_S (cm)
d_D (cm)
W_A (kgf)
W_L (kgf)
W_{THN} (kgf)
d_{GA} (cm)
d_{GL} (cm)
d_{GTHN} (cm)
M_C (kgf·cm)
d_W (cm)
d (cm)

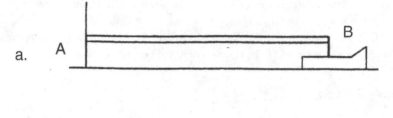

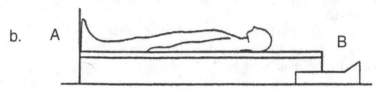

FIGURE PW13.1 (a) Reaction board resting horizontally with knife edge support B resting on the weighing scales. (b) Reaction board resting horizontally with knife edge support B resting on the weighing scales with the subject lying on the board.

6 The subject lies on the board with arms by sides and soles of feet against the foot block, i.e. with the soles of the feet in the vertical plane containing knife edge support A (Figure PW13.1b).

7 Record in Table PW13.1 the vertical force S_2 (kgf) exerted on end B.

8 Using the centimetre scale on the side of the board, record in Table PW13.1 the horizontal distances (cm) between the plane of the soles of the feet (reference zero) and the following points on the left side of the body (see Figure PW13.2): lateral malleolus (d_M), greater trochanter (d_H), styloid process of the ulna (d_U), shoulder joint (d_S), vertical plane through the top of the head (d_D).

Data analysis

1 Calculate the horizontal distance d between the plane of the soles of the feet and the plane containing the CG of the body by the direct method using equation PW13.1 and record the result in Table PW13.1.

$$d(\text{cm}) = \frac{l(S_2 - S_1)}{W} \quad \text{Eq. PW13.1}$$

2 Calculate the horizontal distance d_W between the plane of the soles of the feet and the plane containing the CG of the body by the indirect method (segmental analysis method):

   i   Calculate the weight (kgf) of each upper limb W_A, the weight of each lower limb W_L and the weight of the combined trunk, head and neck W_{THN}.

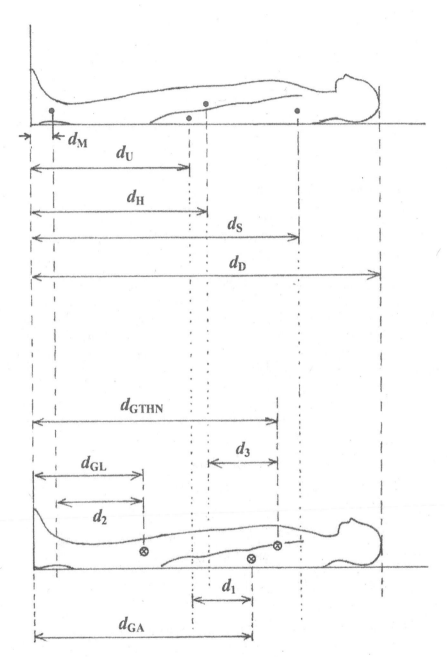

FIGURE PW13.2 Location of the segmental centres of gravity.

Record the results in Table PW13.1. Use the Plagenhoef *et al.* (1983) data for segment weight percentages in Table 6.1 for men and Table 6.2 for women, i.e.

Men: $W_A\,(\text{kgf})=0.0577 \times W$

$\quad W_L\,(\text{kgf})=0.1668 \times W$

$\quad W_{THN}\,(\text{kgf})=0.551 \times W$

Women: $W_A\,(\text{kgf})=0.0497 \times W$

$\quad W_L\,(\text{kgf})=0.1843 \times W$

$\quad W_{THN}\,(\text{kgf})=0.532 \times W$

ii Calculate the moment arms, about end A of the board, of the centres of gravity of each upper limb (d_{GA}) (assume that the moment arms are the same for the left and right upper limbs), each lower limb (d_{GL}) (assume that the moment arms are the same for the left and right lower limbs) and the combined trunk, head and neck (d_{GTHN}). See Figure PW13.2. Record the results in Table PW13.1. Use the Plagenhoef *et al.* (1983) data for segment centre of gravity loci in Table 6.1 for men and Table 6.2 for women, i.e.

Men: $d_{GA}\,(\text{cm})=d_U+d_1=d_U+0.50(d_S-d_U)$

$\quad d_{GL}\,(\text{cm})=d_M+d_2=d_M+0.564(d_H-d_M)$

$\quad d_{GTHN}\,(\text{cm})=d_H+d_3=d_H+0.434(d_D-d_H)$

Women: $d_{GA}\,(\text{cm})=d_U+d_1=d_U+0.514(d_S-d_U)$

$\quad d_{GL}\,(\text{cm})=d_M+d_2=d_M+0.580(d_H-d_M)$

$\quad d_{GTHN}\,(\text{cm})=d_H+d_3=d_H+0.397(d_D-d_H)$

iii Calculate the combined moment (M_C) about end A of the board of the five segments of the body (two upper limbs, two lower limbs, combined trunk, head and neck). Record the result in Table PW13.1.

$M_C\,(\text{kgf·cm}) = 2(W_A \times d_{GA}) + 2(W_L \times d_{GL}) + W_{THN} \times d_{GTHN}$

iv Calculate the moment arm of total body weight (d_W) about end A by the principle of moments. Record the result in Table PW13.1.

$$d_W \text{ (cm)} = M_C/W$$

v Compare d with d_W. If the anthropometric data (segmental masses and mass centre loci) used in the calculation of M_C were accurate, then d and d_W should be exactly the same. This is unlikely since the anthropometric data were estimated from mean data obtained by volumetric analysis. Nevertheless, the anthropometric data is accurate enough for most analyses of human movement.

Presentation of results

1 Present your individual results in Table PW13.1.
2 Present the results for all of the subjects in your group and the group mean data in Table PW13.2.

TABLE PW13.2 Individual and group results

Subjects	h (cm)	W (kgf)	d (cm)	d (%)*	d_W (cm)	d_W* (%)	$d_W - d$ (cm)	$d_W - d$ (%)*
Women								
1.								
2.								
3.								
4.								
5.								
Mean								
SD								
Men								
1.								
2.								
3.								
4.								
5.								
Mean								
SD								

* % of h.

Example results

Example results are shown in Tables PW13.3 and PW13.4. The group mean data show that the indirect result was greater than the direct result for both the women and the men by an average of 2.4 cm (1.5% of height) and 4.1 cm (2.3% of height), respectively.

TABLE PW13.3 Individual results

Subject	Pamela
W (kgf)	57
h (cm)	165.8
l (cm)	198.8
S_1 (kgf)	13
S_2 (kgf)	40.5
d_M (cm)	8
d_H (cm)	86
d_U (cm)	91
d_S (cm)	139
d_D (cm)	168
W_A (kgf)	2.9
W_L (kgf)	9.2
W_{THN} (kgf)	32.8
d_{GA} (cm)	114.4
d_{GL} (cm)	52.1
d_{GTHN} (cm)	118.5
M_C (kgf·cm)	5509
d_W (cm)	96.6
d (cm)	95.9

TABLE PW13.4 Individual and group results

Subjects	h (cm)	W (kgf)	d (cm)	d (%)*	d_W (cm)	d_W* (%)	$d_W - d$ (cm)	$d_W - d$ (%)*
Women								
1. Pamela	165.8	57	95.9	57.8	96.6	58.3	0.7	0.4
2. Jane	164.2	52	96.5	58.8	99	60.3	2.5	1.5
3. Susan	172	66	102.4	59.5	106.7	62	4.3	2.5
4. Sally	160.3	49	91.8	57.3	95.8	59.8	4.0	2.5
5. Fiona	155.5	55	90.4	58.1	91.1	58.6	0.7	0.5
Mean	163.6	55.8	95.4	58.3	97.8	59.8	2.4	1.5
SD	6.2	6.5	4.7	0.9	5.7	1.5	1.7	1.0
Men								
1. Stuart	169.3	68.5	91.7	54.2	96.3	56.9	4.6	2.7
2. Paul	176.5	77	103	58.4	108.9	61.7	5.9	3.3
3. John	170.2	71	99.6	58.5	100.4	59	0.8	0.5
4. Graeme	184.8	79.5	102.9	55.7	109.2	59.1	6.3	3.4
5. Richard	181.3	76	109.2	60.2	111.9	61.7	2.7	1.5
Mean	176.4	74.4	101.3	57.4	105.4	59.7	4.1	2.3
SD	6.8	4.5	6.4	2.4	6.6	2.0	2.3	1.2

* % of h.

PRACTICAL WORKSHEET 14

Determination of take-off distance, flight distance and landing distance in a standing long jump

Objective

To video a person performing a standing long jump and to determine the take-off distance, flight distance and landing distance components of the jump distance by analysis of the video.

Location

Motion analysis laboratory

Apparatus and equipment

Video camera and computer with appropriate video analysis software

Method

Subject's clothing and preparation of the subject

In the analysis of the video it is necessary to record the sagittal plane X (left to right) and Y (vertical) coordinates of the approximate positions of the following points and joints on the right side of the subject: shoulder joint, elbow joint, wrist joint, hip joint (greater trochanter), knee joint, ankle joint (lateral malleolus), heel, great toe. Consequently, the subject should wear tight-fitting shorts, a tight-fitting sleeveless top and shoes without socks so that the points can be easily identified and marked as shown in Figure PW14.1. The points should be marked with pieces of coloured tape of approximately 1.5 cm^2.

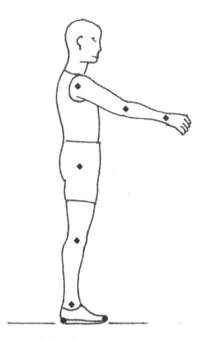

FIGURE PW14.1   Preparation of the subject.

Mass and height of the subject

The mass (kg) and height (cm) of the subject are measured with the subject standing upright without shoes. The mass and height are recorded in Table PW14.1.

Video recording of standing long jump

1   A white line approximately 2.5 m long is marked on the floor parallel to and approximately 1 m from a suitable vertical non-reflective background.

2   The camera is set up at a distance of approximately 10 m from the line with the optical axis of the camera perpendicular to the line and passing through the centre of the line.

3   With respect to the camera, the subject stands at the left end of the line with the line in the median plane of the subject.

4   The subject performs two or three practice trials of a standing long jump while attempting to jump along the line (left to right in relation to the camera view) and trying to maintain symmetrical movements of the arms and legs. As the subject performs the practice trials, the camera operator should observe where the subject lands and adjust the zoom of the camera to ensure that all of the movement will be visible in the recorded trials.

TABLE PW14.1 Individual results

Name of subject:					
Mass of subject (kg):					
Height of subject h (cm):					

Coordinates of the segmental model

	Take-off			Landing	
Segmental model	X (cm)	Y (cm)		X (cm)	Y (cm)
Shoulder					
Elbow					
Wrist					
Hip					
Knee					
Ankle					
Toe T_{TX} and T_{TY}					
Heel H_{LX} and H_{LY}					

Coordinates of the whole body centre of gravity

Take-off		Landing	
CG_{TX} (cm)	CG_{TY} (cm)	CG_{LX} (cm)	CG_{LY} (cm)

	Distance (cm)	Distance as a proportion of D (%)	Distance as a percentage of h (%)
Jump distance $D = H_{LX} - T_{TX}$		100	
Take-off distance $TD = CG_{TX} - T_{TX}$			
Landing distance $LD = H_{LX} - CG_{LX}$			
Flight distance $FD = D - TD - LD$			
$CG_Y = CG_{TY} - CG_{LY}$			

T_{TX}, X coordinate of toe at take-off; T_{TY}, Y coordinate of toe at take-off; H_{LX}, X coordinate of the heel on landing; H_{LY}, Y coordinate of the heel on landing; CG_{TX}, X coordinate of the CG at take-off; CG_{TY}, Y coordinate of the CG at take-off; CG_{LX}, X coordinate of the CG on landing; CG_{LY}, Y coordinate of the CG on landing; CG_Y, vertical displacement of the CG at take-off relative to landing.

5   A metre stick is placed along the line with the centre of the stick over the centre of the line. The picture of the subject standing at the left end of the line ready to jump and the metre stick is recorded for 1–2 s. The metre stick is then removed.

6   On the command from the camera operator the subject then performs a maximal effort standing long jump which is recorded. Two more trials are recorded
with a recovery period of approximately 30 s between trials.

Video analysis

1   Using the playback facility of the motion analysis system in use, select one of
the trials for analysis. The selected trial should be one in which the subject
demonstrates a high level of symmetry in the movement of the arms and legs.

2   Use the origin function to set the origin for the measurement of the X and
Y coordinates of points in the display to the left of and just below the feet of
the subject in the stationary starting position. The location of the origin may
be set automatically or manually depending upon the motion analysis system
in use.

3   Using the reference distance function, identify and record the coordinates of
the left end of the metre stick followed by the right end of the metre stick.
Input the reference distance, i.e. 1 m.

4   In the selected trial, identify the take-off frame, i.e. the last frame in which
the right toe is still in contact with the floor before take-off. The accuracy
with which this instant can be determined will depend upon the sampling
frequency of the camera (the number of frames per second), but 50 Hz should
be adequate.

5   In the take-off frame, digitize the following points on the subject, as in Figure
PW14.2, and record the X and Y coordinates of the points in Table PW14.1.
   • Shoulder
   • Elbow
   • Wrist
   • Hip
   • Knee
   • Ankle
   • Toe.

6   In the selected trial, identify the landing frame, i.e. the frame in which the heels
first make contact with the floor. The accuracy with which this instant can be
determined will depend upon the sampling frequency of the camera, but 50 Hz
should be adequate.

7   In the landing frame, digitize the following points on the subject, as in Figure
PW14.2, and record the X and Y coordinates of the points in Table PW14.1.
   • Shoulder
   • Elbow
   • Wrist
   • Hip
   • Knee
   • Ankle
   • Heel.

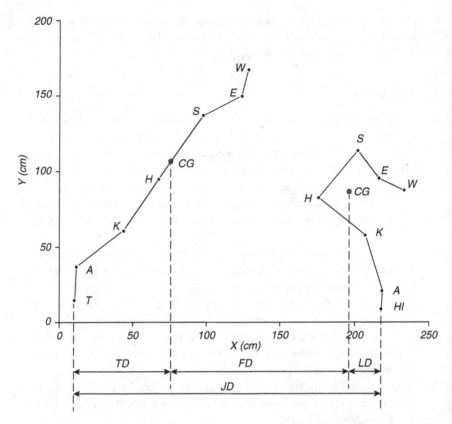

FIGURE PW14.2   Position of the body at take-off and landing in a standing long jump. *W*, wrist joint; *E*, elbow joint; *S*, shoulder joint; *H*, hip joint (greater trochanter); *K*, knee joint; *A*, ankle joint (lateral malleolus), *HI*, heel; *T*, great toe; *JD*, jump distance; *TD*, take-off distance; *FD*, flight distance; *LD*, landing distance; *CG*, whole body centre of gravity.

Determination of jump distance, take-off distance, flight distance, landing distance and vertical displacement of the centre of gravity in the jump

1   Use the Plagenhoef *et al.* (1993) data for segmental masses and mass centre loci (Tables 6.1 and 6.2) and the X-Y coordinate data in Table PW14.1 to determine the X-Y coordinates of the centre of gravity of the body in the take-off frame and the landing frame. Record the coordinates in Table PW14.1.

2   Use the segmental model coordinates and the centre of gravity coordinates in Table PW14.1 to determine the jump distance (*D*), take-off distance (*TD*), landing distance (*LD*), flight distance (*LD*) and the vertical displacement of the centre of gravity at take-off relative to landing (*CG*$_Y$). Record the data in Table PW14.1.

Presentation of results

1 Present your individual results in Table PW14.1.
2 Present a stick figure, as in Figure PW14.2, showing the position of the body and the centre of gravity of the body in the take-off and landing frames.
3 Present the results for all of the subjects in your group and the group mean data in Table PW14.2.

TABLE PW14.2 Individual and group results

Subjects	h (cm)	D (cm)	D_h (%)	TD (cm)	TD_D (%)	FD (cm)	FD_D (%)	LD (cm)	LD_D (%)	CG_Y (cm)	CG_Yh (%)
Women											
1											
2											
3											
4											
5											
6											
Mean											
SD											
Men											
1											
2											
3											
4											
5											
6											
Mean											
SD											

h, height; D, jump distance; D_h (%), jump distance as a percentage of h; TD, take-off distance; FD, flight distance; LD, landing distance; TD_D, take-off distance as a percentage of D; FD_D, flight distance as a percentage of D; LD_D, landing distance as a percentage of D; CG_Y, vertical displacement of CG at take-off relative to landing; $CG_Yh = CG_Y$ as a percentage of h.

Example results

Example results are shown in Tables PW14.3 and PW14.4. The stick figure corresponding to the data in Table PW14.3 is shown in Figure PW14.2. The group mean data show that the average jump distance of the men as a percentage of height (120.3%) was much greater than that of the women (96.9%). However, the average take-off, flight and landing distance components as a percentage of jump distance were similar for the men (32.6%, 54.8%, 12.6%) and women (30.2%, 56.3%, 13.6%).

TABLE PW14.3 Individual results

Name of subject: Ross
Mass of subject m (kg): 75.4
Height of subject h (cm): 171.5

Coordinates of the segmental model

Segmental model	Take-off		Landing	
	X (cm)	Y (cm)	X (cm)	Y (cm)
Shoulder	98.0	136.7	203.0	111.8
Elbow	123.8	148.8	216.7	93.7
Wrist	129.0	166.0	233.9	86.0
Hip	67.9	94.6	176.3	80.8
Knee	43.9	60.2	208.1	55.9
Ankle	12.0	36.1	219.3	19.8
Toe T_{TX} and T_{TY}	11.2	14.6		
Heel H_{LX} and H_{LY}			218.4	8.6

Coordinates of the whole body centre of gravity

	Take-off		Landing	
	CG_{TX} (cm)	CG_{TY} (cm)	CG_{LX} (cm)	CG_{LY} (cm)
	76.5	106.4	198.0	85.4

	Distance (cm)	Distance as a proportion of D (%)	Distance as a percentage of h (%)
Jump distance $D = H_{LX} - T_{TX}$	207.2	100	120.8
Take-off distance $TD = CG_{TX} - T_{TX}$	65.3	31.5	38.0
Landing distance $LD = H_{LX} - CG_{LX}$	20.4	9.8	11.9
Flight distance $FD = D - TD - LD$	121.5	58.6	70.8
$CG_Y = CG_{TY} - CG_{LY}$	21.0	10.1	12.2

T_{TX}, X coordinate of toe at take-off; T_{TY}, Y coordinate of toe at take-off; H_{LX}, X coordinate of the heel on landing; H_{LY}, Y coordinate of the heel on landing; CG_{TX}, X coordinate of the CG at take-off; CG_{TY}, Y coordinate of the CG at take-off; CG_{LX}, X coordinate of the CG on landing; CG_{LY}, Y coordinate of the CG on landing; CG_Y, vertical displacement of the CG at take-off relative to landing.

TABLE PW14.4 Individual and group results

Subjects	h (cm)	D (cm)	D_h (%)	TD (cm)	TD_D (%)	FD (cm)	FD_D (%)	LD (cm)	LD_D (%)	CG_Y (cm)	CG_Yh (%)
Women											
Natalie	165.5	205.1	123.9	54.2	26.4	123.6	60.3	27.3	13.3	11.5	6.9
Pamela	165	169	102.4	54	32	94	55.6	21	12.4	11	6.7
Fiona	155.5	93.3	60	44.3	47.5	29.5	31.6	19.5	20.9	16.5	10.6
Janet	176	171	97.2	39.6	23.2	113	66.1	18.4	10.8	12.9	7.3
Hazel	172	173	100.6	50.3	29.1	99.3	57.4	23.4	13.5	21.1	12.3
Donna	176	171	97.2	39	22.8	114	66.7	18	10.5	12.9	7.3
Mean	168.3	163.7	96.9	46.9	30.2	95.6	56.3	21.3	13.6	14.3	8.5
SD	7.94	37.12	20.66	6.9	9.19	34.09	12.9	3.55	3.8	3.84	2.35
Men											
Ross	171.5	207.2	120.8	65.3	31.5	121.5	58.6	20.4	9.8	21.0	12.2
Kevin	173.5	221	127.4	74	33.5	111	50.2	36	16.3	5.5	3.2
Robert	188	162	86.2	52	32.1	103	63.6	7	4.3	24	12.8
Carl	180.5	190.5	105.5	62.1	32.6	101	53	27.4	14.4	7.4	4.1
Michael	169	247	146.2	73.5	29.8	141	57.1	32.5	13.2	26.5	15.7
Nicholas	185	250.7	135.5	90.1	35.9	116.9	46.6	43.7	17.4	18.9	10.2
Mean	177.9	213.0	120.3	69.5	32.6	115.7	54.8	27.8	12.6	17.2	9.7
SD	7.73	34.01	21.61	12.96	2.05	14.66	6.14	12.88	4.84	8.75	5.01

h, height; D, jump distance; D_h (%), jump distance as a percentage of h; TD, take-off distance; FD, flight distance; LD, landing distance; TD_D, take-off distance as a percentage of D; FD_D, flight distance as a percentage of D; LD_D, landing distance as a percentage of D; CG_Y, vertical displacement of CG at take-off relative to landing; $CG_Yh = CG_Y$ as a percentage of h.

PRACTICAL WORKSHEET 15

Measurement of the moment of inertia of the human body

Objective

To measure the moment of inertia and radius of gyration of the human body about a vertical axis while in a seated position.

Location

Motion analysis laboratory

Apparatus and equipment

1   A turntable with a radial pointer extending from the turntable.
2   A stool which can be placed on the turntable with the vertical axis through the centre of the stool in line with the spindle of the turntable (Figure PW15.1).
3   A pulley-based gravitational load system to apply an angular impulse to the turntable.
4   A timer linked to two sets of photo-cells to record the duration of the angular impulse (time for the load to descend from its starting point to the floor).
5   A timer linked to two sets of photo-cells defining an arc of one radian within the field of the pointer.
6   A set of weighing scales.

Method

Subject's clothing

Shorts, shirt and training shoes

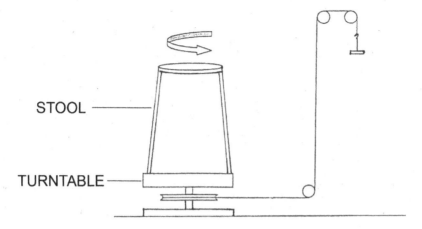

FIGURE PW15.1   Turntable and pulley-based gravitational load system.

Data collection

1   Record the mass (kg) of the subject in Table PW15.1.
2   With the stool resting on the turntable and the whole system at rest, a load is allowed to descend from its starting point to the floor. As the load descends, it applies, via the pulley system, an angular impulse to the turntable and stool about the vertical axis a_Y through the spindle of the turntable. The angular impulse generates a certain amount of angular momentum of the turntable and stool about a_Y, i.e.

$M \cdot t = I \cdot \omega$ (equation 6.12 where $\omega_1 = 0$) Eq. PW15.1

where

F = load (N)
d = moment arm (m) of F about a_Y
$M = F \cdot d$ = moment (N·m) exerted on turntable and stool about a_Y
t = duration (s) of the angular impulse
I = moment of inertia (kg·m²) of turntable and stool about a_Y
ω = angular velocity (rad/s) of the turntable and stool about a_Y resulting from the angular impulse

3   The duration of the angular impulse t_1 is the time taken for the load to descend from rest to the floor (over a distance of about 1 m; see Figure PW15.1). After the load contacts the floor (at which point the string applying the load to the turntable disconnects from the turntable), the turntable and stool will continue to rotate about a_Y. If there is no friction around the spindle of the turntable, the turntable and stool will rotate with constant angular velocity as angular momentum would be conserved. However, friction around the spindle will

gradually reduce the speed of rotation. Consequently it is important to measure ω as soon as possible after the end of the angular impulse, i.e. after the load has contacted the floor. ω is measured from $\omega = 1/t_2$ where t_2 is the time for the pointer to sweep through the arc of one radian after the string has disconnected from the turntable. Record F, d, t_1 and t_2 in Table PW15.1. In the example results in Table PW15.3, $F = 4.905$ N (0.5 kgf) and $d = 0.235$ m.

4   Repeat steps 2–3 with the subject sitting on the stool. Record F, d, t_1 and t_2 in Table PW15.1.

TABLE PW15.1 Individual results

Name of subject:

Mass of subject (kg):

	F (N)	d (m)	M (N·m)	t_1 (s)	$M \cdot t_1$ (N·m·s)	t_2 (s)	ω (rad/s)	I_1 (kg·m²)
Turntable and stool								
	F (N)	d (m)	M (N·m)	t_1 (s)	$M \cdot t_1$ (N·m·s)	t_2 (s)	ω (rad/s)	I_2 (kg·m²)
Turntable, stool and subject								
			I_3 (kg·m²)			k (m)		
Subject								

Data analysis

1   Calculate the turning moment M and the impulse of the turning moment $M \cdot t_1$ for the turntable and stool and for the turntable, stool and subject. Record the results in Table PW15.1.

2   Calculate $\omega = 1/t_2$ for the turntable and stool and for the turntable, stool and subject. Record the results in Table PW15.1.

3   Calculate the moment of inertia I_1 of the turntable and stool about a_Y and the moment of inertia I_2 of the turntable, stool and subject about a_Y from equation PW15.1, i.e. $I = (M \cdot t_1)/\omega$. Record the results in Table PW15.1.

4   Calculate the moment of inertia I_3 of the subject about a_Y from $I_3 = I_2 - I_1$. Record the result in Table PW15.1.

5   Calculate the radius of gyration k of the subject about a_Y from $k = \sqrt{(I_3 / m)}$ where m = mass of the subject. Record the result in Table PW15.1.

Presentation of results

1   Present your individual results in Table PW15.1.
2   Present the results for all of the subjects in your group and the group mean results in Table PW15.2.

TABLE PW15.2 Individual and group results

Subjects Women	Mass (kg)	I_1 (kg·m²)	I_2 (kg·m²)	I_3 (kg·m²)	k (m)
1.					
2.					
3.					
4.					
5.					
Mean					
SD					
Subjects Men	Mass (kg)	I_1 (kg·m²)	I_2 (kg·m²)	I_3 (kg·m²)	k (m)
1					
2					
3					
4					
5					
Mean					
SD					

Example results

Example results are shown in Tables PW15.3 and PW15.4. The group mean results show that the average moment of inertia (I_3) and average radius of gyration (k) of the men (3.549 kg·m², 0.219 m) were very similar to those of the women (3.321 kg·m², 0.235 m), even though the average mass of the men (73.3 kg) was much greater than that of the women (60.6 kg).

TABLE PW15.3 Individual results

Name of subject: Dan
Mass of subject (kg): 66.0

	F (N)	d (m)	M (N·m)	t_1 (s)	$M·t_1$ (N·m·s)	t_2 (s)	ω (rad/s)	I_1 (kg·m^2)
Turntable and stool	4.905	0.235	1.153	0.910	1.049	0.171	5.848	0.179

	F (N)	d (m)	M (N·m)	t_1 (s)	$M·t_1$ (N·m·s)	t_2 (s)	ω (rad/s)	I_2 (kg·m^2)
Turntable, stool and subject	4.905	0.235	1.153	3.751	4.325	0.826	1.210	3.571

	I_3 (kg·m^2)	K (m)
Subject	3.392	0.227

TABLE PW15.4 Individual and group results

Subjects Women	Mass (kg)	I_1 (kg·m^2)	I_2 (kg·m^2)	I_3 (kg·m^2)	k (m)
1. Fiona	52.2	0.179	3.336	3.157	0.246
2. Jennifer	63.9	0.179	3.347	3.168	0.223
3. Natalie	59.7	0.179	3.843	3.664	0.248
4. Lynne	68.2	0.179	3.641	3.462	0.225
5. Sarah	59.1	0.179	3.333	3.154	0.231
Mean	60.6	0.179	3.500	3.321	0.235
SD	5.96	0	0.232	0.232	0.012

Subjects Men	Mass (kg)	I_1 (kg·m^2)	I_2 (kg·m^2)	I_3 (kg·m^2)	k (m)
1. Dan	66.0	0.179	3.571	3.392	0.227
2. Stuart	69.6	0.179	3.131	2.952	0.206
3. Richard	78.2	0.179	3.650	3.471	0.211
4. Paul	74.8	0.179	4.016	3.837	0.226
5. Ross	77.9	0.179	4.270	4.091	0.229
Mean	73.3	0.179	3.728	3.549	0.219
SD	5.35	0	0.437	0.437	0.011

PRACTICAL WORKSHEET 16

Determination of human power output in stair climbing and running up a slope

Objectives

To determine the power output of the human body (rate of increase in gravitational potential energy) in stair climbing and running up a slope.

Location, apparatus and equipment

Stair climbing

It is unlikely that a purpose-built stairway will be available, but any suitable stairway indoors or outdoors will suffice for the test. In the test, the subject is required to run up a stairway or part of a stairway as fast as possible. The time to complete a particular number of steps, involving a certain vertical displacement of the body, is measured by a timer linked to pressure mats placed on specific steps or photo cells placed at the sides of the stairway (Figure PW16.1). The average power output P_a of the body (rate of increase in gravitational potential energy) is given by

$$P_a = m \cdot g \cdot h / t \text{ Eq. PW16.1}$$

where m = mass of the subject (kg),
g = acceleration due to gravity = 9.81 m/s^2,
h = vertical displacement (m) of the whole body centre of gravity in time t.

For example, if m is 70 kg, the height of each step is 0.15 m, and the time to complete four steps is 0.5 s, P_a is given by

$$P_a = (70 \text{ kg} \times 9.81 \text{ m/s}^2 \times 4 \times 0.15 \text{ m})/0.5 \text{ s} = 824 \text{ W}$$

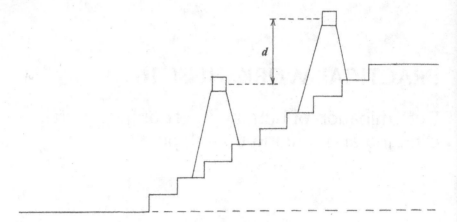

FIGURE PW16.1   Location of photo cells in relation to the stairway.

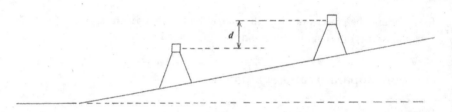

FIGURE PW16.2   Location of photo cells in relation to the slope.

Running up a slope

Any even slope of approximately 25 m in length that is not too steep should be suitable. In the test, the subject is required to run up the slope as fast as possible. The time to complete a particular distance up the slope, involving a certain vertical displacement of the body, is measured by a timer linked to photo cells placed at the sides of the runway (Figure PW16.2). The subject begins her or his run about 5 m before the start of the test region and slows down after completing the test distance. The average power output P_a of the body (rate of increase in gravitational potential energy) is measured in the same way as in the stair climbing test. For example, if the angle of the slope is 5° and the test distance up the slope is 10 m, then the vertical displacement $h = 10$ m $\times \sin 5° = 10$ m $\times 0.0871 = 0.87$ m. If the mass of the subject m is 60 kg and the time to complete the test distance = 1.8 s, then P_a is given by

$$P_a = (60 \text{ kg} \times 9.81 \text{ m/s}^2 \times 0.87 \text{ m})/1.8 \text{ s} = 284.5 \text{ W}$$

Method

Subject's clothing

Shorts, shirt and trainers

Data collection and analysis: stair climbing

1   Ensure that each set of photo cells is at the same height (approximately waist height) above the target steps.
2   Reset the timer.
3   Have the subject perform a trial, i.e. from a 5 m rolling start, the subject runs up the stairs between the sets of photo cells (Figure PW16.1) as quickly as possible.
4   Record the time for the trial in Table PW16.1.
5   Repeat stages 2–4 for 5 more trials.
6   Record the subject's mass (kg) in Table PW16.1.
7   Record the vertical displacement d between the photo cells in Table PW16.1.
8   Calculate the average power P_a in each trial, by using equation PW16.1. Record P_a in Table PW16.1 in watts (W) and watts per kilogram of body mass (W/kg).
9   Calculate the mean and standard deviation of P_a and record the data in Table PW16.1.

TABLE PW16.1 Stair climbing test

Name of subject:
Mass (kg):
d (m):

Trial	Time (s)	P_a (W)	P_a (W/kg)
1			
2			
3			
4			
5			
6			
Mean			
SD			

Data collection and analysis: running up a slope

1   Ensure that each set of photo cells is at the same height (approximately waist height) above the slope.
2   Reset the timer.
3   Have the subject perform a trial, i.e. from a 5 m rolling start, the subject runs up the slope between the sets of photo cells (Figure PW16.2) as quickly as possible.

4   Record the time for the trial in Table PW16.2.
5   Repeat stages 2–4 for 5 more trials.
6   Record the subject's mass (kg) in Table PW16.2.
7   Record the vertical displacement d between the photo cells in Table PW16.2.
8   Calculate the average power P_a in each trial, by using equation PW16.1. Record
     P_a in Table PW16.2 in watts (W) and watts per kilogram of body mass (W/kg).
9   Calculate the mean and standard deviation of P_a and record the data in Table PW16.2.

TABLE PW16.2 Running test

Name of subject:
Mass (kg):
d (m):

Trial	Time (s)	P_a (W)	P_a (W/kg)
1			
2			
3			
4			
5			
6			
Mean			
SD			

Group results

1   Record the mean data for all of the subjects in your group in both tests in Table
     PW16.3.
2   Calculate the group mean and standard deviation for P_a for the subjects in your
     group in both tests and record the results in Table PW16.3.

TABLE PW16.3 Individual means and group mean results

Name	Mass (kg)	Stair climbing test			Running test		
		Time (s)	Pa (W)	Pa (W/kg)	Time (s)	Pa (W)	Pa (W/kg)
1							
2							
3							
4							
5							
Mean							
SD							

Presentation of results

1   Present your individual results for both tests: Tables PW16.1 and PW16.2.
2   Present the group results for both tests, using Table PW16.3.

Example results

Example results are shown in Tables PW16.4–PW16.6. The group mean results in Table PW16.6 show that absolute average power output in the stair climbing test (846.0 W) was 2.55 times the absolute average power output in the running test (331.1 W). Even when normalized with respect to body mass, the average power output in the stair climbing test (12.03 W/kg) was 2.57 times the average power output in the running test (4.68 W/kg). In contrast, the average time in the stair climbing test (0.495 s) was 0.27 times the average time in the running test (1.824 s). These results are to be expected for two reasons:

1   When maximal effort is exerted for the duration of the exercise, average power output of the human body is inversely proportional to the duration of the exercise, i.e. the shorter the duration of the exercise the higher the power output. These example results are consistent with the example results presented at the end of Practical Worksheet 17 which is concerned with the determination of peak power output and average power output in a vertical jump.
2   The change in gravitational potential energy in running up a slope is likely to be a much smaller proportion of the total work done by the body than when running upstairs. See the section on internal and external work in Chapter 7.

TABLE PW16.4 Stair climbing test

Name of subject: John
Mass (kg): 61.7
d (m): 0.6 m

Trial	Time (s)	P_a (W)	P_a (W/kg)
1	0.528	687.8	11.14
2	0.491	739.3	11.98
3	0.453	801.3	12.98
4	0.471	770.7	12.49
5	0.484	750.0	12.15
6	0.469	774.0	12.54
Mean	0.483	753.8	12.21
SD	0.026	38.8	0.63

∗ Height of each step = 0.15 m. 4 steps × 0.15 m = 0.6 m.
Depth of each step = 0.2 m.

TABLE PW16.5 Running test

Name of subject: John
Mass (kg): 61.7

d (m): 0.87 m

Trial	Time (s)	P_a (W)	P_a (W/kg)
1	1.890	278.6	4.51
2	1.864	282.5	4.58
3	1.870	281.6	4.56
4	1.902	276.9	4.49
5	1.879	280.2	4.54
6	1.877	280.5	4.55
Mean	1.880	280.0	4.54
SD	0.014	2.03	0.03

∗ 10 m test distance on a 5° slope: vertical displacement = 0.87 m

TABLE PW16.6 Individual means and group mean results

Name	Mass (kg)	Stair climbing test			Running test		
		Time (s)	Pa (W)	Pa (W/kg)	Time (s)	Pa (W)	Pa (W/kg)
1. John	61.7	0.483	753.8	12.21	1.880	280.0	4.54
2. James	82.1	0.565	854.9	10.42	1.901	368.5	4.49
3. Stephen	71.9	0.539	784.7	10.89	1.748	351.0	4.88
4. Callum	70.1	0.463	891.8	12.74	1.812	330.2	4.71
5. David	67.9	0.423	945.1	13.89	1.777	326.0	4.79
Mean	70.7	0.495	846.0	12.03	1.824	331.1	4.68
SD	7.43	0.06	77.9	1.40	0.07	33.3	0.16

PRACTICAL WORKSHEET 17

Determination of human power output in a countermovement vertical jump

Objectives

To determine the peak power output and average power output of the human body during the upward propulsion phase of a countermovement vertical jump.

Location

Motion analysis laboratory

Apparatus and equipment

Force platform system

Method

Subject's clothing

Shorts, shirt and trainers

Data collection

Record the vertical component of the ground reaction force acting on a subject when performing a countermovement vertical jump on a force platform.

1   Each subject should practice the jump a number of times before any trials are recorded. The jump is a countermovement jump without the use of the arms. The subject adopts a relaxed standing position on the force platform with hands

on hips (to eliminate the use of the arms) and feet shoulder width apart. The subject stands as still as possible for at least two seconds before the jump and then, in a single continuous movement, flexes the hips, knees and ankles (the countermovement) to move into a half squat position (knee angle approximately 90°) and immediately follows the half squat with a vertical jump for maximal height to land back on the force platform. The hands remain on the hips throughout the entire movement.

2   After two or three practice trials, two trials are recorded.
3   On a signal from the force platform system operator, the subject steps onto the platform. After the subject has adopted the start position, the system operator starts recording the vertical component of the ground reaction force at 1000 Hz. On another signal from the system operator, the subject performs a jump. When the subject regains a stationary standing position after landing, the system operator stops the recording and signals to the subject to step off the platform. After a 30 s recovery period, a second trial is recorded.
4   The trial with the longer flight time (which is likely to be associated with a higher peak power) is selected for analysis.

Data analysis

1   Data analysis will be described in relation to the example results shown in Table PW17.1 and Figure PW17.1.
2   The force-time graph of the jump should be displayed and the weight W (N) of the subject should be determined by averaging a 0.5 s section of the force-time recording during the period when the subject was standing still before the jump (see Figure PW17.1). Record the weight of the subject in an Excel spreadsheet as shown in Table PW17.1.
3   Calculate the mass m of the subject where m (kg) = $W/9.81$. Record the subject's mass as shown in Table PW17.1.
4   The force-time graph should be time-sliced to retain the force-time data from about 0.2 s before the start of the countermovement to just after landing. The time-sliced force-time data should be copied into the first two columns of the Excel spreadsheet as shown in Table PW17.1. In the example results in Table PW17.1 the period of the time slice is 0.92 s (from 4.3 s to 5.2 s). With a sampling frequency of 1000 Hz, a time period of 0.92 s would require 920 rows in the Excel spreadsheet (920 × 0.001 s = 0.92 s). In the example results in Table PW17.1, the sampling frequency has been reduced from 1000 Hz to 50 Hz so that the example analysis can be presented more concisely. Consequently, there are 46 rows of data (46 × 0.02 s = 0.92 s) in Table PW17.1. The reduction of the sampling frequency to 50 Hz decreases the accuracy of the analysis; peak power and average power are reduced by about 4% and 10% respectively, compared to an analysis based on a sampling frequency of 1000 Hz.

5　The subject's weight should be copied into all of the cells in column 3 of the spreadsheet as in Table PW17.1.

6　In column 4 of the spreadsheet, the resultant vertical force acting on the centre of gravity (CG) of the subject at each instant in time is calculated by subtracting body weight (column 3) from the vertical component of the ground reaction force (column 2). A negative resultant force indicates downward acceleration of the CG or upward deceleration of the CG. A positive resultant force indicates downward deceleration of the CG or upward acceleration of the CG.

7　In column 5 of the spreadsheet, the impulse of the resultant vertical force in each time interval is calculated by multiplying the average resultant force in the time interval by the length of the time interval. In the first time interval in Table PW17.1 (between 4.3 s and 4.32 s) the resultant force at the start of the time interval is −1.07 N. The resultant force at the end of the time interval is −1.00 N. Consequently, the average resultant force over the time interval is −1.035 N and the impulse of the average resultant force in the time interval is −1.035 N ×0.02 s = −0.0207 N·s.

8　In column 6 of the spreadsheet, the cumulative impulse of the resultant vertical force is calculated by summing the impulses in column 5 from the start to the end of the time slice. At the end of the first time interval the impulse is −0.0207 N·s, i.e. 0 + (−0.0207) N·s = −0.0207 N·s. At the end of the second time interval (4.32 s to 4.34 s) the cumulative impulse = −0.0207 N·s + (−0.0254) N·s = −0.0461 N·s.

9　In column 7 of the spreadsheet, the cumulative vertical velocity of the CG is calculated by dividing the cumulative impulse data in column 6 by the mass of the subject. As expected, the data in column 7 shows that the velocity of the CG was zero (to three decimal places) as the subject was standing still before the jump (4.3 s to 4.44 s). After the start of the countermovement (at 4.44 s) the CG accelerated downward (increasing downward velocity) and reached a maximum velocity downward of −1.37 m/s at 4.8 s. This was followed by a period of downward deceleration, in which the downward velocity of the CG was reduced to zero (the lowest point in the countermovement) at approximately 4.93 s. This was followed by a period of upward acceleration of the CG culminating in a maximum upward velocity of 2.85 m/s at 5.14 s and a take-off velocity of 2.65 m/s at 5.18 s (see Figure PW17.1).

10　In column 8 of the spreadsheet, the power output of the body at each instant in time from the start of movement to take-off is calculated by multiplying the ground reaction force by the cumulative velocity. For example, at 4.46 s the power output of the body was 762.85 N ×−0.01 m/s = −7.63 W. The negative value indicates negative power, i.e. the rate at which the body was losing energy (decrease in the combined total of gravitational potential energy, translational kinetic energy and rotational kinetic energy). The body experiences negative power during the whole of the countermovement; see Table PW17.1 and Figure PW17.1. The body produces positive power (rate of increase in the combined total of gravitational potential energy, translational kinetic energy and rotational kinetic energy) during the whole of the period of upward propulsion (from the lowest point in the countermovement to take-off). Table PW17.1 shows that peak positive power was 4625.28 W (at 5.1 s); see Figure PW17.1.

11 The average positive power output is the average of the instantaneous power values in the period of upward propulsion. In Table PW17.1, the period of upward propulsion was from approximately 4.93 s to take-off. Consequently, average power output was approximately 2439.6 W (average of the instantaneous power values in the period 4.94 s to 5.18 s).

12 Peak positive power (W and W/kg), average positive power (W and W/kg) and propulsion time (s) are recorded in Table PW17.1.

13 The weight (N), mass (kg), propulsion time (s), peak positive power (W and W/kg) and average positive power (W and W/kg) are recorded for all subjects in Table PW17.2.

TABLE PW17.1 Analysis of the vertical ground reaction force-time recording of the performance of a countermovement jump (hands on hips) by a young adult male sports science student (sampling frequency of the ground reaction force = 50 Hz)

Name of subject: Brian　　　Weight (N): 799.05　　　　　　　Mass (kg): 81.45
Peak positive power (W): 4625.28　　　　Average positive power (W): 2439.6
Peak positive power (W/kg): 56.79　　　　Average positive power (W/kg): 29.95
Propulsion time (s): 0.25

Time (s)	GRF (N)	BW (N)	GRF – BW (N)	Impulse (N·s)	Cum Imp (N·s)	Cum Vel (m/s)	Power (W)
4.3	797.98	799.05	−1.07	0	0	0	0
4.32	798.05	799.05	−1	−0.0207	−0.0207	0	0
4.34	797.51	799.05	−1.54	−0.0254	−0.0461	0	0
4.36	798.78	799.05	−0.27	−0.0181	−0.0642	0	0
4.38	799.35	799.05	0.3	0.0003	−0.0639	0	0
4.4	799.39	799.05	0.34	0.0064	−0.0575	0	0
4.42	799.26	799.05	0.21	0.0055	−0.052	0	0
4.44	799.13	799.05	0.08	0.0029	−0.0491	0	0
4.46	762.85	799.05	−36.2	−0.3612	−0.4103	−0.01	−7.63
4.48	713.89	799.05	−85.16	−1.2136	−1.6239	−0.02	−14.28
4.5	654.35	799.05	−144.7	−2.2986	−3.9225	−0.05	−32.72
4.52	581.66	799.05	−217.39	−3.6209	−7.5434	−0.09	−52.35
4.54	494.14	799.05	−304.91	−5.223	−12.7664	−0.16	−79.06
4.56	382.55	799.05	−416.5	−7.2141	−19.9805	−0.25	−95.64
4.58	302.89	799.05	−496.16	−9.1266	−29.1071	−0.36	−109.04
4.6	259.49	799.05	−539.56	−10.3572	−39.4643	−0.48	−124.56

Time (s)	GRF (N)	BW (N)	GRF – BW (N)	Impulse (N·s)	Cum Imp (N·s)	Cum Vel (m/s)	Power (W)
4.62	258.75	799.05	−540.3	−10.7986	−50.2629	−0.62	−160.43
4.64	320.22	799.05	−478.83	−10.1913	−60.4542	−0.74	−236.96
4.66	328.37	799.05	−470.68	−9.4951	−69.9493	−0.86	−282.4
4.68	372.26	799.05	−426.79	−8.9747	−78.924	−0.97	−361.09
4.7	412.75	799.05	−386.3	−8.1309	−87.0549	−1.07	−441.64
4.72	440.17	799.05	−358.88	−7.4518	−94.5067	−1.16	−510.6
4.74	520.03	799.05	−279.02	−6.379	−100.8857	−1.24	−644.84
4.76	541.43	799.05	−257.62	−5.3664	−106.2521	−1.3	−703.86
4.78	654.22	799.05	−144.83	−4.0245	−110.2766	−1.35	−883.2
4.8	777.3	799.05	−21.75	−1.6658	−111.9424	−1.37	−1064.9
4.82	988.94	799.05	189.89	1.6814	−110.261	−1.35	−1335.07
4.84	1303.28	799.05	504.23	6.9412	−103.3198	−1.27	−1655.17
4.86	1643.57	799.05	844.52	13.4875	−89.8323	−1.1	−1807.93
4.88	1970.25	799.05	1171.2	20.1572	−69.6751	−0.86	−1694.42
4.9	2175.1	799.05	1376.05	25.4725	−44.2026	−0.54	−1174.55
4.92	2233.01	799.05	1433.96	28.1001	−16.1025	−0.2	−446.6
4.94	2180.73	799.05	1381.68	28.1564	12.0539	0.15	327.11
4.96	2095.19	799.05	1296.14	26.7782	38.8321	0.48	1005.69
4.98	2032.53	799.05	1233.48	25.2962	64.1283	0.79	1605.7
5	1971.18	799.05	1172.13	24.0561	88.1844	1.08	2128.87
5.02	1938.57	799.05	1139.52	23.1165	111.3009	1.37	2655.84
5.04	1907.75	799.05	1108.7	22.4822	133.7831	1.64	3128.71
5.06	1889.94	799.05	1090.89	21.9959	155.779	1.91	3609.79
5.08	1887.42	799.05	1088.37	21.7926	177.5716	2.18	4114.58
5.1	1887.87	799.05	1088.82	21.7719	199.3435	2.45	4625.28
5.12	1715.98	799.05	916.93	20.0575	219.401	2.69	4615.99
5.14	1158.97	799.05	359.92	12.7685	232.1695	2.85	3303.06
5.16	210.71	799.05	−588.34	−2.2842	229.8853	2.82	594.2
5.18	0	799.05	−799.05	−13.8739	216.0114	2.65	0
5.2	0	799.05	−799.05	−15.981	200.0304	2.45	0

Presentation of results

1 Present your individual force-time analysis as shown in Table PW17.1.
2 Present your individual force-time, velocity-time and power-time graphs as shown in Figure PW17.1.
3 Present your individual and group results as shown in Table PW17.2.

Example results

Example results are shown in Tables PW17.1 and PW17.2 and Figure PW17.1. Table PW17.2 shows that the group mean propulsion time was 0.27 s, group mean peak power was 3942.87 W and 48.24 W/kg and group mean average power was 2142.91 W and 26.24 W/kg. The results for average power are consistent with the example results for average power in stair climbing and running up a slope presented at the end of Practical Worksheet 16, i.e. the shorter the period of maximal effort, the higher the average power output.

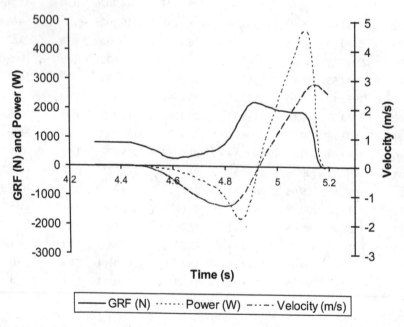

FIGURE PW17.1 Vertical ground reaction force-time graph and corresponding vertical velocity-time and vertical power-time graphs of the performance of a countermovement jump (hands on hips) by a young adult male sports science student (data in Table PW17.1).

TABLE PW17.2 Individual and group results for peak and average power output in a countermovement jump (hands on hips) for 12 young adult male sports science students (sampling frequency of the ground reaction force = 1000 Hz)

Subjects	Weight	Mass	Propulsion time	Peak power		Average power	
	(N)	(kg)	(s)	(W)	(W/kg)	(W)	(W/kg)
1. Brian	799.05	81.45	0.238	4817.81	59.15	2719.07	33.38
2. Leo	694.76	70.82	0.263	3279.73	46.31	1817.93	25.67
3. Sam	849.04	86.55	0.29	3619.15	41.82	2089.87	24.15
4. David	752.72	76.73	0.321	3856.25	50.26	2106.81	27.46
5. Bruce	658.64	67.14	0.235	3878.91	57.77	2235.51	33.3
6. Ieuan	809.72	82.54	0.277	4205.56	50.95	2059.7	24.95
7. Charlie	954.71	97.32	0.296	4304.28	44.23	2415.69	24.82
8. Jack	1083.61	110.46	0.258	3033.12	27.46	1661.11	15.04
9. Chris	877.9	89.49	0.23	4352.34	48.63	2355.05	26.32
10. George	830.81	84.69	0.261	4205.47	49.66	2254.35	26.62
11. Kevin	672.18	68.52	0.286	3479.37	50.78	1899.25	27.72
12. Ben	809.23	82.49	0.301	4282.45	51.91	2100.63	25.47
Mean	816.03	83.18	0.27	3942.87	48.24	2142.91	26.24
SD	115.66	11.79	0.03	492.93	7.83	271.16	4.46

PRACTICAL WORKSHEET 18

Determination of the reliability of distance jumped in a standing long jump

Objective

To determine the reliability (reliability coefficient and standard error of measurement) of distance jumped in a standing long jump.

Location

A flat, dry, wooden surface with court lines marked on the floor and enough space (at least 3 m × 5 m) to safely perform standing long jumps with an arm swing.

Equipment

Steel measuring tape

Method

Subject's clothing

Shorts, shirt and trainers

Data collection

1 A start line on the floor is selected that is perpendicular to another line running in the intended direction of the jump. At the start of a trial, the subject stands with feet behind the start line, one foot either side of the intended jump direction line and toes in line with the back edge of the start line. The subject then performs a standing long jump with arm swing. Each jump consists of a countermovement phase and a jump phase. In the countermovement phase, the

subject flexes the shoulders (backswing of the arms), hips and knees and dorsi-flexes the ankles, to adopt a body position from which to forcefully project the body forwards in the jump phase. In the jump phase, the subject should try to jump along the intended jump direction line, maintain symmetrical movements of the arms and legs and land on the feet.

2　When a subject lands from a jump, an observer marks the position of the rear-most heel on the floor. The length of a jump is measured, with a steel tape, from the back edge of the start line to the heel-mark, on a line that is perpendicular to the start line.

3　After sufficient practice, each subject performs two trials (test and retest) with 30 s rest between trials. The jump distances are recorded.

Data analysis

1　Table PW18.1 shows the test-retest scores for groups of men ($N = 25$) and women ($N = 25$) sports science students.

2　The scattergrams for both groups of subjects are shown in Figure PW18.1.

3　For each group, the reliability coefficient (r) of the test is calculated using the method shown in Table 2.3. The results are shown in Table PW18.2.

TABLE PW18.1 Test and retest scores for distance jumped in a standing long jump with arm swing (cm) for men ($N = 25$) and women ($N = 25$) sports science students. SD, standard deviation.

Subject	Men		Women	
	Test	Retest	Test	Retest
1	205	200	156	162
2	200	190	162	154
3	190	184	146	155
4	186	200	168	182
5	218	212	195	189
6	205	210	162	175
7	196	204	165	160
8	192	198	142	153
9	236	224	155	150
10	217	222	145	142
11	174	181	149	157
12	183	175	165	164
13	174	172	183	188
14	182	194	186	190
15	215	205	153	158

(Continued)

TABLE PW18.1 (Continued)

Subject	Men		Women	
	Test	Retest	Test	Retest
16	230	236	180	176
17	192	194	175	186
18	197	208	190	188
19	223	230	133	140
20	197	193	155	145
21	212	225	138	132
22	227	220	168	172
23	210	214	172	164
24	185	182	151	155
25	223	212	178	185
Mean	202.76	203.40	162.88	164.88
SD	17.76	17.39	16.68	17.25

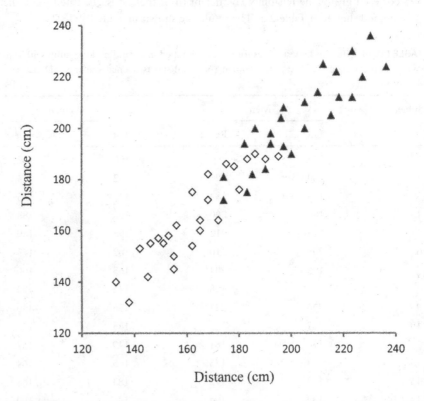

FIGURE PW18.1 Scattergrams for test (x axis) and retest (y axis) scores for a standing long jump with arm swing for men (N = 25, ▲) and women (N = 25, ◊) sports science students.

TABLE PW18.2 Reliability coefficient (r), standard deviation of all of the test and retest scores (s), standard error of the measurement (SEM) and 95% confidence limits (CL_{95}) for distance jumped in a standing long jump with arm swing for men ($N = 25$) and women ($N = 25$) sports science students. $SEM = s\sqrt{(1-r)}; CL_{95} = \pm1.96 \times SEM$.

	Men	Women
r	0.888	0.909
s (cm)	17.31	16.82
SEM (cm)	5.78	5.073
CL95 (cm)	±11.33	±9.94

4   For each group, the standard deviation of all of the test and retest scores (s) is calculated using the method shown in Table 2.2. The results are shown in Table PW18.2.

5   For each group, the standard error of measurement (SEM) is calculated using the equation, $SEM = s\sqrt{(1-r)}$. The results are shown in Table PW18.2.

6   For each group, the 95% confidence limits (CL_{95}) of the test are calculated using the equation, $CL_{95} = \pm1.96 \times SEM$. The results are shown in Table PW18.2.

Presentation of results

1   Present the test and retest scores of all of the subjects (men and women separately) as shown in Table PW18.1.

2   For each group, present the reliability coefficient (r), standard deviation of all of the test and retest scores (s), the standard error of measurement (SEM) and 95% confidence limits as shown in Table PW18.2.

Example results

Example results are presented in Table PW18.1, Table PW18.2 and Figure PW18.1 for groups of men and women sports science students. The subjects were well-practised and, not surprisingly, the means and standard deviations of the test and retest scores for each group were quite similar (Table PW18.1). The reliability coefficient of the test for the men ($r = 0.888$) was slightly lower than that for the women ($r = 0.909$) and the standard deviation of all of the test and retest scores for the men ($s = 17.31$ cm) was slightly higher than that for the women ($s = 16.82$ cm). Consequently, the standard error of measurement (men 5.78 cm; women, 5.073 cm) and 95% confidence limits (men, ±11.33 cm; women, ±9.94 cm) were higher for the men than for the women (Table PW18.2).

PRACTICAL WORKSHEET 19

Determination of the concurrent validity of distance jumped in a standing long jump as a predictor of peak instantaneous power in a countermovement vertical jump

Objectives

To determine the concurrent validity of distance jumped in a standing long jump with an arm swing as a predictor of peak instantaneous power in a countermovement vertical jump with hands on hips.

Location

Standing long jump:

> The location should be a flat, dry, wooden surface with court lines marked on the floor and enough space (at least 3 m × 5 m) to safely perform a standing long jump with an arm swing.

Countermovement vertical jump:

> The location should be a motion analysis laboratory with a force platform system, or an area that can accommodate a portable force platform system, such as a sports hall or gymnasium.

Apparatus and equipment

Force platform system
   Steel measuring tape

Method

Subject's clothing

Shorts, shirt and trainers

Data collection

Standing long jump:

1   The method of administering a standing long jump with an arm swing, and measuring distance jumped, is described in Practical Worksheet 18.
2   After sufficient practice, each subject performs two trials with 30 s rest between trials. The jump distances are recorded. The longest distance is recorded as the field measure (X) for the purpose of calculating concurrent validity, as shown in the second column of Table PW19.1.

Countermovement jump:

1   Peak instantaneous power output in a countermovement jump with hands on hips is determined by integration of the corresponding vertical force-time record as described in Practical Worksheet 17.
2   After sufficient practice, each subject performs two trials with 30 s rest between trials. The force-time recording with the longest flight time (which is likely to be associated with a higher peak instantaneous power) is selected for analysis.

Ideally, the standing long jump trials and countermovement jump trials should be performed in a single testing session.

Data analysis

1   Peak instantaneous power in the countermovement jump is recorded as the criterion measure (Y) for the purpose of calculating concurrent validity, as shown in the third column of Table PW19.1.
2   The mean ($\overline{X}$) and standard deviation (σ_X) of the field test scores (distance jumped) are calculated and recorded, as shown in Table PW19.1. The method of calculating the mean and standard deviation is shown in Table 2.2.
3   The mean ($\overline{Y}$) and standard deviation (σ_Y) of the criterion test scores (peak instantaneous power) are calculated and recorded, as shown in Table PW19.1.
4   The validity coefficient (r) of the field test with respect to the criterion test (correlation between the field test scores and the criterion test scores) is calculated and recorded, as shown in Table PW19.1. The method of calculating the validity coefficient is shown in Table 2.3.

TABLE PW19.1 Determination of the simple regression equation and standard error of the estimate (*SEE*) for predicting peak instantaneous power in a countermovement jump with hands on hips (criterion test) from distance jumped in a standing long jump with arm swing (field test). The subjects were 25 young, physically active men.

Subject	Jump distance (X)	Power (Y)	Predicted power (Y')	$d = Y - Y'$	d^2
	(cm)	(W)	(W)	(W)	(W^2)
1	205	4652	4512.60	139.39	19430.97
2	198	4223	4322.27	−99.27	9854.14
3	191	4298	4131.93	166.07	27578.91
4	200	4646	4376.65	269.35	72549.42
5	218	4809	4866.09	−57.09	3259.04
6	211	5114	4675.75	438.25	192062.19
7	204	4273	4485.41	−212.41	45119.71
8	193	4096	4186.31	−90.31	8156.44
9	236	5188	5355.53	−167.53	28064.96
10	222	5176	4974.85	201.15	40460.52
11	181	3654	3860.02	−206.02	42444.65
12	183	4257	3914.40	342.59	117372.70
13	174	3673	3669.68	3.32	10.99
14	196	3923	4267.89	−344.89	118946.35
15	215	4363	4784.51	−421.51	177674.89
16	232	5526	5246.76	279.24	77973.86
17	197	4441	4295.08	145.92	21293.52
18	208	4758	4594.18	163.82	26837.65
19	229	4925	5165.19	−240.19	57690.75
20	175	3562	3696.87	−134.87	18191.26
21	225	5188	5056.42	131.57	17311.98
22	221	4889	4947.66	−58.66	3441.11
23	214	4853	4757.32	95.68	9153.89
24	184	3843	3941.59	−98.59	9720.78
25	223	4757	5002.04	−245.04	60046.07
	$\overline{X} = 205.40$	$\overline{Y} = 4523.48$			$\sum d^2 = 1204646.78$
	$\sigma_X = 18.08$	$\sigma_Y = 540.30$			

$r = 0.9099$

$$Y' = \overline{Y} + r\frac{(\sigma_Y)}{\sigma_X}(X - \overline{X}) = 27.191X - 1061.55$$

$$SEE = \sqrt{\frac{\sum d^2}{N}} = \sqrt{\frac{1204646.78}{25}} = \sqrt{48185.87} = 219.51 \text{ W}$$

95% confidence limits: $\pm 1.96 \times SEE = \pm 430.24 \text{ W}$

5   The simple regression equation for predicting peak instantaneous power (Y') in the countermovement from distance jumped in the standing long jump (X) is calculated and recorded, as shown Table PW19.1.

6   The standard error of the estimate (*SEE*) of the prediction of peak instantaneous power in the countermovement from distance jumped in the standing long jump is calculated and recorded, as shown Table PW19.1.

7   The 95% confidence limits of the prediction of peak instantaneous power in the countermovement jump from distance jumped in the standing long jump are calculated and recorded, as in Table PW19.1.

Presentation of results

1   Present a scattergram of the field test (x axis) and criterion test (y axis) scores.

2   Present the corresponding simple regression equation, as in Table PW19.1.

3   Present the corresponding standard error of the estimate and 95% confidence limits, as in Table PW19.1.

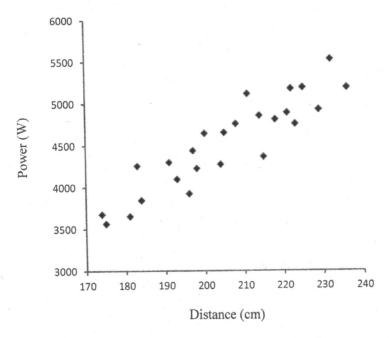

FIGURE PW19.1   Scattergram of distance jumped in a standing long jump with arm swing (field test) and peak instantaneous power in a countermovement with hands on hips (criterion test) for 25 physically active young men.

Example results

Example results for 25 young, physically active men are shown in Figure PW19.1 and Table PW19.1. Figure PW19.1 shows a scattergram of the field test (x axis) and criterion test (y axis) scores presented in Table PW19.1. The scattergram shows a clear trend for peak instantaneous power to increase as standing long jump distance increases. This trend is reflected in the validity coefficient between the field test and criterion test scores ($r = 0.9099$). Table PW19.1 shows the simple regression equation for predicting peak instantaneous power (Y') in the countermovement jump from distance jumped (X) in the standing long jump ($Y' = 27.191X - 1061.55$) together with the standard error of the prediction (219.51 cm) and the 95% confidence limits of the prediction (±430.24 cm).

INDEX